THE INTERNET IN THE WORKPLACE: HOW NEW TECHNOLOGY IS TRANSFORMING WORK

The Internet, and all the netcentric innovations that emerge from it, has transformed the workplace and our working lives in a very short time. The net added a window to the world on worker's desks, and made 24 by 7 connectivity to the workplace a reality – blurring the line between work and time off. It triggered new styles of teamwork, new leadership challenges, new modes of communicating, new job roles and employer–employee relationships, and new, alarmingly effective tools for workplace surveillance. The capabilities offered by netcentric technologies might seem to eliminate the need for a physical workplace altogether, but the workplace remains, and in fact, the physical appearance of a typical office looks about the same. Nevertheless, the psychological characteristics of the workplace have changed considerably. Workers, from the mail room clerk to the CEO, are learning new skills – to capitalize on the net's power, but avoid the egregious blunders that the net so dramatically amplifies. In *The Internet in the Workplace*, Wallace shows how netcentric technologies touch every kind of workplace, and explores the challenges and dilemmas they create.

Patricia Wallace, Ph.D., is Senior Director, Information Technology and Distance Programs at the Center for Talented Youth, Johns Hopkins University.

The **Internet**
in the
Workplace:
How New Technology Is
Transforming Work

PATRICIA WALLACE
Johns Hopkins University

CAMBRIDGE
UNIVERSITY PRESS

PUBLISHED BY THE PRESS SYNDICATE OF THE UNIVERSITY OF CAMBRIDGE
The Pitt Building, Trumpington Street, Cambridge, United Kingdom

CAMBRIDGE UNIVERSITY PRESS
The Edinburgh Building, Cambridge CB2 2RU, UK
40 West 20th Street, New York, NY 10011-4211, USA
477 Williamstown Road, Port Melbourne, VIC 3207, Australia
Ruiz de Alarcón 13, 28014 Madrid, Spain
Dock House, The Waterfront, Cape Town 8001, South Africa

http://www.cambridge.org

First published 2004

Printed in the United States of America

Typefaces Stone Serif 9/13 pt. and Futura   *System* LaTeX 2_ε [TB]

A catalog record for this book is available from the British Library.

Library of Congress Cataloging in Publication Data

ISBN 0 521 80931 2 hardback

For Rhea, Chris, and John, and in memory of Loretta and Julian Wallace

Contents

Preface

The workplace and our working lives have been transformed by the Internet and the netcentric innovations it has brought. Although the new gadgets that connect to the net are part of the transformation, they form only one element in a major transition that affects the nature of work in an organization and the employee's role. Oddly, the transformation may not even be apparent from a quick glance at the physical office. Most offices have not changed very much and an office worker transported from the early twentieth century would easily recognize most of the room's features. Even the computer would not seem entirely strange, because the keyboard looks so much like a typewriter's keys. However, the fundamental nature of the workplace – from communication patterns to management styles, and from approaches to teamwork to employer–employee relationships, have changed dramatically.

Netcentric technologies bring a host of new tools and capabilities to workers, especially in the areas of information access, communications, and collaboration. People can open a window to the digital world on their desktops or laptops, and they have access to a limitless supply of information and business intelligence. Twenty-four-hour connection to coworkers, clients, and the information resources of the workplace itself is commonplace. Team members can use collaborative technologies to work together regardless of physical location. E-learning enables workers to improve their skills and earn degrees without commuting to classes. These new capabilities bring extraordinary advantages to employees and their organizations, but as their use grows, we see their disadvantages emerge. Constant connectivity, for example, blurs the line between work and nonwork and has implications for work-life balance.

Beyond the new capabilities the Internet offers, netcentric technologies create fundamental changes in the economic context of work, and the need for certain kinds of companies, skills, or occupations. They created a wave of disruption that changed what employees – and the organizations in which they work – must do to add value to a product or process. The demand for certain kinds of work and particular skills is skyrocketing, but many occupations, companies, and whole industries have all but disappeared. More will follow as netcentric innovations reach further into every industry. These waves trigger other kinds of changes in the workplace, such as more job instability, new organizational forms, and looser relationships between employees and employers.

The Internet in the Workplace examines the many ways in which netcentric technologies have transformed our working lives, and presents both the positive and the negative consequences to employees and their organizations. The influence is not one-way, however, and people have many opportunities to influence and guide future technological developments, as well as the policies that govern how netcentric capabilities are used within the organization.

Acknowledgements

The many people who contributed to the development of this book deserve much thanks. Hundreds of colleagues offered insights, shared research results, described case studies, or recalled relevant anecdotes. Special thanks go to friends and colleagues at The Johns Hopkins University, the Robert H. Smith School of Business at University of Maryland, College Park, and the University of Maryland University College. People in government and in business around the world have also been extraordinarily helpful, and many provided very detailed information about the impact of the Internet on their working lives. Many people in universities, government, and business were helpful by sharing workplace insights, providing examples, commenting on the manuscript, or offering other kinds of contributions, including Joe Arden, Mike Ball, Joseph Bailey, Kathryn Bartol, Ramon Barquin, Sandor Boyson, Alan Carswell, Loretta Castaldi, James Cramer, Sam Donaldson, Christine Fabella, Samer Faraj, Howard Frank, Nathan Gessner, Larry Gordon, Prakash Gupta, Cooper Graham, Calvert Jones, Julian Jones, P. K. Kannan, Kim Kelley, Rhea Kittredge, Ted McKeldin, Don Riley, Lemma Senbet, Sudhakar Shenoy, Yolan So, Susan Taylor, Peter Wayner, and Lea Ybarra. My students, many of whom were seeking a career change precisely because of the Internet's wave of creative destruction, deserve a great deal of thanks. I also want to thank the anonymous reviewers for their thoughtful comments, and Cambridge University Press team for the excellent support and encouragement, especially from my editors, Julia Hough and Phil Laughlin.

Patricia Wallace, Ph.D.
Center for Talented Youth
The Johns Hopkins University
Baltimore, Maryland
August, 2003

1 The Internet Transforms the Workplace

"What people have not grasped is that the Internet will change everything."
— John Chambers, CEO of CISCO

The Internet was virtually unknown among business leaders in the 1970s, confined as it was to the arcane academic and government research domains. By the late 1980s, though, and especially in the 1990s after the World Wide Web made its debut, the Internet set off a wave of creative destruction that affected business around the world. John Chambers, chair of what was once an obscure networking company that made the routers for the Internet's infrastructure, rapidly became one of the most widely quoted visionaries in the new era. Developing an "Internet strategy" became the battle cry for many organizations, as their anxious leaders watched infant net companies like Amazon.com and eBay rise to spectacular heights on Wall Street and in the public consciousness. The leaders of these newcomers, along with the hosts of techno-savvy entrepreneurs who were attracting so much investment capital, seemed to "get it." Yet when most of the dot-coms crashed at the end of the decade, it became very clear that competing effectively in the Internet age is far more difficult than anyone thought. Riding the Internet wave and truly understanding its impact and underlying role in massive changes turned out to be more complex than just "getting it."

The Internet's dramatic effects on business models and strategies have captured the headlines, and business leaders have been struggling through some very turbulent times as they experiment with ways to exploit the net to achieve competitive advantage. The changes the Internet has brought to the workplace itself, however, have received much less notice in the rush to e-business. Most of us are now working in a *netcentric* environment, one in which the influence and capabilities of the Internet permeate our work lives.

1

We are only beginning to understand the nature of the changes and how dramatically they alter the organizations in which we work and our roles within them. We are just learning, for example, what "virtual leadership" is and how internal power relationships change when any employee from the kitchen staff to the board of directors can send an email to the CEO or launch a Web site that criticizes the company. We are only beginning to glimpse the effects that around-the-clock access to email, the Web, and wireless devices has on the lives of employees and their families. In offices around the world, workers have desktop access to every Internet corner, whether work-related or not. The tools to monitor and control their activities are widespread and easily implemented, and businesses are adopting those tools without fully understanding how this kind of surveillance affects productivity or the psychological characteristics of the workplace.

Internet in the Workplace: A Brief Tour

In *The Internet in the Workplace*, we explore the many changes this shift to netcentricity has triggered. Some of those changes are dramatic, but others are quite subtle. Most office workers, for example, already had seen their dumb terminal retired by the early 1990s and welcomed the new microcomputer on their desks that they could use for far more tasks. They could not only still access the company's mainframe database, but also do word processing, spreadsheets, statistical analysis, and presentations. Most were also connected to a local or wide area network and could share files, printers, and send email and documents to one another. Adding the required telecommunications equipment and the connection to the Internet would not contribute any remarkable physical changes to the typical office or cubicle. Yet this imperceptible alteration opened a gateway to the outside world – beyond the walls of the corporation – that has had, and will continue to have, far-reaching effects.

Though the Internet as a "desktop gateway to the world" is probably the most obvious change from the worker's point of view, the Internet's effects on the workplace go far beyond that. It changed the context of work, the context of business in general, and the context of entire industries. The Internet became a catalyst for new business models, strategies, and organizational structures. It introduced new factors that affected the competitive landscape, new rivalries, new competitors, and new pressures that many business leaders were not prepared to address. It triggered new ways of thinking about how to do business, some of which fared well and some of which failed miserably. It also led to surgery on the components of many value chains. The kinds of work that make a contribution to the value chain changed, making the roles that many people were playing along that chain obsolete – often rather suddenly.

The Internet's role as a catalyst for technological innovation is another signficant feature in its effects on the workplace, and it is the subject of the second chapter. The net's architecture was designed to support all kinds of innovative add-ons, some of which have already found their way to the landfill, the flea market, or to the online auctions. The Internet itself and the evolving standards and protocols that make it up form a stage on which considerable innovation can develop, though not all the new gadgets and software will make it much beyond a single season. Netcentric technologies have, however, certainly made their way into the workplace, and this book examines their effects as well.

The Internet changed the business landscape, making it far more competitive and the workplace considerably more fast-moving. It also hastened the advent of widespread twenty-four-hour connectivity, particularly through netcentric technologies such as cell phones and wireless devices that can receive and send email. Together, these factors led to a reconceptualization of what constitutes the "workday" or the "workweek." The concept of work–life balance has gained new meaning in a highly competitive, netcentric, global economy, in which each worker is accessible any time, any place, and employees can access their colleagues, documents, and data from just about anywhere. For many people, this "always on" mode has become second nature, and it has emerged as one of the major advantages or drawbacks of the Internet's effects on the workplace, depending on your point of view.

By the late 1990s, the volume of email traffic surpassed the volume of telephone traffic, marking a milestone in the Internet's influence on our patterns of communication. Instant messaging has grown rapidly as well, along with several other forms of communication that rely on netcentric technologies. Although neither the business letter nor the interoffice memo has become extinct, their roles in and between organizations, and between the organization and its customers, have changed considerably. Yet the long history and common understanding about how letters and memos should be written and used do not yet exist for the new communication styles, so blunders, misunderstandings, and missteps are frequent. In this book, we will also look closely at the new modes of business communication and explore case studies that demonstrate how they have been integrated into the workplace.

Management and leadership have also been affected by the Internet. Managing groups of people in the netcentric age brings new opportunities and challenges, especially for people whose management skills were honed in a more traditional face-to-face environment. How are managers adapting their styles to an organization in which much of the interaction occurs over the network, often in choppy, asynchronous rhythms? One management challenge that arises from this new environment involves the ease and frequency with which employees can use – or overuse – the cc: or the bcc: features during email exchanges. Many employees now include their managers in very routine conversations, though they would rarely have included them in these exchanges in person, by phone, or by memo when those methods were the only alternatives. The leaders of the organization are also confronted with new challenges. How can a leader who relies on a charismatic, personal style to effect change and communicate a vision take advantage of the Internet?

Another impact of the net in the workplace involves access to information and the growing realization that more is not necessarily better. Access to the Internet has had an enormous influence on the kind and amount of information that can reach every employee's desktop. Intranets can give employees access to voluminous and up-to-date internal information, and the Internet provides access to vast quantities of business intelligence. Email among employees often contains significant bits of knowledge that would help new employees and veteran colleagues avoid reinventing wheels. Taking advantage of this wealth of information, however, and turning it into useful knowledge that can help the worker solve problems or increase productivity have been far more difficult than most people anticipated. Although the field of "knowledge management" was in progress before the Internet became widespread, the net certainly made it clear that access to more and more raw, unfiltered information did not necessarily lead to productive "knowledge." We explore the young field of knowledge management in this book and describe how some of the initiatives to harness knowledge in organizations have fared. The challenges involve far more than technology, and knowledge management efforts have met with mixed success because they frequently encounter organizational resistance.

The Internet has enabled distance education and "e-learning" and altered the ways in which many organizations provide training and professional development to their employees. Distance education programs have grown at a startling rate, with the emergence of numerous virtual universities, online learning consortia, and endless partnerships among publishers, educational institutions, commercial training programs, in-house development efforts, and technology companies offering distance learning environments. The advantages of distance programs in the workplace are powerful, if they are successful, because they can dramatically reduce travel expenses and time away from work. They can also offer just-in-time learning on the job in ways that were not feasible when most training was conducted in classroom settings and had to be scheduled well in advance. As you will see in this book, a variety of e-learning approaches have emerged, and many studies have been conducted to determine how effective these programs are compared to more traditional, face-to-face classroom settings.

The value of teamwork became clear long before the Internet permeated the workplace, but most of the time team members were physically collocated. Meetings, brainstorming sessions, after-hours relaxation, and formal team briefings to the boss occurred in the face-to-face mode. The Internet, however, and the collaborative technologies that have been built to take advantage of the global network, raised the possibility of virtual, global teams. You will see later in this book how virtual teams are faring and how group dynamics unfold in a setting in which team members may never actually meet one another in person. Trust, in particular, is a key ingredient to the success of any team, and virtual teamwork requires innovative strategies to develop trust among team members.

One of the most controversial aspects of the Internet's role in the workplace is the issue of workplace surveillance and employee privacy. Although employers have always had extensive legal rights to monitor behavior in the workplace, the netcentric environment vastly increases the scope and ease with which they can perform such surveillance. Digital documents – including email – are stored and may remain accessible for years, and software tools to track net-surfing activity, downloads, and virtually any keystroke are widely available. Small, inexpensive digital cameras can become Webcams, generating video images that can be accessed anywhere in the world from the Web. In this book, we examine the reasons underlying the increase in surveillance by employers and also look at the ethical and legal issues involved.

The impact that technological advances have on employment and job displacement has been an important subject of debate for centuries. In Chapter 10, we examine these historical debates and then zoom in on the recent past, in which the Internet's rapid growth initiated a wave of dislocations, disintermediations, and astonishing changes in compensation packages. For example, many organizations are placing people trained in information technology into special, privileged categories because of workforce shortages. Certain types of IT workers continue to be in high demand and short supply, and human resource managers have responded with special compensation plans. While shortages in some areas exist, some other jobs and whole business units become candidates for disintermediation and phaseout because of the Internet. This chapter explores these trends and their implications for equity, retention, and career planning.

Finally, we look to the future of the workplace, given the growing extent and influence of netcentricity around the globe. The Internet itself is a vivid reminder of how quickly trends come and go, and of how frequently predictions are made, even by very knowledgeable people, that are far off the mark. For example, IBM Chairman Thomas Watson's remarks are very easy to find on the net. In 1943, he predicted, "I think there is a world market for maybe five computers." Instead of making predictions about the next-generation workplace, I propose various alternative futures, ones that will have pros and cons based on what we now know about netcentricity and on the psychological and sociological effects it can have on human beings in the workplace.

The Context of Change: The Evolving Netcentric Economy

A substantial portion of the Internet's effects on the workplace arise from the economic environment itself, an environment that has been affected a great deal by the growth of the digital network. Although we are not yet conducting business at the speed of thought, as Bill Gates suggested, the pace of business is fast – largely because large quantities of information can be transmitted and processed so much more quickly. Equally important, the cost of transmitting information has dropped precipitously, making it possible to send it farther, to more people, and to almost any place on the globe.

We hear about "Internet time," a phrase that has been applied to many different business processes. The time allotted to product development, for example, has been compressed so businesses can create new products and market them much faster. Systems development has also undergone some remarkable time compressions. Companies that want to bring up e-commerce applications so their customers can reach them and transact business on the Web do not want to wait through the old-fashioned "waterfall" method of life-cycle systems development, in which the many phases – from feasibility study to requirements analysis to software development to implementation – follow one another in sequence. This methodology was always slow, but in the Internet age it could lead to disaster. Given how fast companies are changing their strategies to respond to customer needs and new competition, the application under development would be obsolete before it made it to the second phase. An alternative is to bring up applications quickly in rougher form, even when they have not been tested thoroughly on many different browsers, for example, or with different computer platforms. Web users are very familiar with this approach – it is never much of a surprise when an online application doesn't seem to work properly, or even causes the computer to freeze. Also, the "under construction" icon on Web sites is very familiar. Imagine how appalling that approach would be in other technology contexts, such as in a kitchen appliance. A consumer who read "under construction" on the digital readout of a new coffeemaker when trying to operate the bean grinder would immediately return the product, not shrug his shoulders and come back later.

Clearly, the intensity of competition among firms has risen. At the same time, the strategies companies use to deal with these new competitive pressures are immature and not well tested. Let's take a look at some of the underlying forces that make the new business landscape so tense and examine some of the strategies corporations are using to address those forces.

Information Asymmetries

The ease with which consumers can now obtain information about competing products, prices, features, repair histories, and company profiles is a major contributor to the change in the context of business. *Information asymmetries* have, in the past, been part and parcel of the business landscape. In any business exchange, it is not uncommon for one party to have more information than the other, and that inequity changes the power equation. For example, when a retailer decides how to market a particular product, the retailer would know that many customers would not take the time or effort to do a comprehensive and exhaustive comparison of all the pros and cons of similar products offered by many different vendors, including the product's features, price, service agreements, or reliability histories. That would require a lot of research and entail much driving, parking, or at least telephoning. It would just be too much trouble, so most customers would settle for a quick survey, or a check of one or two competitors. Though the net has not had much effect on information asymmetries in some contexts, it has become a major leveler of information for an important quantitative variable: price. Here, the analytical power of the net's computers can be put into action.

INFORMATION ASYMMETRY AND INTERNET PRICES: EARLY EXPERIMENTS

Information asymmetries associated with pricing have been especially affected, and reduced, by the Internet, particularly for products that are offered via e-commerce. A consumer can now, with very little effort, check out the prices of a product from multiple vendors around the country, or even around the world, by using one of the many shopping bots (shopbots) or price comparison engines. These scour the Web for product prices and organize them into tables for ease of comparison. The products can be sorted by vendor, price, model, or other variables, and the consumer can easily draw comparisons. A recent search on MySimon, for example, revealed that the same printer was selling for prices that differed by as much as $100 through different outlets. A consumer could just click on the "buy now" button next to the lowest priced offering and go right to that vendor's e-commerce site to conduct the transaction. This dramatically reduces search costs for the consumer and makes the competition very fierce among businesses selling similar products.

In principle, the lower cost of comparison shopping associated with the reduction in information asymmetry should make these electronic markets more efficient, so prices for products available through the Internet should be lower than those sold through conventional channels. This could be a great advantage to the consumer, though it also changes the intensity of competition among businesses in the same industry. As it turns out, though, pricing is more complicated than this. Research on this subject suggests that businesses have been struggling with different strategies and appear to be unsure of how to deal with the new information asymmetries or with their own competitors. As we see several times throughout this book, we are in an early period of e-commerce, and experimentation is common, often with painful results. There is little research or history to help companies understand how the digital economy actually works or to predict how their actions will affect consumers, competitors, or their own bottom line.

Joseph P. Bailey of the University of Maryland's Robert H. Smith School of Business followed the prices of a shopping basket of books, CDs, and software sold on the Internet and also through conventional stores in the mid-1990s.[1] Surprisingly, he found that the prices of these products on the net were actually higher than they were in the stores, even though the products themselves were exactly the same. He argued that the results could have been due to the immaturity of the electronic markets. Given how new these markets were at the time, it would have been premature to assume that they would not eventually be more efficient, with lower prices for the consumer. It was more likely that the companies were experimenting,

---

[1] Bailey, J. P. (1998). Electronic commerce: prices and consumer issues for three products: Books, compact discs, and software. Organization for Economic Co-Operation and Development, *OCDE/GD*(98)4.

not completely sure how consumers or competitors would behave. After all, the companies had to invest in the technology infrastructure to offer their products online, and the higher prices were an attempt to recoup those initial investments. The companies may also have reasoned that the convenience of online shopping warranted a little premium that customers would be willing to pay.

In 1997, Bailey found evidence for more experimentation, this time during the period in which Amazon.com – the main online outlet for the shopping basket goods, faced competition from a very worthy competitor – Barnes and Noble. When Barnes and Noble opened their online channel, Amazon reacted dramatically. During the three months after their March 19 debut, Amazon dropped its prices by 10 percent to match their competitors.

MARKET EFFICIENCIES AND FRICTION

Later in the decade, the electronic markets began to show the increased efficiency economists predicted. Eric Brynjolfsson and Michael Smith of the MIT Sloan School of Management compared the prices of books and CDs, collecting over 8,500 price observations over a period of fifteen months in 1998 and 1999 in both online and conventional retail settings.[2] They found that the prices for these products online were nine to sixteen percent lower than they were in the stores, even after considering shipping, handling, and local sales taxes. The electronic market may not be totally without any friction, but it does appear that goods can be sold at lower costs online than they can in stores, or at least they are offered for lower prices, perhaps because of the brutal competition and easy switching by the customers.

Another intriguing finding from this investigation was that the Internet retailers were making many tiny price adjustments to their online offerings, in some cases as small as a penny. The costs for making such changes, called menu costs, are much lower online than they would be in a conventional outlet. For online products, the retailer need only change the price in the central database and the new price will appear immediately whenever shoppers bring up the details for the product. In contrast, a conventional retailer must relabel the products on the shelves in all the stores.

The low menu costs make it easier for online retailers to experiment with pricing strategies, but they also make it easy for companies to respond very

---

[2] Brynjolfsson, E., & Smith, M. (2000). Frictionless commerce? A comparison of Internet and conventional retailers. *Management Science, 46*(4), 563–586.

quickly to any price cuts by their competitors. In fact, Hal Varian, Dean of the School of Information Management and Systems at the University of California at Berkeley, points out that thanks to the low menu costs, the effects of the comparison shopbots can work both ways. They reduce information asymmetry for consumers and help lower friction in the markets, but they can also, in some circumstances, lead to higher prices rather than to lower ones.[3] This is partly because the shopbots reveal the competition's pricing as soon as it occurs. A price cut is most effective in gaining new business if enough new customers are drawn to the retailer before the competitor responds with its own price cut. But if competing firms can move even faster than the consumers, there is no advantage to cutting prices. This is another example of what "Internet time" is all about, and how it has created a blindingly fast business climate.

Price is not the only factor consumers use to decide which company to patronize, and for many, it is not the main one. The vendor with the lowest price online does not necessarily have the largest market share because consumers are influenced by other variables, such as brand name and reputation. This has certainly drawn many big players into e-commerce, even when their online business competes with physical stores. It has also launched ferocious competition for valuable online "real estate," so customers can easily find you, a competition that has unleashed technological attempts to un-level the playing field and introduce more market friction.

For example, figuring out what key words a customer might use to search for vendors of a product, and then designing Web sites that will be considered "highly relevant" by the search engines and listed on the first page, has turned out to be an extremely important task. The widely used search engine Google uses a ranking algorithm that takes into account a site's "popularity" in terms of how many other sites contain links to *it*.[4] A more popular site containing the user's key words would be listed before a less popular one when the matches are retrieved. Google considers this a fair metric to include in the ranking process, analogous to word-of-mouth recommendations. However, to artificially manipulate popularity level without waiting for outsiders to add links to their site, designers build "link farms." These are groups of circular Web sites that link back and forth to each other for the sole purpose of optimizing their rankings. Google doesn't publish all of its criteria and warns Web site designers not to use tactics like link farms to rig

---

[3] Varian, H. R. (2000). Market structure in the network age. In E. Brynjolfsson & B. Kahin (Eds.), *Understanding the digital economy.* Cambridge, MA: MIT Press.

[4] Grimes, B. (2003). Fooling Google. *PC Magazine, 22*(8), 74.

the system and jockey for position. They even threaten to drop persistent offenders from Google's index entirely. The link farms, after all, introduce a new kind of market inefficiency that prevents customers from making the most informed choice. They also diminish the public's faith in the trustworthiness and fairness of the search engine's results.

Disintermediation along the Value Chain

Arguably, the longest and most unpronounceable word associated with the netcentric economy is also one of the most feared. The Merriam-Webster Collegiate Dictionary defines *disintermediation* as the diversion of savings from savings accounts with low fixed interest rates to direct investment in high yielding instruments. The word has been redefined in the Internet era to refer to the bypass of a wide variety of middlemen, or intermediaries, that have been traditionally part of the value chain that led from the actual suppliers or manufacturer of a product to the consumers who buy it to use. Middlemen serve many different roles along this process. For example, they might bring together a party in search of a particular service with the firms that provide the service, or they might aggregate many buyers to create a larger volume of demand. Intermediaries might serve a filtering role, qualifying various products or companies to save the buyers the time required to do this themselves. They also might serve in the capacity of distributor of many related products, so their creators or manufacturers need not attempt to market or distribute individually.

A key ingredient in the wave of creative destruction that the Internet brought about involves various kinds of disintermediation, and entire industries have been shaken to their foundations by the process. After the meltdown of dot-coms in the late 1990s, the fears abated somewhat, especially as many of those who served intermediary roles found new ways to add value to the value chain within the context of the emerging digital economy. Nevertheless, the Internet fundamentally changes what the value chain looks like and what kinds of activities add value to it.

Authors, for example, can in principle reach out directly to their readers and fans through the Internet, bypassing editors, printers, layout artists, publishers, distributors, bookstores, promoters, and other kinds of intermediaries involved in the industry. Stephen King was the first best-selling author to publish one of his books through the Internet before it ever appeared in print. In the first forty-eight hours, an estimated half-million people downloaded the e-book *Riding the Bullet*, and King says he has made almost a half-million dollars in royalties. The cost of the e-book was low for consumers, but publishers are offering authors higher royalty rates because they don't have to bear the burden of actually publishing a print version. Random House, for example, announced that e-book authors would receive 50 percent of sales revenue, which is considerably higher than the usual 10 to 15 percent that authors usually receive.[5] On the extreme end, an author can just publish his or her own book on a Web site and offer it for sale, or for free. Whether anyone notices it, or pays money to read it, is another question, of course.

THE VANISHING INTERMEDIARIES

Intermediaries have played key roles in many industries, such as insurance, real estate, travel, and financial services. Another example of disintermediation occurred when E*Trade began offering consumers the opportunity to research stocks online and conduct their own transactions to buy or sell stock holdings. The broker's role and the broker's commission were dramatically affected.

In the travel business, the independent agent's role as an intermediary between the traveler and the airlines has also been traumatized by the net. The airlines actively promote online ticket purchases, offering special "Internet only" deals and discounts for customers who will skip the travel agent or the phone call to make a reservation. They also make it easier for travelers who use e-tickets. At Los Angeles airport, for example, while my colleagues who attended a conference with me waited half an hour in a long line to check in, I went to an e-ticket kiosk with no line to get my boarding pass.

Consumers can now do considerable research and comparison shopping for their vacation deals online. Their information searches can also go well beyond the glossy advertisements and promotions launched on the Web by the tourist industry and can stretch into online newsgroups and discussion forums populated by travelers who have actually visited the locations and stayed in the hotels. For example, a quick search on the Web for Batopilas, Mexico, brings up dozens of commercial sites, some of which pay the search engine to obtain their top billing. This information is enormously valuable, with listings of accommodations, recreation, major architectural attractions, museums, nightlife, and things for kids to do. This is the kind of information that a traveler would have spent many weeks obtaining in the past. The net offers even more in the way of reducing search costs, however,

[5] Offline? (December 9, 2000). *The Economist, 357*(8200), 93.

and rebalancing that information asymmetry. A search for Batopilas in the discussion forums brings up some intriguing postings by actual tourists who describe their own experiences and give advice. Many will happily answer email queries from people who are interested in visiting the same place.

In the academic world, disintermediation is also on the horizon. Consider the high price of journal subscriptions that universities pay. These journals have very small distribution, mainly to academic libraries, and the authors of the articles, their reviewers, and the journal's editors are paid little or nothing. Yet the journal subscriptions are extremely expensive, crushing the library's budget and forcing librarians to make very difficult choices about what to buy each year. One university librarian lamented that faculty foolishly give away their intellectual output to the academic journal publishers, who then sell it back to the university at extremely high prices in the form of journal subscriptions.

Economist Manfredi La Manna of St. Andrews University in Scotland proposed the launch of an alternative academic journal distribution system, based on the Internet. He is starting the Electronic Society for Social Scientists, which will pay authors, reviewers, and editors small honoraria for their work and then distribute the articles via the Web for subscription charges that are half what the academic journal publishers now charge. He sees this organization as a template for academic publishing that will eventually replace the current model and disintermediate the academic journal publishers. Universities are slow to change, but more than a thousand scholars had signed up with the project.[6]

Disintermediation of pieces in the value chain that no longer add much value may seem like an obvious way to reduce friction and lower prices, but sometimes surprising obstacles surface. In this case, the journal publisher seems to be an obsolete appendage, but one of the barriers to moving in the online journal direction involves the way faculty are evaluated by their peers and by the committees that decide whether to grant tenure. Publishing in peer-reviewed journals is an essential ingredient of success, and some journals are more highly regarded than others. In fact, some departments maintain lists of journals in which an assistant professor must publish in order to be evaluated favorably by a tenure committee. These lists do not include any upstart online journals such as the ones La Manna is attempting to launch. Instead, they include the journals that are published by the same academic journal publishers whose contribution to the value chain is

---

[6] Payne, D. (2001). A revolutionary idea in publishing. *Chronicle of Higher Education*, *47*(26), 39–40.

under attack. To add fuel to this fire, and further complexity to any analysis of the value chain, the rankings of a university department can be affected by the journals in which its faculty publish. *U.S. News and World Report*, for example, publishes rankings of business schools each year. In 1999, the magazine announced that its rankings would add "intellectual capital" to the criteria by which it determines a business school's rank. This controversial new dimension judges the quality of the faculty's intellectual output by their publications and the potential influence and reach of their papers and books. For example, the quantitative measure includes not only a tally of book reviews in the major business journals but also the number of papers that are published in a select list of favored academic journals. Not surprisingly, these favored academic journals are not online journals – they are published by the academic journal publishers. A value chain, such as this one, is a complex mix of economic, historic, and psychological factors.

DISINTERMEDIATION IN RELATIONSHIPS BETWEEN BUSINESSES

We've seen examples of how the business-to-consumer relationship (B2C) has been touched by disintermediation and the rise of the Internet and of how university-to-business connections may be affected. Many economists predict that the most important economic changes will occur behind the scenes, at least with respect to the consumer, and will involve the way businesses interact and communicate with one another (B2B). These changes are not invisible to the worker, however, because the workplace is undergoing significant changes as a result of B2B e-commerce.

Some areas in which businesses can gain advantage from electronic communication with one another include procurement, inventory management, and logistics. For example, an online florist who takes orders from customers via the Web can dramatically improve its service by automating and coordinating the logistics of delivery. One company called Proflowers sells flowers online for delivery anywhere in the country, and the flowers are shipped directly from the grower rather than from a retail florist. Proflowers has a B2B relationship with FedEx such that the shipping process is automatically initiated when the customer makes the online order, including the creation of a shipping label that is downloaded to one of the growers. The whole process occurs in less than 5 seconds.[7] The growers who tend the farms and nurseries are connected directly to their consumers via this B2B e-commerce transaction, and the workers who formerly would have

---

[7] Boyson, S., & Olian, J. (1999). *Harnessing the power of netcentricity*. College Park, MD: Robert H. Smith School of Business, University of Maryland, College Park.

facilitated this process are, of course, no longer needed for much more than troubleshooting problems when the electronic supply chain breaks. The disintermediated list would include the retail florists, and it would also include those who coordinated contacts with the growers and supervised the logistics for the customers.

Another way in which B2B relationships are facilitated through the Internet involves the electronic marketplace in which many sellers can interact with many buyers in a hub. For example, Sciquest.com is one of these online marketplaces that specializes in the life science industry, providing a place to find and buy various scientific and laboratory products. A number of different kinds of organizations use this service, including pharmaceutical houses, biotech research firms, and educational organizations. (Like many such electronic marketplaces and other Internet "pure plays," this one had a turbulent ride in the late 1990s. By the time of this writing, it had not yet turned a profit.)

FROM EDI TO THE INTERNET

Electronic communication between businesses along the supply chain is not new, and many companies have used electronic data interchange (EDI) since the 1970s to reap some of the rewards. This system, which some consider to be the first form of e-commerce, was created to enable companies to transmit information electronically to one another – about inventory levels of various products, for example. One goal was to keep inventory levels low by ensuring the supplier knew when products were needed. Developing an EDI relationship between two companies involved negotiation, customized programming, and often the launch of two databases containing synchronized product information, one at each location. Also, the relationship depended on a proprietary value-added network (VAN) that charged for each byte of data transmitted, because the concept predated the Internet and its flat fees.

One of the differences between EDI and Internet-based B2B relationships involves their openness, and the ease with which companies can switch suppliers or new and smaller companies can join in a supply chain relationship. Because EDI relationships generally involved two companies who worked together to create the link, the investment in the relationship and the infrastructure needed to support it was larger. Because of this up-front investment, companies did not do much switching once they had things in place and working properly. As companies move to electronic marketplaces on the Internet, switching costs are lowered and relationships will be more volatile and competitive.[8] We see again that the Internet introduced a new level of tension and competition for businesses – this time by making electronic supply chain relationships far easier to establish – or break.

Technological innovation has always had significant effects on the employment picture, as we discuss in a later chapter, and it is nothing new for automation to replace the work of human beings. Also, those whose economic livelihoods are affected try to find means to protect their futures, through such avenues as unionization, retraining, or restructuring of work. In the next section, we examine some of the strategies people use when their role in the value chain is reduced or eliminated.

The Disintermediated Fight Back

Li and Fung is a company in China that formerly had a thriving business introducing western retailers of clothes, toys, and other goods to the many family-operated shops of China. This intermediary role was essential at the time, because retailers would have little time or capability to perform the kind of research and make the contacts one would need in order to deal with so many little shops and home-based factories. By the end of the twentieth century, however, the company's role was no longer needed because suppliers and retailers could find one another online. Its intermediary position was eclipsed by the major western trading houses and by the disintermediation brought about by the Internet.

INVENTING NEW LINKS FOR THE VALUE CHAIN

Rather than quit, the two brothers who now run the family business, Victor and William Fung, reinvented their role in the age of the Internet. They *reintermediated* their contribution to the value chain by specializing in the coordination of some extremely complex supply chains, ones that are getting more complicated all the time. For example, a clothes retailer in Europe might want to order thousands of items, and the supply chain might be very convoluted indeed. The yarn may come from South Korea, and factories in Taiwan may be the best place to dye it and weave it into cloth. A zipper factory in Japan may be called upon to deliver the zippers at the right time in the process. Because of the growth of sewing factories in Thailand, the final products may be created in several locations throughout that country. Li and Fung now specialize in providing coordination for this intricate web of precise timing and business relationships. They also search out

---

[8] Williams, M. L., & Frolick, M. N. (2001). The evolution of EDI for competitive advantage: The Fedex case. *Information Systems Management, 18*(2), 47–54.

new suppliers throughout Asia, including the little sewing machine cottages in Bangladesh where the women are not (yet) using the Internet. The company has a staff of 3,600 people who travel through thirty-seven countries, with a "machete in one hand, laptop in the other."[9]

THE RISE OF THE INFOMEDIARY

Another way in which the disintermediated are fighting back and altering their roles is by capitalizing on precisely what moved them out of the intermediary business in the first place. The Internet has dramatically reduced search costs, so the intermediary is not as important for helping consumers or businesses find the suppliers. But the immense volume of information available through the net, a volume that is growing all the time, has paved the way for another type of intermediary. This is the one who sorts, filters, qualifies, and provides value by solving the information overload problem. John Hagel and Marc Singer introduced the concept of the *infomediary*, and this is a role that may become increasingly important.[10] Consumers and businesses seeking suppliers are confronted with a glut of information, an overload, that may be best solved by the use of a trusted and unbiased infomediary.

The shopbots perform a simple infomediary service by sorting products according to price. Many other Web sites provide review and evaluation services, such as tables of current mortgage rates by financial institutions. Another Web site compares credit card offerings, allowing visitors to search for credit cards that have the lowest interest rates, offer the most frequent flyer miles, or have other kinds of reward programs. The credit card issuers do not appear to have reduced their direct marketing efforts to attract customers, judging from the number of "You are already approved!" envelopes that flood the post office. However, the canny consumers can easily use one of the online infomediaries to find the credit card that best meets their needs.

Another role these infomediaries might play is as a guardian of the consumer's privacy. Increasingly, companies are collecting profiling information about individuals who buy products or just visit their Web sites, and as we see later in this book, the technology to do this has become incredibly sophisticated. Personal information, such as buying patterns and customer preferences, has considerable value, judging by the eagerness with which corporations are attempting to collect and analyze it. Varun Grover, of the

---

[9] Links in the global chain. (2001). *The Economist, 359*(8224), 62–63.

[10] Hagel, J., & Singer, M. (1999). *Net worth: Shaping markets when customers make the rules.* Boston, MA: Harvard Business School Press.

University of South Carolina, and Pradipkumar Ramanlal, of the University of Central Florida, argue that infomediaries whose role is to protect, aggregate, and leverage the value of personal information, will flourish in the digital age.[11] These customer-oriented infomediaries will be the custodians and brokers of personal information, drawing their revenue from the businesses who want the information and sharing it with the consumer.

SEEKING PROTECTION FROM CREATIVE DESTRUCTION

The candidates for disintermediation are also trying to protect their economic livelihoods and the role of their links in the value chain by seeking government intervention and legislation. Historically, legal relief has been a common means of redress when groups are displaced by new technology or business strategies. For example, people whose livelihood depended on the use of the horse in transportation created organizations in the early twentieth century to lobby for laws to restrict trucks and automobiles. Horseshoers, hay growers, horsebreeders, and others involved in the horse industry built organizations and campaigned to limit trucks on public roads and to restrict parking on public streets. More recently, gas station employees attempted to pressure state legislatures to make self-service gas stations illegal.

Robert D. Atkinson of the Progressive Policy Institute in Washington, DC, points out ways in which the drive to seek protection may cause problems elsewhere, especially for cases in which consumer choice is limited by attempts to enact restrictive legislation on e-commerce activity.[12] For example, car dealers have lobbied successfully for legislation to restrict any direct selling of automobiles by car manufacturers in their states. Wine wholesalers have actively protested against direct selling of wine on the Internet by the wineries. The American Optometrist Association has fought back as well to promote restrictions on the sales of contact lenses over the net. Optometrists conduct the eye exam, and in the past, the patients were required to purchase their contact lenses from the optometrist. The price of contact lenses, however, can be considerably lower when consumers buy through online sellers. The optometry associations have used a number of strategies to keep the optometrist in the loop for contact lens sales and maintain this revenue stream, including lobbying against any legislation that would require optometrists to provide patients with their own prescriptions and passing laws that make it more difficult for the patient to obtain lenses

---

[11] Grover, V., & Ramanlal, P. (2000). Playing the e-commerce game. *Business and Economic Review, 47*(1), 9–15.

[12] Atkinson, R. D. (2001). Middlemen fight consumer choice. *Consumers' Research Magazine, 84*(4), 10–16.

through other outlets. One such law, for example, requires online companies to obtain an original, hand-signed copy of the prescription rather than a faxed version.

Extreme Disintermediation: The Case of Digital Products

Reducing the role of intermediaries can be especially dramatic in industries in which the product itself is digital and the Internet can be the main player in the supply chain. For King's book, for example, the product could be downloaded directly from the Web site to the customer. This differs from supply chains in which a physical product is involved, and something must be constructed from parts, maintained in a warehouse, shipped, and unloaded. For information products, the Internet can actually deliver the goods right to the customer, rather than just create the transaction that is fulfilled through other distribution channels.

Digital products include anything that can be stored digitally, such as books, music, movies, software, photographs, and – of course – information. Each of them is surrounded by a long-standing set of supporting players, and the Internet can fundamentally alter the role it plays. The key ingredient for these products is that the trappings of a physical product are not needed, though they might be included for a variety of reasons – to make them more difficult for shoplifters to stuff them in a pocket, for example. Most of us have purchased software in a box and discovered that the box is many times too large for the small disk it contains. Its contents are mainly cardboard and air, and even a manual is missing because it is included on the disk.

Napster was probably the most publicized example of an Internet-distributed digital product in the late 1990s. The electronic music-swapping service bypassed a host of players in a single sweep. Although Napster did not appear to reduce the sale of CDs initially, the potential was certainly there. Other swapping services emerged after Napster was shut down, and the downloading continued. When CD sales fell 9 percent in 2002, commentators blamed the free downloads for the decline, though the slow economy may also have played a role.[13] Nevertheless, protests by the industry players, especially the Recording Industry Association of America (RIAA), were intense. When Lars Ulrich of Metallica sued Napster for copyright infringement, attention was drawn to the intellectual property issue and the

---

[13] Green, H., Grover, R., & Hof, R. D. (2003). Music merchants rush in where labels have failed. *Business Week, 3819*, 36–39. Retrieved February 28, 2003, from Business Source Premier.

fact that artists would not receive royalties from such swapping. However, many other economic issues were also at stake that had little to do with infringement of intellectual property rights and the cost to artists. After all, the artist receives only a very small portion of the revenue from CD sales in the form of royalties; the rest goes to all the other players involved in the music industry from the music retailer to the factories that make the jewel boxes to the stock clerk who keeps the shelves in order.

Companies that specialize in digital information products have an especially difficult time in the Internet age because consumers have become accustomed to obtaining things for free online. The recording industry has had limited success in persuading people to pay to download music, for example, and various music subscription schemes have not fared well. Also, to build market share, many companies have given away goods online that formerly would have been available only for a fee. The online financial services enterprises, for example, provide very detailed information about corporations, stocks, mutual funds, and other financial issues, and the ease with which consumers can pull up charts and analytical tools is quite remarkable. These services cost money in the past. Many newspapers and magazines are widely available online for free, though their printed counterparts still carry a subscription fee.

These tactics and e-commerce strategies have reinforced the consumer view that digital products distributed over the Internet should be free. They hint that the content itself is not worth much, and consumers are left with the message that digitally distributed information products should be essentially free to all. An important difference between digital information products and physical products is that the cost to create the first copy of a digital information product is high, but the marginal cost to create and distribute additional copies is absurdly low. Consumers know that that marginal cost is almost nil, so they resist attempts to charge for digital products delivered on the net. Creating business strategies that can recoup the initial high cost of creation, and educating customers that there has to be some economically viable plan in place to recover the initial cost, will not be easy. The workers, whoever they are and whatever role they play in this volatile value chain for digital products, will continue to have a rough economic ride ahead.

Business Models, Strategies, and Industry Competition

The 1990s was a phenomenal decade, one that not only closed out a millennium but also gave birth to a technology that many believe will be one of the most revolutionary in human history. Hyperbole aside, it is clear that the Internet created both extraordinary opportunity and blurred vision in the business world during those years, as the roller coaster ride of the markets amply demonstrates. During the height of frenzy, the tech-heavy NASDAQ exchange crossed the 5,000 mark. A little more than a year later, the index plunged to the 2,000 level, wiping out trillions in net worth.

The terms "new economy" and "old economy" described the business models that distinguished those companies that were getting on the Internet bandwagon from those that were either tied down by investments in physical assets or simply lacked the vision to see what the Internet might mean. Within the new economy were the Internet *pure plays*, the new companies that had little or no investment in existing inventories, warehouses, or commercial buildings, and whose strategy emphasized meeting unique online needs. Amazon.com was probably the most visible early example of a pure-play e-tailer. Thousands of others adopted the model, including the online eBay auction house, electronic marketplaces, CDNow, and online banks with no physical branches for customers to visit. The venture capital poured into these business startups, despite the fact that few startups ever turned a profit. On Wall Street and in university business schools, the valuation of these companies was almost a separate science, with heavy emphasis on total revenue, rather than on bottom-line profits, which were nonexistent, number of Web site visitors, or number of pages downloaded. A professor of finance told me at the time, "What else can we look at? They aren't making any money. They're just spending it."

Michael Porter of the Harvard Business School points out, in retrospect, that some of the blurred vision was due to distorted market signals that misled business leaders about the value of the companies, their business strategies, or their bottom lines. To some extent, this distortion was self-inflicted.[14] For example, the sales figures that people were using to valuate these companies were misleading and unreliable as indicators of a company's future success, partly because so many companies were giving away or subsidizing the purchase of their own products to gain market share. Buyers got a very good deal at the time, because they were obtaining products for free or well below the cost to make them.

Another ingredient in the distortions involved the way many of these startups embedded stock options and equity as part of their compensation packages, recruiting top talent for lower salaries than other companies were

---

[14] Porter, M. E. (2001). Strategy and the Internet. *Harvard Business Review, 79*(3), 62–80.

offering. This blurs the actual cost of doing business, and it also becomes a real cost to shareholders whose shares lose value.

THE FIVE FORCES MODEL

Business students are very familiar with Michael Porter's five forces model, widely used to analyze the structural attractiveness and competitiveness of different industries and to help business leaders develop strategies appropriate to the setting.[15] He proposed that the major forces that contribute to an industry's attractiveness include:

- The intensity of rivalry among existing competitors
- The barriers to entry for new competitors
- The threat of substitute products or services
- The bargaining power of suppliers
- The bargaining power of buyers.

For example, an industry is more attractive for existing players if new competitors have a difficult time getting into it, often because it requires considerable capital investment that the current competitors have already made. Another industry may be more competitive, and less attractive, if suppliers have a great deal of power. Oil executives eagerly press for new sources of oil because OPEC's power as a supplier makes their industry particularly competitive. The position of buyers, too, affects how competitive an industry may be. When buyers lack bargaining leverage, perhaps because it is relatively difficult for them to switch to a competitor's product, the industry is more attractive. In the proprietary world of mainframe computing, switching costs were historically extremely high, weakening the power of buyers. Once companies chose their platform, whether it was IBM, DEC, Hewlett-Packard, or some other brand, they began to acquire software, databases, applications, compatible hardware, networks, and other kinds of supporting infrastructure. It was all tied to the platform they chose, and the personnel the company hired or trained were also specialized in that platform. Sometimes years of training and experience were required to fully qualify someone to administer a mainframe database. The size of the investments in the proprietary IT infrastructure snowballed year after year, making it extremely costly and difficult to switch. Companies eventually began to demand more open architectures, interchangeable parts, and more compatibility and standardization. As a result, buyer power increased.

---

[15] Porter, M. E. (1980). *Competitive strategy: Techniques for analyzing industries and competitors*. New York: The Free Press.

FIVE FORCES IN THE INTERNET AGE: COMPETITION INTENSIFIES

How does the Internet affect the structural attractiveness of most industries? It offers a great many new opportunities; but how do the five forces that determine the structural attractiveness of particular industries play out? We have already seen that the Internet has added much frenetic activity to some types of business, but Porter proposes that, overall, the technology increases competitiveness and reduces attractiveness in most industries across the board.

For example, the reduction in information asymmetry we discussed earlier is one of the ingredients that raises the power of buyers, according to Porter's five forces model. This bolsters their bargaining power, adds to the intensity of competition, and makes the industry less attractive. With respect to barriers to entry, the Internet is also adding to the tension. Because corporations can now do much of their selling online, new entrants do not need to hire or train a sales force. In fact, one of the most extraordinary enabling features of the net is that any mom and pop shop can set up to sell online with very little capital, and their reach can potentially extend around the globe. Reduced switching costs also help lower the barriers to entry. It is not too costly to move the mouse about and click on a different vendor's "add to cart" button if the buyer perceives an advantage, even a slight one.

In the business-to-business arena, the Internet should also help reduce the barriers to entry for companies upstream, partly by reducing switching costs. As I mentioned, EDI has been an important development in the technology used to streamline B2B relationships, but the Internet is making this kind of relationship more "plug and play." Those large investments that were needed to launch an electronic relationship and to create customized program code and proprietary communications networks under EDI will be much reduced.

RIVALRY RISES, INDUSTRY LINES BLUR

The net has had the effect of increasing rivalry among firms, partly because the sheer number of firms competing in the same space has grown. With the breakdown of geographic barriers, firms compete against any company in the same business, regardless of where they may be located. This has dramatically affected higher education, because students can obtain degrees completely online from many institutions, and the geographic home base of that institution is irrelevant. Recently, when I released a request for proposals from companies interested in developing software for an educational CD-ROM, I received a proposal from a firm in Pune, India.

Rivalry has also increased because the boundaries among industries have blurred, and business leaders have great difficulty predicting where the next threat will come from. Amazon began as an online book seller, competing against the likes of Borders, Barnes and Noble, and the many smaller chains and independent stores. Soon it added related products, such as videos, CDs, small electronics, and software; thus, it began competing against the empires of Blockbuster, Tower Records, and CompUSA. It added Sears, Walmart, and Kmart to its list of competitors when it began selling home appliances, kitchenware, backyard grills, and picnic chests, and then Toys-R-Us when it added toys, games, and baby gear. It also offers an online auction for person-to-person selling, competing against eBay.

The New York Times foreign affairs correspondent Thomas Friedman, author of *The Lexus and the Olive Tree*, describes in vivid detail how the lines defining the space in which a particular business competes have become very blurry. In the past, a bank was a bank, and their CEOs did not lose sleep at night worrying about competition from, for example, a software company. Yet Microsoft has entered that arena with a variety of online financial services. The same company, widely known as the "software giant," also attempted to enter the real estate business, with an online service in which agents would receive less than the usual 6 percent commission. And Microsoft is not the only giant interested in moving into real estate. A featured link on www.realtor.com reads, "Keep Banks out of Real Estate – "The Big Grab." The intensity of competition increased not only because geographical barriers were breaking down, but also because the lines that separated industries from one another were redrawn.

Porter recognizes that not all of the Internet's effects are negative, nor are they mostly negative in some industries. Many companies, for example, gain more power over the channels they use to distribute their products because they now have more choices. A manufacturer can sell directly to consumers, and the lobbying that some industry associations are conducting to prevent this, which I described earlier, is an indication of how significant it may become. Overall, however, the Internet has made most industries more competitive and rivalries more intense and unpredictable.

The Workplace in the Middle

The workplace has not been immune from the Internet's effects on the business environment. All of the trends I described in this chapter form a context in which people work, build their careers, look for jobs, save for the future, and cope with pink slips. The context touches every aspect of the nature of the workplace, from its physical dimensions and architectural styles, to its psychological characteristics. Consider Frank T., an office worker in a large architectural firm, whose role is procurement manager. He works with many different suppliers to buy products his company needs, mostly office supplies and equipment. His productivity was greatly enhanced by the microcomputer on his desk, which appeared in the early 1980s. The PC replaced the video display terminal that had been there since he started working in 1974, and once he began using some of the software, he was amazed at the new kinds of tasks he could perform. He still has fond memories of the kudos he received when he created a report on office supply expenditures, complete with graphs, charts, and projections.

In the late 1980s, the company moved to larger quarters in the suburbs and also decided to use office landscaping rather than private offices. Frank was very dismayed by the longer commute, and though the "landscape" may have been attractive to an architect, his own cubicle's lack of status was troubling. But by the mid-1990s, the company had an Internet connection and his PC was one of the first to access it – mostly because he could now do a much better job of comparison shopping for supplies. He used email constantly to work with suppliers, and when the electronic marketplaces began to emerge, he was one of the first to use them to get the best prices for his company. He joined discussion forums for buyers and experimented with one of the auctions to unload some obsolete equipment. Despite the open-plan cubicles, he seems to see his fellow workers less and less and communicates more by email, even with those whose cubes are quite close. He once used his office email and instant messaging to communicate with family and friends but quit after he heard the company might be monitoring it.

His company was doing extremely well during the late 1990s, with many new office buildings for the dot-coms underway. The architects were especially enthusiastic because the young CEOs wanted innovation, large open spaces, team-oriented environments, and new features that would support their new organizational forms. However, things began to change when the downturn came and layoffs skyrocketed. Even some projects already underway were abandoned, and companies were seeking every possible way to reduce costs and increase profitability. Now Frank occasionally uses the Internet to check the online want ads.

How has the Internet transformed Frank's workplace, and how will those transformations proceed in the future? Frank's job is not what anyone would call high tech, but the Internet has had major effects on his working life anyway. In the foreground, the Internet created many new ways to do business that Frank uses daily. It changes the way he interacts with coworkers inside the company, with suppliers outside, and with other buyers around the country who can form their own community of practice, independent of any corporate ties. Further behind the scenes, the Internet is enabling changes that affect the kinds of workplaces people need, and even whether they need any stable physical location at all. It's creating an environment in which companies both experiment with new strategies and business models and rise and fall with breathtaking speed. The net is changing the value and need for different kinds of work, even of entire businesses and industries. Procurement, for example, is one of those business functions that may need far less human intervention or judgment in the future. As companies develop their electronic supply chains, low inventory will trigger automatic shipments from suppliers, purchased through software agents that scour the suppliers' prices and service agreements to find the best deals.

In the next chapter, we look more closely at the netcentric technologies and the ways in which they are being integrated into the workplace. Email was the killer Internet app, and it still is for most organizations. But there are many others that will contribute to the Internet's effects on the workplace, especially as the pipes to carry the bits of information grow.

2 The Netcentric Technologies Emerge

When Internet access began spreading to homes and businesses, the pace of innovation for net-related technologies quickened considerably. The introduction of the Mosaic browser began the launch of the World Wide Web, the technology that triggered the net's advance and acceptance throughout the world. However, many more technologies have been launched that affect the workplace and that link to Internet capabilities and resources.

In this chapter, we look at the Internet first as the trigger for a wave of change and compare it to previous technologies that have had similar broad-based effects on the way we live and work. We will see how the Internet's clever design features made it possible for inventors and developers to not only dream up but also implement a huge variety of new technologies. Next, we focus on the Internet itself as a technology, and we survey some of the most important advances and ancillaries that have emerged because of the net's existence. Together, these form the framework for the netcentric world in which we now find ourselves, and they have initiated a host of changes in organizational structures, working patterns, family relationships, and even the commute to work.

Waves of Technological Transformation

The scholars of many civilizations have been interested in charting cycles, especially long-term ones that might be used to predict the future. The Mayans, for example, proposed cycles for agricultural events that occurred every fifty-two years. Economists have examined many sources of data to find patterns in the last centuries, using prices, inflation, employment information, and whatever statistical aids are available. Minute details about the state of the current business cycle and predictions about when a new one will start are no longer just for economists. Nightly news programs feature these details for the public in their scrolling banners, providing viewers with updates on the tiniest changes in all the metrics used to assess the state of the economy, from the index of consumer confidence to the number of new housing starts.

One of the best known theories of economic cycles in recent times that involves technology comes from the Russian economist Nicolai Kondratiev, who relied on data from prices, wages, interest rates, foreign trade, and other sources since the late eighteenth century. He was less interested in the tiny ups and downs, and instead proposed a theory of "long waves," in which technology-driven cycles that affect the swings in economic indices occurred about every fifty to fifty-four years. The technology involved in these cycles began with the Industrial Revolution, with the introduction of mechanization. The upswing for the next wave during the Victorian age coincided with the spread of steam power and railroads, and also with the telegraph and its lines that followed the railroad tracks. The third fifty-year cycle, peaking in the 1920s, was associated with the growing use of steel and electricity. The fourth was a postwar prosperity that benefited from access to vast energy sources and mass production.

Why do these waves start, and how does their timing relate to technological innovation? Gerhard O. Mensch analyzed the time frames and clusters of basic innovations and found their peaks generally coincided with these waves, occurring at or near the bottom of each cycle.[16] Each time, the burst of innovation occurred around the time of an economic depression. It seems that a groundswell of new thinking during a depression can gather momentum and lead to new inventions. Those inventions can then become the tools for expansion as the next wave begins.

THE NETCENTRIC FIFTH WAVE

If we can rely on the continuation of the Kondratiev cycles, the heart of the fifth wave is computerization and netcentricity. There is no question that these technologies triggered explosions of innovation that are gathering momentum, changing organizational structures, and altering many components of the business landscape, as we saw in the last chapter. Nevertheless, grasping the shape, direction, and speed of a wave is very difficult from the point of view of the swimmers inside it, and debates are common –

---

[16] Mensch, G. O. (1982). The co-evolution of technology and work-organization. In G. Mensch & R. J. Niehaus (Eds.), *Work, organizations, and technological change*. New York: Plenum Press.

especially about timing. Are we at the end of the fifth wave, in the middle or is the wave just getting underway?

One reason the timing question can be difficult to answer is that the technologies that start a wave can affect their speed of diffusion. For example, from its introduction into the market, it took thirty-eight years for radio to reach fifty million users, and sixteen years for PCs to achieve the same benchmark. However, the Internet diffused much more quickly, extending to fifty million users in just four years. This kind of explosive growth was unknown for previous waves.

The nature of the technologies that trigger a wave varies from one wave to the next, and their characteristics can affect what that wave looks like. Netcentric technologies share many similarities with technologies that helped trigger previous cycles, but they also differ in important respects. The telegraph, for instance, was a revolutionary invention that dramatically changed the nature and speed of communication. It was an important force in Kondratiev's second wave because people and businesses could transmit information within minutes rather than days or weeks and messages could be sent at any time to multiple recipients. This represented a qualitative leap in communication efficiency compared to regular mail and Pony Express.

Initially, this basic innovation in communication was not appreciated. Tom Standage, author of *The Victorian Internet*, which details the history of the telegraph,[17] points out that most thought the device was more of a conjuring trick than a means of communication. When Samuel Morse attempted to obtain funding from the U.S. Congress to advance the technology in 1842, one representative ridiculed the invention by comparing it to a funding request for mesmerism. The Congress did provide some funding eventually, but by a narrow margin and with considerable skepticism. The Internet, in contrast, was supported with government funding from the beginning. Once it caught on, and businesses learned of the advantages they could obtain through use of the telegraph, it spread quickly. From 1846, when the only line in the United States was the experimental one that Morse built between Baltimore and Washington, to 1852, the telegraph network grew more than 600-fold, with 23,000 miles of line in operation, and another 10,000 miles under construction.

Alexander Graham Bell received the patent for the telephone in 1876, entitling his patent "Improvements in Telegraphy." This was far more than a slight improvement, however, and it became one of the basic innovations

---

[17] Standage, T. (1998). *The Victorian Internet*. New York: Berkeley Books.

that helped launch the next wave. The major advantages over the telegraph became obvious quickly. It required no skilled operator to transmit signals with a telegraph key using Morse code, and its transmission rates were faster. Most important of all, it allowed people to communicate in a much more natural fashion, using their own voices. By 1880, more than 30,000 telephones were in use.

Though the timing of this fifth wave is debatable, the fundamental innovations that are triggering it are not. The next wave has, at its core, the computer and Internet technologies. What distinguishes this wave from the previous ones in terms of its technological driving forces?

The Internet at the Core: Design Principles

The Internet's infrastructure can combine many technologies that were formerly separate, and can support new ones that were never before possible. It can be used to distribute broadcast images and also as a telephone. It can distribute the organization's newsletter via email, and it can provide remote access to a virtual whiteboard for group presentations and discussions involving people from anywhere on the planet. From a ski lift or from a beach, employees can check their email, see whether their client placed any orders, or track the status of a package they sent to headquarters.

At the core of this diversity is the Internet infrastructure itself, which is an interconnected set of computer networks around the globe and the telecommunications links among them, creating what appears to be a single, uniform network. The original architects of the Internet embedded a number of design principles that helped to make this a revolutionary technology and also a phenomenal innovation, one that could support incredible growth in number of users.[18] These principles make the Internet somewhat different from earlier technologies.

HOURGLASS ARCHITECTURE

The most important design feature for the Internet was the "hourglass" architecture (see Figure 2.1). The way to achieve flexibility and simplicity was to make the work the Internet actually did relatively simple, and also very open. The network provides only a very basic level of service – transmitting data in the form of bits using standardized protocols. The real "intelligence" of the network is at both ends of the hourglass, which represent the service

[18] Computer Science and Telecommunications Board, National Research Council. (2001). *The Internet's coming of age.* Washington, DC: National Academy Press.

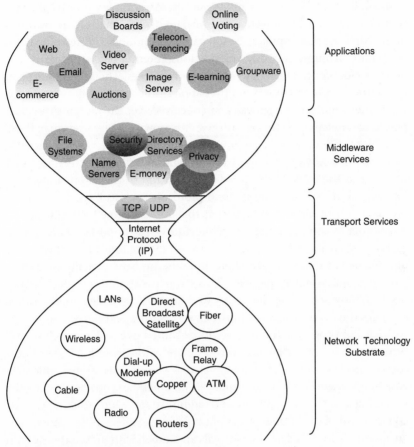

Figure 2.1. The Internet's Hourglass Architecture.
Adapted from Computer Science and Telecommunications Board (CSTB), National Research Council (1994). Realizing the Information Future: The Internet and Beyond. Washington, DC: National Academy Press.

providers and users on one end and the transmission media and routing infrastructure on the other. The innovation occurs at the *edges* of the network, rather than in the center, and as long as the innovative applications or services use the standard protocols to transmit data, they can continue to grow and invent.

In the bottom half of the hourglass, for example, various communication technologies were implemented well after the Internet was up and running on copper telephone lines, but they could be integrated into the network as long as the transmissions themselves followed the rules. Examples included asynchronous transfer mode (ATM), frame relay, and the use of the radio spectrum to transmit wirelessly. We also see explosive innovation in applications that were never imagined when the Internet was first designed, those that populate the top part of the hourglass. Streaming video and audio, e-commerce, worldwide auctions, Internet-based telephony, and desktop videoconferencing are just a few examples. Though an old timer in Internet terms, email was another application that was not envisioned when the Internet's design was first conceived, yet the design easily supported its implementation and astonishing growth. Many users may think of the World Wide Web as synonymous with the Internet, but in fact this was another innovation supported by the hourglass architecture, one that occurred in the early 1990s. It is layered on top of the Internet and uses its own set of evolving standardized protocols such as hypertext transfer protocol or http, those familiar letters that appear before Web addresses.

Another reason the hourglass architecture was so important in creating a platform to spark so much innovation was that the innovators themselves did not need to know much about how the network actually worked to add new applications at the edges. Also, the network administrators did not need to know what the innovators were up to. A provider could create a specialized database of journal articles with search and retrieve functions without knowing how the bits would be routed over the network to and from the end users or having to coordinate with network administrators for technical support or changes to network design. This layered approach, which separates transport from application, unleashes considerable creativity and also unburdens the network administrator who would always be concerned about how one new application might affect all the others that are out there. At the edges, a great deal can happen without interfering with the Internet's operation, including the introduction of new kinds of devices that attach to the net in different ways. As you will see later in this chapter, the wireless devices are some of those innovations at the edge, and they have introduced considerable change in the workplace.

The hourglass architecture makes the Internet different from the public-switched telephone network, and makes it far more adaptable and supportive of new ideas. The telephone network was designed for relatively dumb edge devices – telephones – with the intelligence built into the central facilities. For decades, the phone itself did little more than to provide a way to transmit a series of numbers, and to ring. After the breakup of AT&T and the introduction of market competition, a number of new capabilities were added to phones, such as answering machines, speed dialing, cordless capabilities, and in-house intercoms. However, these add-ons pale in comparison to what happened in the world of the Internet. As a platform for creative innovation, it is unsurpassed.

ROBUSTNESS

Another critical design decision involved robustness, which means that the Internet should be able to accommodate changes such as lost hosts, dropped messages, broken edge devices, changes in routes, or any number of unpredictable events that can occur in a network with no central control or authority and much innovation at the edges. In the imperfect world of telecommunications, the Internet was built so that the sender of information should take a conservative route in packaging its information, conforming to standards as explicitly as possible. The receiver, however, should be very liberal and should interpret whatever comes along as broadly as possible. If you ever designed a Web page yourself, writing your own HTML, you know that your Web page will be received even though your code has scattered coding errors. This is an example of robustness in action.

The way packets of information are routed from one place to the next illustrates another example of the net's robust design. Each packet is transmitted separately and may take a different route from that of its predecessor if one of the routers suddenly goes down or traffic congestion appears. When packets can reach their destination along any number of routes, they are much less vulnerable to a failure at any single point on the network.

LACK OF CENTRAL CONTROL AND THE REWARDS OF INTERCONNECTION

Design decisions spring not only from the architects' notions of what will work best for the application but also from the values of the architects themselves, most of whom were scientists and engineers who treasured openness, research, sharing of information, and broad access. Another key design decision was that there should be no central authority to control the Internet's evolution or access to it. Even the organizations that develop standards consider them voluntary. Interconnection is its own reward, and much of the Internet's value for workplace productivity, information sharing, marketing, communications, and commerce comes from the *network effect*. This principle states that the value in connecting people and services is proportional to the square of the number of connected people. Complying with standards that help make this happen is the way to exponentially grow the net's value.

Although the design principles of the Internet itself emphasized the lack of central control, the businesses that launch services and applications are often at odds with the principle. They seek greater market share and sometimes introduce proprietary and incompatible services that limit access to their own users. The spat between Microsoft and AOL over the instant messenger services illustrates the tension between openness and proprietary control. AOL offers an instant messaging (IM) application that lets users see which buddies are online at any time and send a quick text based message to him or her. Commercial help desks, sales people, and even librarians began using the service as well, so that end-users could quickly send a text message and receive a reply. Based on the network effect, the value of instant messenger services rises dramatically as more users take advantage of it, but AOL was unwilling to allow Microsoft's IM users to talk to the AOL IM users for fear Microsoft would capture their users in other markets.[19] The result was that the two pools of IM users could only talk to others within their own pool, unless they installed both applications.

AN EXCEPTION TO LACK OF CENTRAL CONTROL: ADDRESSES

The three most important characteristics of real property are location, location, and location. Virtual property is not that different, and location is highly valued. The one exception to the Internet's lack of central control involves the assignment of addresses and names. The underlying communications protocol is called TCP/IP, for transmission control protocol/Internet protocol, and each device connected to the net must have a unique IP address. The uniqueness of these addresses makes it possible for packets to be transmitted correctly, so it was not possible to leave this in the hands of the users or devices at the edge.

These addresses consist of a sequence of four numbers separated by dots, such as 128.40.33.39. The hierarchical structure supports about 4.3 billion unique addresses, which seemed like quite enough at the time. Nevertheless, the world's entire population surpassed 6 billion in 1999. Although no one expects each human to need a unique address any time soon, the pressure for additional addresses is coming from another source. Continued miniaturization of chips is leading to a push to embed them in anything people might want to track and connect to the Internet. Analysts predict a big spike in the demand for IP addresses as chips are installed in cars, trucks, cell phones, toys, watches, or people.[20] An upgrade to the Internet Protocol itself is underway (IPv6), which will vastly increase the number of unique addresses available and make other improvements as well.

The unique numerical addresses usually map to a unique domain name that is easier for people to remember, such as www.myhome.com. In 1998, the Internet Corporation for Assigned Names and Numbers (ICANN) took

---

[19] Guglielmo, C. (2001). Microsoft, AOL, wrangle over IM, digital media. *Interactive Week, 8*(23), 13.

[20] Anthes, G. H. (2003). Internet Protocol Version 6. *Computerworld, 37*(3), 33. Retrieved March 2, 2003, from Business Source Premier Database.

on the responsibility of managing the technical architecture for the domain name system and the allocation of IP addresses.

Managing addresses and domain names can be difficult for many reasons, because prime locations in cyberspace have become valuable commodities. Contentious debates arise over who should be allocated how much address space and what criteria should be used to assign (or deny) domain names. The practice of "cybersquatting," for example, became a thorny problem in the 1990s. Individuals speculated in domain names, registering those they thought might become very valuable in the future. The names often contained company trademarks, and when the company tried to register it for themselves they were asked to pay a kingly sum to the speculator. The Anti-Cybersquatting Consumer Protection Act was passed in the United States in 1999 to prevent this kind of speculation, but domain name assignment remains a sensitive area. ICANN has also established a "Uniform Domain-Name Dispute Resolution Policy" that can be used to settle arguments over who should get particular names.[21]

Technologies at the Edge

The technologies that emerged during the netcentric wave have had dramatic effects on business models, on our workplaces, and on our working lives. They have changed the timing of our workplace interactions and of their volume. They have changed the fifty-foot rule that dominated in organizations as a yardstick to estimate which colleagues would tend to interact and work efficiently as teams. People tended to run into each other if their offices were less than fifty feet apart, and that influenced their teamwork. The technologies have also influenced how managers manage, and how employees voice their concerns. Let's take a look at some of these technologies at the edge that have been especially important in transforming the workplace.

CHANGES AT THE DESKTOP

As the netcentric wave emerged, the physical configuration of the desktop has seen fewer changes than the applications themselves, but it has seen a few changes that affect the workplace. In the late 1970s, some businesses began buying stand-alone microcomputers, even though very little commercial software was available to run on them. A notable exception was

[21] Internet Corporation for Assigned Names and Numbers (ICANN) Web site. Retrieved March 1, 2003, from http://www.icann.org/udrp/

VisiCalc, the ground-breaking electronic spreadsheet program and great-grandfather of modern versions such as Excel or Lotus 123. Many businesses purchased an Apple microcomputer in the late 1970s simply to run this single program, which was so useful in doing calculations of the "what if" type.

In the 1980s, organizations began retiring the familiar terminal and keyboard that interacted only with the mainframes to which it was connected. They began installing PCs, especially after 1981 when IBM released its first microcomputer. IBM, after all, stands for International Business Machines, and their entry into the microcomputer business was a strong signal that the machines were not toys. These monochrome models could function as terminals to connect to the mainframes, but they also had significant processing power of their own, including some storage capability for local files.

The next physical change in the desktop environment was the introduction of devices that permitted direct manipulation of graphical objects such as the sketch pad and light pen. The mouse, however, invented by Douglas Engelbart in the 1960s, was the device that eventually became almost universal on workplace computers. He called it an "x-y position indicator," and it became the means by which people could interact with the computer in a graphical way, by moving the cursor around and clicking mouse buttons rather than by typing commands.[22]

Another addition to the microcomputer that occurred in some organizations was the support for multimedia, which meant speakers and, in some cases, microphones. The speakers were not welcome everywhere, and many corporations even toss them out because they can be distracting to nearby workers. Tiny eyeball-shaped video cameras have also been added to the frame of monitors to support desktop interactive video conferencing.

Although most desktops in offices continue to use the microcomputer, with the familiar monitor, desktop or tower CPU, keyboard, and mouse, some have taken advantage of a netcentric approach. This approach relies on "thin clients," meaning that the device at the desktop needs fewer accessories or capabilities, because the functions they once performed can be handled by servers. On the office desktop, the device typically has a monitor, mouse, and keyboard, but the large CPU is missing. Instead, the user runs applications from the server and stores all files on the server's disks, so no local file storage is needed.

---

[22] Myers. B. A. (1998). A brief history of human computer interaction technology. *ACM Interactions, 5*(2), 44–54.

Some of these devices are especially designed for business settings that need special support for *hot desks*. These are desks with computer and network connections that can be shared by any number of employees. With the growth of telecommuting and the need to conserve office space, many organizations offer their employees shared facilities instead of dedicated desks or offices. Moving everyone's files onto a server and prohibiting local storage saves some space at the desktop, and it also provides other advantages. Employees don't have to worry about backing up their own locally stored files, because the server's disks would be backed up routinely. The thin clients also reduce other kinds of problems from the standpoint of managers, such as the tendency of employees to install their own software, some of which may be illegal, incompatible with corporate systems, or not work-related. If the thin clients lack any local file storage – even a CD-ROM drive – they also reduce the possibility that employees might download sensitive information and walk out the door with it on a floppy disk or CD. The security over data theft provided by the absence of disk drives was somewhat short-lived, however. Storage technologies continued to evolve, and tiny, portable storage devices became available that workers can plug into commonly available ports on the computer.

Some people who use these hot desks with thin clients are very pleased with the arrangement, especially if they can quickly tell the server who they are so the server can launch their personalized desktops. For example, swiping a smart card at such a desk can authenticate the user and launch that employee's favorite settings, files, calendars, and recent work. Others, though, object to losing their personal PC and its flexibility. They see it more as a step backward to a mainframe-like environment in which employees' activities were tightly controlled and they had little say about the applications they could use.

The wireless boom has affected many office desktop environments as well. Many people who are on the road a great deal choose to trade in the desktop computer for a laptop that can be docked in a station on the desk when they work in the office, so they can connect directly to the corporate network. Rather than having to transfer recent files, the employee can continue to work on the same computer whether in the home office or on the road. People who use Palm Pilots or other personal digital assistants (PDA) may add one additional gadget to their desktop – a cradle. This lets them back up whatever is on the tiny information appliance to their hard drive and synchronize their calendar with their office scheduling system.

Though a few items may have changed, the desktops of most office workers do not look very much different from the way they looked a couple of decades ago. They are still dominated by a monitor, keyboard, and mouse, though the flat-panel, slimmed-down monitors have helped reduce the bulky versions that hogged so much room. Most desks are still covered with what some hoped would soon become obsolete: papers, folders, envelopes, letters, pens, and pencils. The coffee cup is still there, and the telephone is still a separate device with its own keypad and usage instructions. Yet appearances can be deceiving. The tools that underlie the netcentric age are not obvious physically, but they have important effects on how we work and what kind of work we do.

COMMUNICATIONS AND COLLABORATIVE TECHNOLOGIES

The network effect has played out most dramatically in the communications arena. Originally, the Internet was designed for computer communication rather than for human communication, especially to allow researchers to log on to computers in distant locations, run programs on those remote computers, and share technical resources. Email among the scientists was not on the radar screen. However, Ray Tomlinson wrote a primitive email software program in 1971 and the program quickly caught on. It was awkward and difficult to use, but the application was very compelling because it supported scientific collaboration in ways that had not before been possible.[23]

Email has become the Internet's "killer app," the application that is so popular that it, alone, can drive people to buy a computer and get connected. This fact demonstrates how important the net has become for staying in touch, but email is not the only technology that supports communications and collaborative work. I mentioned instant messaging (IM) before, and this technology enables people to communicate in real time using text-based chat windows. Its use in corporate environments is growing rapidly, and in many cases, the IT department did nothing to install it or encourage its use. A vice president at a Boston firm pointed out, "Most senior executives don't even know that instant messaging is happening. Once they realize . . . they move from denial to anger because they realize they have no control of applications on their system."[24] Since many senior people associate instant messaging with teenagers and wasting time, they can be

[23] Hardy, I. (1996). *The evolution of ARPANET email.* Retrieved October 24, 2001, from University of California at Berkeley Web site: http://server.berkeley.edu/virtual-berkeley/email_history

[24] MacSweeney, G. (2003). R U Ready 4 IM? *Insurance and Technology, 28,* 36+. Retrieved March 1, 2003, from Business Source Premier Database.

quite resistant to the possibility of productive use. In fact, as I will discuss in more detail in a later chapter, IM has special characteristics that can make it an extremely useful tool in the workplace. Unlike email, it signals the "awareness of presence." It lets you know whether the person is actually around so you don't waste time asking questions of people who aren't in their office.

Another intriguing innovation in the collaboration area was the introduction of *interactive whiteboards*, which allow people to share a virtual whiteboard for graphical presentations. Not all information can be easily communicated with the keyboard and ASCII text, and the whiteboards allow people to draw diagrams, circle important points, write symbols, or make notes next to another person's drawings. Any well-equipped conference room has at least one large whiteboard, and the electronic version serves a similar purpose. Engineers, physicists, and others who need to communicate with mathematical symbols (such as ϕ, Π, Σ, $\subseteq$, λ, or $\cong$) would barely be able to collaborate electronically at all without tools like the whiteboard.

Collaborative technologies have expanded to support an entire portfolio of software to meet a workgroup's needs, including whiteboards, chat areas, discussion rooms, knowledge bases, interactive video, file-sharing spaces, and collaborative document editing. As we see in the chapter on virtual teams, these tools can be used to support a workgroup regardless of the members' geographic location. Email is usually the foundation, but the other tools supplement and enrich the interactions of the workgroup. Research departments have sprung up in universities to expand knowledge relating to *computer-supported collaborative work* (CSCW), and the field has become an important contributor to our understanding of the workplace in the netcentric age.

A special kind of collaborative technology goes by names such as groupware or group decision-making software systems (GDSS). Most of these systems were initially designed for face-to-face meetings in which each participant had access to a computer. They support anonymous brainstorming, voting, ranking, and many other features that help work groups organize their ideas and participate on a more equal basis, without the status effects that are common in face-to-face meetings. We discuss the group dynamics that emerge during these systems in a later chapter.

Communication for employees can extend outside the working group, and the Internet can be used for communication to anyone who has access, not just for those in the same company. One of the important developments during the 1990s was the emergence of *communities of practice* with participants from anywhere on the planet, drawn together by a common interest in a particular subject. The linking thread for many of these virtual communities is a professional field, or an obscure branch of one, such as C++ programming, cost accounting, genetic engineering, linguistics, or the biology of bats. A person who runs an e-commerce Web site for a particular corporation built with a specialized software tool, for example, might have more in common with a counterpart in another corporation who knows the ins and outs of the same set of software tools than they would with the marketing manager down the hall. If the person runs into an undocumented software bug, there is probably no one in the company who can help at all, but that person can turn to his or her community of practice for help. Mailing lists, organizational Web sites, and discussion forums support these communities.

These professionally oriented communities that span corporate and organizational boundaries have blossomed, though sometimes tension exists. Corporate loyalties and professional interest can sometimes conflict, especially because the communities foster considerable information sharing. A manager might view such sharing as leaks and consider an employee who actively helps competitors in this way as a time waster at best and disloyal at worst.

INFORMATION DISSEMINATION AND RETRIEVAL

The Internet and the World Wide Web created possibilities for workplace information dissemination and retrieval that far exceed what any in-house newsletter or employee handbook could ever accomplish. This kind of information is not generally intended to be public, but the ease of creating Web pages that can be easily accessed inside the corporation, and also outside by employees from home or on the road, became an important enabler for organizational communications. *Intranets* – the corporate Web sites intended for employees only – quickly gained popularity in the mid-1990s. The corporate intranet has become the starting place on the Web for many people, and organizations have struggled to make this into a welcoming home that provides workplace information, news, discussions, birthday greetings, software tools, and access to corporate data.

Technically, there is little difference between an intranet and a publicly accessible Web site except that it typically resides behind a layer of security to prevent nonemployees from entering. Functionally, an intranet can aggregate and organize an enormous amount of information important to employees and make updates instantly available to everyone. Organizations have used their intranets in a variety of ways, including as a free-for-all for employee discussions and personal pages. They grew so fast that many lacked thoughtful governance or organization, so some became a kind of "Wild West" in which anything goes.

By the late 1990s, *portal* became the buzzword and simple corporate intranets began to evolve in that direction. Unfortunately, the term came to mean a great many things so there is much confusion about what a portal actually is. In the context of internal corporate communications, the *enterprise portal* is the grandchild of the intranet. The information technology research organization called Gartner Group identifies three major features of the portal[25]:

- Aggregates content and delivery of information relevant to the audience.
- Provides support for collaboration and community services.
- Offers access to services and applications for the target audience, delivered in a highly personalized manner.

To some extent, the earlier intranets did these things, but to expand the capabilities of the intranet much new software has been developed. In fact, more than 100 companies leaped into the market, offering various kinds of portal technology and adding to the confusion for managers and intranet designers.

One key feature of the portal software offerings was support for the *single sign-on* for each employee, one that would authenticate the user for many different kinds of applications that had separate logins in the past. Most employees have numerous logins and passwords at work, and each new application may require yet another username and password. The reason for this is that security systems have typically been built into the application, so each one has its own set of authenticated users who are granted access to specific capabilities within the application. For example, you might have separate logins for your network, for the corporate intranet, for your email, for the accounting system, and for your company's marketing data. When you log in to your network, your login identifies which directories you can access and what you can do with the files in them. When you log in to your accounting system, your login identifies which screens you can see and what kinds of data you can add, delete, or edit.

Creating a single sign-on that would authenticate you and all your access capabilities across all of these applications is not a trivial task. It is an

---

[25] Phifer, G. (2000). Management update: Do you really know what the term 'portal' means? InSide Gartner Group, October 18, 2000.

important one for organizations, though, partly because the more user-names and passwords you have, the less able you are to commit them to memory. You are then more likely to write them all on Post-it® notes and paste them onto your monitor, creating a security problem. Also, the single sign-on makes it easier to add or delete the access capabilities of new employees or ones that leave.

From the employee's point of view, a single sign-on for all Internet services – not just the work-related ones – would seem, on the surface, to be a great advantage. Now, people are asked to create user IDs and passwords for dozens, perhaps hundreds, of different services, from their online banking to their records at the motor vehicle administration. In the interest of profiling customers and Web site visitors, many services where you do not maintain any personal account prompt you to create a user ID and password anyway, so they can track your activity and present information and ads that are more customized based on your previous behavior. Services such as Microsoft Passport or Sun One have attempted to become the gateways for such a single sign-on, at least for participating sites and services, but concerns about trust and privacy are very great.

Another new feature offered by portal technology is the ability for employees to personalize their gateway to the vast resources lying behind. Rather than opening the browser with the generic "Welcome to Company X Intranet," with the same news of the day and links to a variety of applications on the front page, employees can design their own entry page and identify their own *channels*. Each channel can contain information and links to resources that are most important to them. For example, a marketing manager might choose one channel that presents a graph summarizing real-time marketing data from the corporate database, another that lists today's corporate headline news, and a third that continually updates their company's price on the stock market. Portals can include channels that aggregate external as well as internal information, so the manager might dedicate a small piece of screen real estate for the local weather, drawn from an online weather service.

EXTRANETS AND THE SUPPLY CHAIN

The Internet, with its standardized transmission protocols and globally accessible Web-based applications, has been the major force in the emergence of another kind of netcentric technology. Just as intranets enabled companies to more easily distribute information and interact with employees, extranets are doing the same thing for the company's external partners, including their customers and suppliers.

An *extranet* refers to the use of Internet technology to serve an extended enterprise, including customers, suppliers, or other partners. It is typically behind a firewall, just as an intranet usually is, and closed to the public (a "closed user group"), but is open to the selected partners, unlike a pure intranet. Information dissemination is a key reason to launch an extranet, but there are many others that have created considerable advantages for the companies that use them. For example, a supplier may be granted direct access to a customer's inventory database and may be authorized to ship products whenever the inventory reaches a certain low point. This extranet application can mean, for example, that no one at the customer's location needs worry about the supply of inkjet paper, or fill out orders when new paper is needed. Running out of paper would be a thing of the past. Also, allocating warehouse space to hold a large inventory of paper would not be necessary. Dell Computer uses this kind of extranet to manage its PC parts' inventories so they never have to stock more than a few days' worth of parts.

Granting access to operational data to customers through Web-based interfaces is another extranet function, one that can be very valuable. People can track the movements of their shipped packages very precisely, for example. Each time a package's bar code is scanned during shipping, the information on its location is entered into a database, and that information can be viewed by both shipper and recipient.

Convergence toward the Web's user interface is not difficult to understand, for intranets, extranets, and applications in general. It is easy to use and accessible from any computer with a browser and net connection. Once you learn how to use a few buttons and understand what links are, you can usually make your way around almost any Web site, even if clumsily. Its ease of use is partly because it represents a highly standardized front end – a contrast from older interfaces that required end users to learn idiosyncratic navigation schemes, new icons, and new processes with each new application. I recall a client–server application that attempted to use "user-friendly" icons on buttons for functions such as print, save, edit, search, and go to next page. One tiny picture nestled on the menu bar showed a red and white life preserver ring, and I asked several of my colleagues what they thought might happen if they clicked that button. One said, "It will bring up the help screen." Another said it would probably go back to an earlier version of the data, ignoring whatever was entered most recently and "saving" you from saving your mistakes. A third didn't recognize the icon as a life preserver at all – she said it must be a button to change the color of the font she was using to red, for emphasis. Inconsistent and puzzling user interfaces add up to long learning curves, mistakes, and lowered productivity.[26]

The advantage of the Web as a user interface is driving another software
trend – "webification" of the interfaces to the older legacy systems.[27] A range
of software tools became available to help IT staff accomplish this, so that
people could use their Web browsers to access live corporate data from any
computer that had Internet access rather than loading special client software
onto their computers. As of 2000, more than 70 percent of the corporate
data still resided inside legacy systems, so this webification effort was very
fruitful.

WIRELESS TECHNOLOGIES

Remarkable innovation has been occurring in the wireless category of netcentric technologies, facilitated by that hourglass architecture that puts few
restrictions on the actual means of transmission. If we can use telephone
wires, coaxial cable, or fiber to transmit information using TCP/IP, then
why not electromagnetic waves?

Despite the obvious disadvantage of tiny screen size, some analysts predict that the cell phone will become the most prevalent means of accessing
the Internet, outstripping the microcomputer in a short time. In some ways,
the mobile Internet access market may be in the same phase that land-line
Internet access was in, in 1995, poised on the brink of an explosive growth
phase.[28] The Internet-enabled cell phone may also be in a position similar to
the telephone, which was initially conceived as a "speaking telegraph." Although PCs abound in industrialized countries, they are far less common in
many parts of the world, and certainly more difficult to use and expensive to
buy compared to a phone. The cell phone with Internet capabilities may be
a means to distribute Internet access far wider than has been possible in the
past. This kind of optimism may have prompted the billions spent by network operators around the world to obtain licenses to run third-generation
(3G) wireless networks, which involve advanced technology that supports
much greater data speeds than the current wireless networks do.

Wireless technologies are in a very fragmented state now, with many
types of devices on the market using a variety of connection strategies, often

---

[26] In fact, the designers intended the button to signal "save."

[27] Bajgoric, N. (2001). Internet technologies for improving data access. *Information Systems Management, 18*(3), 30–42. Retrieved January 15, 2002, from EBSCO
Database.

[28] The Internet, untethered [Electronic version]. (2001). *The Economist, 361*(8243),
3. Retrieved February 1, 2002, from EBSCO Database.

incompatible with one another. They can be grouped into three general categories, based largely on the distance the signal needs to travel: personal area, local area, and wide area.[29]

In the wireless personal area network arena, a key goal is to develop ways for devices to synchronize and interact with one another without short-run cables. A technology called Bluetooth is an important ingredient here, and many predict that it will replace a good portion of the cabling infrastructure that clutters office desks, connecting computers to printers, personal digital assistants, and cell phones.

For local area networks, wireless technologies offer another set of attractions, especially for laptop users. Wireless access points can be placed in various locations of a building, and those with laptops and wireless LAN cards can log in to the network from any nearby location. This is becoming very popular for public spaces that would be difficult to configure with data jacks, such as large conference rooms, libraries, airports, and outdoor patios or gardens. Office workers can take their laptops to the balcony and enjoy some sunshine as they continue to access the network. Wireless LANs are also becoming popular in homes, particularly for people who have a high-speed Internet connection and more than one computer, but don't want to punch holes in their walls for the wiring.

Wide area wireless networks offer many different opportunities for the workplace, including the Internet-enabled cell phones and personal digital assistants. Retrieving your email from your PDA while waiting in line at the airport is not difficult with these devices, and we discuss the implications of this kind of anywhere/anytime access in a later chapter. The speed of connection is typically slow, but these devices work well for simple text.

The "last mile" has been an obstacle to the delivery of high-speed Internet access, especially to remote areas. Wireless wide area networks offer opportunities here as well. It is very expensive to deploy new wiring to every office or residence, but constructing towers with transmitters that can service wider areas is more feasible. Satellites can also be used to serve large geographic areas. In Alaska, for example, satellites are being used to provide Internet connectivity to libraries, schools, and municipalities in remote areas of the state.

Though wireless technology is still in a fragmented state, the drive to develop the capabilities is compelling. Becoming untethered from the desktop

---

[29] Richardson, P. (2001). Personal to global: Wireless technologies, 2005–2010. Gartner Group Dataquest Perspective, Feburary 23, 2001. Retrieved November 3, 2001, from DataQuest.

can offer considerable advantages, though it can also introduce problems for people trying to balance work and home lives, as we will see in the next chapter.

INFORMATION APPLIANCES

The microcomputer is a multipurpose device, one that can handle many different kinds of chores, and it has been dominant as the way to connect to the Internet. However, as you have already seen, many other kinds of devices can access the Internet, and the term *information appliance* is used to identify them. There is no consensus about what an information appliance is, except that it has an Internet connection and is not a microcomputer or server. The netcentric thin clients and wireless devices I mentioned earlier fall into this category, and the term covers many other innovations, including TVs, eyeglasses, watches, copiers, and many other things to which an IP address might be applied.

In the mid-1990s, the high cost of the microcomputer led some man-ufacturers to introduce lower cost single-purpose information appliances that would allow users to surf the Web, send and receive email, and not much more. The TV was pressed into service as a Web-surfing information appliance, followed by the PDAs and cell phones.

The development of wearable computers is an active area for research in another kind of information appliance. The MIThril project at MIT, for example, is focusing on a lightweight, context-sensitive design involving "memory glasses" that clip to the user's own glasses and a vest containing the equipment.[30] The name MIThril comes from J. R. R. Tolkien's *Hobbit* and *Lord of the Rings*. The light silvery steel was made into a tunic by the elves and Frodo wore it under his clothing for protection.

Copiers and fax machines are getting access to IP in businesses, especially to enable office workers to send jobs to these devices from their desktops. A print run for the copier, for example, can be sent from anywhere in the world in digital format and then printed, sorted, collated, and stapled at the location where the documents are needed.

Innovations for the home are on the horizon as well, as appliances get their own Internet connections and the home network expands to incorpo-rate security systems, lighting, televisions, sprinkler systems, and kitchen appliances. Some vendors are now promoting the Internet refrigerator.

---

[30] DeVaul, R. W., Schwartz, S. J., & Pentland, A. S. (2001). MIThril: Context-aware computing for daily life. May 16, 2001. Retrieved October 28, 2001, from the Massachusetts Institute of Technology Media Laboratory Web site: http://lcs.www.media.mit.edu/projects/wearables/mithril/mithril.pdf

Observing that the refrigerator door, covered in magnets and notes, has been "information central" for many homes, refrigerator manufacturers are adding a flat-panel display to the doors and connecting it to the net. Notes entered onto this display would be accessible from any location.

Even when the object itself might not be an obvious tool for information access, it might benefit from an onboard chip for tracking purposes. Initiatives are underway to make just about anything large enough to carry a tiny chip an information appliance of sorts, with its own unique address so that it can identify itself to scanners, report its own history, and store new information. E-tags on cars already use this kind of auto-identification technology, and many more uses are on the horizon, such as on cereal boxes and other grocery store items, if chip cost can be reduced enough. In a netcentric world, just about anything can have an IP address and become interconnected.

Whether everything should be interconnected is another question. The life span of many of these information appliances may be short, and some have already vanished due to disinterest. Sony pulled the plug on its eVilla desktop Web-surfing appliance only two months after it was released. Other manufacturers have also retired their offerings and are reevaluating the information appliance market. A few will probably enjoy immense success, however. The significant point is that the Internet's design principles allowed these innovations to occur at breathtaking speed, regardless of their potential or lack of it. The market will determine which ones survive.

Security and Netcentric Technologies

Although security was an important concern during the early development of the Internet, particularly for military and sensitive research applications, the approach that was taken did not keep up with the changes in the net's role over time. The early approach relied heavily on the use of encryption during transmission and specialized hardware to protect confidential information maintained on large servers with robust operating systems, usually housed in secure locations. When the PC entered the picture and the Internet evolved into a public commodity, the old security model didn't work. PCs were initially developed as single-user devices that were not designed to be connected to networks, so their operating systems lacked the rigorous security of, for example, an operating system such as UNIX that was targeted for larger computers to accommodate many users. Also, openness and public access emerged as important goals, and for some, security measures became obstacles that hindered their work. Mischievous and malevolent players found many, many holes they could exploit, and those same players could easily use the open Internet to disseminate what they learned.[31]

For the workplace, the rise in security threats and the need for defensive countermeasures have turned into major headaches and timesinks. The IT staff spend considerable time each day with security issues. But employees must also get involved in security in ways that go far beyond keeping their passwords secure. Hardly a day goes by in which some security issue does not rear its head for almost every employee. What are some of the major security threats affecting the workplace?

EXAMPLES OF SECURITY THREATS

First, the Internet and any services or devices connected to it are susceptible to viruses, worms, and Trojan horses, all of which destroy data, wreak havoc on computers and networks, and consume considerable time in the workplace. A single virus attack might compromise a worker's computer and destroy local files, or it might damage the entire corporation's network. When the Internet was young, viruses and other destructive agents were considered teen pranks, launched by bored but tech-savvy kids who were sometimes rewarded, rather than punished, by the justice system for their cleverness. Now, these activities threaten the integrity of the net and cost considerable sums. The cost to clean up after the Love Bug virus, for example, was estimated at $10 billion.[32]

Another security threat is *denial of service*. Large commercial Web sites depend on 24 by 7 access for their business, and various tactics have been used to overwhelm a Web site so that no one else can visit it, often by children or teens using prewritten scripts they download and install. The attacker bombards the host with network messages, causing it to crash or disrupting traffic so badly that access by legitimate visitors is slowed to a crawl. A more potent form of this activity is the *distributed denial of service* attack, in which the attacker first penetrates other computers on the net, often those with cable or DSL "always-on" service, and installs software on them. These computers become "zombies," which later receive a message from the attacker to bombard a particular Web site all at once. For the victim Web site, the attack appears to be coming from many different directions and the original perpetrator remains veiled behind the zombies.

---

[31] Piscitello, D., & Kent, S. (2003). The sad and increasingly deplorable state of Internet security. *Business Communication Review*, February, 49–53. Retrieved March 3, 2003, from Business Source Premier Database.

[32] McFadden, M. (2000). As virus attacks develop, defenses are evolving. *ENT, 5*(13), 31. Retrieved March 2, 2003, from Business Source Premier Database.

Unauthorized intrusion is another critical security threat. Hosts on the Internet are protected mainly by passwords, and passwords can be cracked, intercepted, guessed, or just handed out, by mistake or deliberately. Computer software and operating systems also may have numerous "holes" that make the computers vulnerable to intrusion and damage, even without intercepting passwords. The Code Red worm that caused so much havoc in 2001 exploited some of these holes in Microsoft's Web Server, spreading from system to system and then triggering an attack on the U.S. White House Web site.

Wireless systems have been especially vulnerable to intrusion, and they illustrate the tense balance between the desire for openness and the concern for security.[33] For example, employees give rave reviews to the development of the wireless network in which they can use their laptops any place near a corporate wireless access point. Corporations have happily set those points up in cafeterias, in the outside gardens, in the auditoriums, and in the conference rooms to untether workers from their desktops and make it easy for people and teams to log in to the network from anyplace on the corporate campus. Yet securing those networks is extraordinarily difficult, and people out in the parking lot or on the street can also access the network with their own laptops.[34] Also "rogue access points" have been hung without the knowledge of the corporation, thus adding unauthorized "doors" into the network.

Security threats are so common that it is easy enough to launch a hoax that frightens people into harming their own computers, under the guise of helping them remove a threat. One such hoax, sent to addresses in the victim's address book, warned that a virus had been infecting all of them and gave precise instructions on how to remove it. There was no virus, but the file that would be removed if the victim followed the instructions was critical to the computer's operating system.

IMPROVING SECURITY

Making the Internet more secure is an enormous task, one that involves IT professionals as well as all Internet users. In the workplace, employee education is a key ingredient to help prevent virus attacks, intrusions, lost data, and unauthorized use. For example, people often use easily guessed

---

[33] Securing the cloud. (2002). *The Economist, 365*(8296). Retrieved March 3, 2003, from Business Source Premier Database.

[34] Gomes, L. (2001). Many wireless networks open to attack. Tech Update, ZDNet. Retrieved March 3, 2003, from ZDNet Web site: http://techupdate.zdnet.com/techupdate/stories/main/0,14179,2713009,00.html

passwords such as their own or their pet's name, and then never change them unless the system automatically requires it. Employees must also continually be educated about the ways in which viruses or worms can spread, often simply by clicking on a seemingly innocuous attachment to an email. Some viruses are spread by exploiting holes in email programs and sending virus-laden messages to everyone in the owner's address book. The dangerous attachment may then appear to be coming from a coworker. Just being cautious about email from strangers is not enough to prevent attack.

On the IT side, a great deal is being done to ramp up security, but the rapid technological advances in the Internet make it a very difficult job. Microsoft, for example, releases dozens of patches to its operating systems each year, which help update the software and close security holes that are discovered after the software is released. Just keeping up with the patches is very time consuming, and often too late. Many companies have added intrusion detection software to their systems, which relies less on closing security holes than on identifying anomalies or odd behavior. This kind of software profiles the normal patterns of use of the programs and end-users and then sends alerts when unusual activity appears to be occurring anywhere on the system.

Firewalls are another important security measure, and their use has spread widely – including to people who work on the road with laptops or at home using high-speed Internet links available through cable or DSL. A *firewall* acts as a gateway between the public Internet and the company's network (or the individual's home computer). It tracks and logs traffic across the gateway and can be configured to prohibit or filter various kinds of traffic, either outbound or inbound.

Security is also needed to build trust in the Internet's messaging systems, and it must occur on several levels. For example, recipients must have confidence that messages are *authentic* – that is, they come from the person listed as the sender and are not electronically forged or altered in some way in transit. Organizations must also have confidence that the message content is secure. Even if it were to be intercepted the message should not be readable. Another important factor for the messaging systems involves *nonrepudiation* and the use of some kind of verification to ensure receipt. Nonrepudiation means that the sender can't deny sending it, and the recipient can't deny receiving it. All of these capabilities exist for our paper documents and packages but it is not easy to create analogous mechanisms for the Internet. Paper documents might require notarized signatures, for example, and they might be encrypted in some way. Shipping services have means to ensure that recipients can't claim the package never arrived by

ware and hardware products introduced, let alone deploy them in the
erprise and train people on their use. Individual workers are bombarded
technology advertising that promises to boost their productivity and
plify their lives. Many of these innovations are boons for productivity
he individual, or for the whole enterprise. Others turn out to be distrac-
s with bugs, terrible documentation, little technical support, and high
. From inside the wave, it is not always easy to predict which is which.
ndividual workers may not understand how or why the workplace has
me more frenzied and competitive, or know why their organizations are
filled with a bewildering and dazzling array of new technologies that
nise to solve all their problems, make them more productive, transform
ness processes, and possibly eliminate their departments and lay them
As Charles Dickens said of another era, "It was the best of times, it
the worst of times." In these first two chapters we have explored the
ground of the Internet in the workplace, and some of the reasons why
entric technologies have had such fundamental effects on our working
. In the next chapter, we move on to the role they play in the structure
ur lives and to their impact on work and nonwork hours.

having someone sign for it when it arrives, thus takii
nonrepudiation issue. Although it has been slow in ge
PKI (public key infrastructure) is likely to be the tech
dress these concerns. This technology involves the use
keys, encryption, and digital signatures.

The spread of so many security threats and the gro
volved in the cat and mouse game of defense have
software industries. Businesses must pay dearly for the
and services and must constantly provide training to
prevent losses. The security threats have also caused l
as important files are corrupted and work must be rec
reduced further by the long list of security-related "to
added to every worker's responsibilities, adding to thei
range from frequent password changes to more time-c
as installing and configuring a firewall for a home cor
corporate network. The list of "tips to stay secure" is
more complicated all the time for the workplace. The
not very supportive of workers whose defenses are dow
or lack of knowledge. For example, software vendors v
with holes tend to blame the victim if they failed to
recent patch to correct the problem, moving the burd
company or down to the worker.

Perhaps the most troubling effect of the growing
the danger these threats may pose to overall trust and
are reluctant to open their email, or they question its
lost and the usefulness of email is reduced. If employee
about using the net's enormous capabilities for collab
tion dissemination, opportunities for virtual teamwoi
employees begin to feel that the burden of holding up
is too big and getting bigger all the time, they may giv

Swimming Inside the Netcentric Wave

The Internet's design principles were more effective in tr
than its architects ever predicted, as you can see from
of some of the new technologies. Now, people in the w
encing what it means to be inside an enormous wave o
transformation. Enormous gains have been made in i
puterization and telecommunications change the way
do business. Yet the IT department can't hope to keep

3 Work, Nonwork, and Fuzzy Lines between Them

The concept of *work–life balance* began attracting considerable attention in the 1990s, partly as a result of what many perceived to be a growing *im*balance. Workers in some segments of the economy told stories of very long working days that extended into evenings, weekends, and holidays, and expanded well beyond the physical confines of the workplace. In a survey conducted by the Families and Work Institute, 46 percent of the respondents said they felt overworked in one way or another, and 28 percent reported feeling overwhelmed.[35] Researchers began exploring the nature of the shifting patterns of work, partly to see whether they truly added up to more work hours in absolute terms or just to feelings of more job pressure. The increasingly fuzzy line between "work" and "nonwork" that was made possible by netcentric innovations also became a prominent concern, and worries about effects on family life grew. Parents who carried their netcentric gadgets to evening PTA meetings so they could be instantly aware of business events were no longer so rare.

In this chapter, we look closely at changes in work, nonwork, and the Internet's role in those changes. Work, and the amount of time we put into it, has changed in complex ways; it is not the same for everyone. The changes have sometimes been very puzzling, especially during the economic boom years of the 1990s when unemployment was low and worker shortages gave many people far more leverage with their bosses than they had previously. Yet some groups worked harder and longer anyway. Why would so many people begin to work so much harder and longer when incomes were rising and workers were in greater demand? As you will see, the factors that

---

[35] Galinsky, E., Kim, S. S., & Bond, J. T. (2001). Feeling overworked: When work becomes too much. Retrieved March 4, 2003, from Families and Work Institute Web site, http://www.familiesandwork.org/

led to the high workloads for some groups are complicated. Some were self-inflicted, but the information revolution and the Internet have played significant roles in these trends.

The Internet's role and the role of the information revolution and netcentric technologies in general are also difficult to pin down, but the changes they have wrought appear to have affected work, nonwork, and the balance between them in several important ways. First, they affected the level of competition and rivalry in business, as I discussed in the first chapter, so the technological changes play a crucial role in the background, by altering the climate and tensions of work. For example, the changing business climate has led to less job security and stability, and more uncertainty – especially for occupational groups that in the past were rarely affected by mass layoffs. At the same time, wage inequalities grew dramatically, raising the stakes for holding onto a position in the fast lane, and increasing the costs for losing that position – especially for American workers. Wage inequalities are also to some extent related to the changes in the business landscape triggered by the netcentric wave.

In the background, then, netcentric technologies have helped to mold a business climate in which working longer and harder can be mandatory for some people and desirable for others. In the foreground, these technologies *enable* people to work as long as they want or need to, around the clock, year-round. The anytime–anywhere connectedness they offer have made it possible for people to do even more work in time slots that previously were not available for much work-related activity, such as the commute. These background and foreground effects reinforce and fuel each other. Managers who know their staff members have access to email at home, for example, will be less forgiving when an employee does not pick up an urgent message in the evening, warning of an emergency meeting at 8 a.m. The coalescing forces have triggered significant changes in the workplace, from transformations of corporate norms about when and where a worker should be accessible to changes in the definition of the "office" itself.

Much of the concern about work–life balance has been sparked by anecdotes – stories of individuals whose work lives have overtaken almost every waking hour and whose families barely see them. One hypothesis is that the stories come mainly from workaholics, Internet entrepreneurs, or people for whom the advice "Get a life!" falls on deaf ears. These people may have chosen long working hours and little personal time regardless of the era, and may have just slept at the office if there was no high-bandwidth connection at home. Let's first look at the data on working hours to see whether people who don't fall into those categories are really working more hours.

Are We Working More?

Disentangling the immense mound of labor statistics on time spent working is not a trivial task. Some sources suggest that working hours have not changed much in recent decades, but others indicate important trends that vary by country and by occupational groups. The International Labour Organization identifies hours worked as one of the key indicators of the labor market, and their analysis shows rather startling differences across the globe.[36] In Germany, for example, the average annual hours worked dropped almost 100 hours a year in the past decade, and France's workers reduced their hours by about 40 during the same period. Their data show that the "workaholic" Japanese have definitely taken a breather as well. They were working more than 2,100 hours per year in 1980, but by the late 1990s, their average annual hours were down to 1,842. Koreans also reduced their working hours, though their averages are so high that they still are among the longest working people on the planet, despite the drop. In 1980 they averaged 2,689 hours per year, but by 2000 their average dropped to 2,474.

Hours worked in other countries, however, showed the opposite trend. The United States, Sweden, and Portugal all show increases in the annual hours worked over the past decade. In the United States, workers added 96 hours per year to their annual tally over a two decade period, putting in an average of 1,979 hours per year by the year 2000. This number is about 30 percent higher than most European countries and adds up to about fifteen more work weeks per year. The implication is that some people are definitely working more than they were twenty years ago, but others – especially in Europe – are gradually reducing their annual working hours and have far more time off. Workers in the Netherlands, for example, work only about 1,365 hours per year.

Average data about hours worked suffer from various methodological problems, and arithmetic averages in general mask the subtleties of

---

[36] Key Indicators of the Labour Market 6: Hours of Work, International Labour Organization. Retrieved December 27, 2001, from http://www.ilo.org/public/english/employment/strat/kilm/table.htm

underlying trends, so it is worth looking more closely at these trends. Especially after the publication of Juliet Schor's *The Overworked American* in 1991,[37] researchers became quite interested in the phenomenon. In the United States, the longer working hours do not appear to be distributed evenly across workers. They are concentrated in certain groups, especially people in professional and managerial roles and those in the upper educational and income brackets. The longer working hours apply equally to men and women in those brackets.[38]

The weight of the evidence suggests that working hours in the United States continued to increase through the 1990s, even during the economic expansion. It seems odd that in times of such prosperity people would be spending more and more hours at work, at least in the United States, particularly people whose incomes were rising very quickly.

Historically, annual working hours were rising and falling during most of the twentieth century, but the general trend was down. Improved productivity helped to reduce the number of hours people worked, but labor movements played their role as well. During the early part of the century, labor organizations worked tirelessly to battle the long workdays imposed by factory production systems, and they were quite successful in most of the industrialized countries. One important goal of this movement was to avoid unemployment and displacement. Samuel Gompers, founder of the American Federation of Labor, said that if even one worker was unemployed, the hours worked by everyone else were too long. In the United States, there was a brief surge in which policymakers were keen to reduce working hours to distribute employment during the Great Depression. For example, both Senate and House passed the Black bill in 1933, which mandated a thirty-hour workweek for all businesses engaged in interstate and foreign commerce. The bill would have been unthinkable before the depression began, but when unemployment soared to over 20 percent and consumers were not able to buy the products filling up in warehouses, legislators supported it enthusiastically, hoping to stimulate consumer demand and get the country back to work. President Roosevelt, however, killed the bill because of his concern for its long-term impact. Though the bill might have positive short-term benefits, restricting business in this way might slow growth down the line and hinder the country's ability to compete in foreign markets.

[37] Schor, J. B. (1991). *The overworked American: The unexpected decline of leisure.* New York: Basic Books.
[38] Golden, L., & Figart, D. (2000). Doing something about long hours. *Challenge, 43*(6), 15–37. Retrieved December 27, 2001, from Academic Search Elite database.

The interest in distributing employment across the population has been especially strong in Europe and has led to much legislation that regulates working hours. In France, the keen concern about distributing employment opportunities has led to a legislated ceiling on the workweek that is mandated to drop to thirty-five hours per week by 2002. Whether Europe is on the same track as the United States, and will eventually relax restrictions about the length of the workweek, is unknown. American business people who attempt to open shop in Europe and try to bring their ideas about how much time workers should be expected to put in are often very frustrated.

Why Are Some People Working Longer Hours?

Although the labor statistics and surveys paint a picture of rising hours in some segments of the population in some countries, the reasons for the trends are more difficult to determine. Personal choice certainly plays a role, but Robert B. Reich, former U.S. Secretary of Labor and now a professor of social and economic policy at Brandeis University, argues that the reasons people are working longer in the United States are more fundamental and have their roots in the changing business environment, caused primarily by the effects of technology, communications, and the information revolution.[39] People make choices in a context, and their choices are affected by the rewards and punishments attached to each option. He began to research the subject of work and nonwork in depth when he found his own work–life balance way out of whack. As a member of the Cabinet, Reich loved his job, could hardly wait to arrive in the morning, and left for home reluctantly. He lost touch with his family and friends and frequently missed tucking his sons into bed at night. One time he called home to say he would yet again be too late to say goodnight, but his son insisted that his dad wake him up when he did get home. When Reich asked why, the boy said he just wanted to know his father was there, at home. At that moment, Reich decided to resign his post and regain some balance.

FRENZY AT WORK: THE ROLE OF THE BUSINESS CLIMATE

Reich's analysis focuses especially on the root causes of longer working days, and a primary one is the change in the business climate brought about by technological innovation, communications, and the information revolution, and the role that consumers play in the change. As we discussed in the first chapter, the netcentric technologies have changed the power equation,

---

[39] Reich, R. B. (2001). *The future of success*. New York: Alfred A. Knopf.

moving power away from businesses and toward the consumer. A consumer can now easily switch to a different supplier of almost any product with little more effort than it takes to click the mouse button. The consumer also has far more power to be informed, by comparing products, checking out prices, or asking networks of friends for recommendations. The sources of information vary widely, and though some of it may be less than accurate, the sheer quantity is immeasurably higher than it was before the Internet. Entire Web sites, such as mySimon.com, are available to help consumers find whatever they want and get the best deal possible. Active discussion groups contain publicly available postings by previous buyers of all kinds of products, many of whom willingly share their experiences.

Most of us are not just consumers, however. We are also producers – the people on the other side of the Web site who are making the goods and performing the services. *The Age of the Terrific Deal*, as Reich dubbed it, is a two-edged sword. On one hand, consumers benefit from better and cheaper products and businesses are highly motivated to compete in the market with innovative offerings. At the same time it leads to fierce competition and tremendous frenzy in the workplace. Products that may have taken a year or more to develop may be introduced into the market, then taken off within just a few weeks because the "buzz" on the street panned them, and information about the product's shortcomings spread very quickly.

Even in prosperous times, the competition for a consumer's eyeballs and dollars has grown white hot, and the workplace has grown more frenzied in response. Today's hot product may be reassuring to the company and its workers who introduced it, but that product may not stay hot for long. Consumers will switch when they find a better deal, and the rivals who will offer them one are only a step or two behind. No one can rest easy or be assured that the business will thrive for very long and that workers can grant themselves a much needed break.

One of the fastest growing categories of software is called "business intelligence" applications, or BI for short. Its emergence was fueled by the Internet and the competitive pressures it created among businesses, who now have dire survival needs for up-to-the-minute information about the response of consumers to their products and the activities of its competitors. This software allows business managers to mine and analyze immense quantities of information available online, whether it resides in corporate databanks, newspapers, annual reports, email, or on the open Internet. It can quickly summarize minute activities such as click-throughs on a Web site and dynamically show graphs and charts to people who are trying to understand and make decisions about business markets and strategy. Much of the data the software analyzes are live, or at least very fresh, appealing to business people trying to work and make decisions on Internet time. Gartner Group forecasts that this segment of the software industry will grow to more than \$8 billion by 2003, and more than one half of the larger enterprises will use BI as the cornerstone for their business.[40]

The growing competition businesses have been facing has led to another factor that forms the context for the choices many people are making about their working hours. In the competition to remain profitable, businesses have had to continually find ways to reduce operating costs, especially costs associated with labor. In particular, they have pursued management strategies that lead to fewer fixed costs associated with a long-term workforce and more flexibility to recruit, hire, and fire as quickly as possible.

JOB INSECURITY

Long-term, secure employment in the same company – the kind that culminates in a retirement party after 30 years, gold watch, and a lifelong retirement check each month – may never have existed as idyllically as the movies of the 1950s would lead one to believe. Nevertheless, most of us know people, our parents or grandparents, perhaps, who enjoyed something like this scenario. My husband's father, for example, born in 1910, worked for General Motors as an engineer his entire working life. His father's father, however, did not have lifelong employment, and probably found it astonishing.

Historically, our concept of employment and of the relationship between employer and employee has changed dramatically over the centuries. In the early nineteenth century, before mass production drew so many away from the farms to factory work, most people were not paid any fixed wage by an employer. Instead, they worked on family farms, in small cottage industries, as craftsmen, fishermen, or tradesmen. As large-scale production grew in the last part of the nineteenth century, more and more workers moved to cities and began working for wages. At the time, the transition was not an easy one. Many considered wages to be demeaning, barely better than slavery, and only a step on the way to financial independence. The company executives gained considerable power over the terms and conditions of employment and could demand long working hours for little pay. The result was the labor movement that led to unionization, collective bargaining,

---

[40] Kempf, E. (2001). Business intelligence: Integrators, prepare your solutions. February 5, 2001, Gartner Advisory. Retrieved January 6, 2002, from Dataquest.

and legislation designed to prevent the worst abuses of the industrial-age employment scene, such as child labor.

By the mid-twentieth century, about one third of the workers in the United States belonged to a union, but a growing cadre of white-collar workers had also appeared. William H. Whyte interviewed many of them for his classic *Organization Man* and found their conception of the relationship between themselves and their company to be a lifelong one. They expected to work for the company until retirement and that their loyalty would be rewarded. After the war, college grads entered the workforce hoping to link up with a major corporation and climb up the ladder inside of it. They were very mindful of the Great Depression's chaos and eager to seek a more secure livelihood. One college senior remarked, "I don't think AT&T is very exciting, but that's the company I'd like to join. If a depression comes, there will always be AT&T."

In 1995, AT&T announced more than 40,000 layoffs, a move that was heralded as the largest layoff in the history of the telecommunications industry. In 2002, AT&T announced an additional 5,000 layoffs, and another 5,000 were subsequently expected to leave the payrolls as their departments were reduced in size. In 2001, more than 2 million workers were laid off, many of them the same kind of white-collar workers who thought there would "always be an AT&T." The young man who made that remark to Whyte may have been one of those laid off, if he had not already retired.

One of those white-collar workers who was unexpectedly laid off in 1996 was Donald Scarry. He bitterly relays his anger about the AT&T layoffs that betrayed his expectations about how AT&T would treat middle managers such as himself, in contrast to production workers for whom layoffs might be expected:

"One of the secret lessons from the AT&T layoff is that this dream, this identification, this lifestyle no longer exists. The layoffs showed us that even those who had it made – and middle managers at AT&T and the like had it made – could now suffer the same fate as mere workers. We could be marginalized instantly by decisions made by our corporations. While most of us through identification with our corporation thought we were insiders, there were real insiders who could make a business decision and cut us loose without much thought. We who had bought the dream, the philosophy and the harshness were now on our own. For many of us it was the first time."[41]

[41] Scarry, D. M. (1996). The economic elite was betrayed. *Business News New Jersey,* 9(6), 28. Retrieved January 6, 2002, from EBSCO Business Wire News.

Downsizing, reengineering, rightsizing, and several other business strategies have been used to reorganize a corporation and make it more competitive in the last part of the twentieth century. These have often involved laying off workers with little notice, even when their performance as an employee was good. Their expectations about their relationship with the company they worked for may have been to hold lifelong employment, but the business climate of the late twentieth century makes that impossible.

Corporations choose layoffs rather than shorter hours partly because of the desire to reduce fixed costs and benefits and remain flexible. Rather than commit to long-term employees (and pay their benefits) through thick or thin, they choose to hold onto a much smaller cadre of full-time employees. In 1962, the manager of employee benefits at General Electric wrote that "Maximizing employment security is a prime company goal."[42] But by the 1990s, it had become smarter business strategy to hire and fire workers as needed on a temporary basis during flush and lean times, responding to the competitive pressures and sudden shifts in consumer demands. For workers, this meant growing job insecurity and an ever-growing concern about a sudden appearance of the dreaded pink slip. Those who cling to a full-time position with benefits are more anxious about keeping their positions and work harder and longer. They do not want to join the growing ranks of underemployed, part-time, and temporary workers.

According to the Bureau of Labor, there have been between 14,000 and 16,000 mass layoff events involving fifty or more employees who were separated from their jobs each year since the Bureau began collecting the data in 1995. In 2001, the numbers were especially troubling because the economy slowed so much, and also because of the events of September 11. In November 2001, for example, mass layoff events were 59 percent higher than they were a year before. These numbers add up to an extraordinarily competitive and volatile business climate in which white-collar workers have every good reason to be concerned for their job security.

CORPORATE NORMS

Combined with a more competitive business climate and less job security, changes in corporate norms also help explain why workers in some segments are working far longer hours. Catherine, for example, was in her

---

[42] Willis, E. S. (1962, April). General Electric's plan for financing retraining. *Management Record, 24*(4). Published in New York by the Conference Board, which was then known as the National Industrial Conference Board. Cited by J. A. Fraser (2001). *White collar sweatshop: The deterioration of work and its rewards in corporate America.* New York: W. W. Norton & Company.

early forties when Jill Andreskey Fraser interviewed her about her working hours.[43] She moved steadily from a junior position at IBM in the 1980s, reaching the ranks of management by the 1990s. In her twenties, she worked twenty hours a day and was often on the road for weeks at a time. When she entered management, she could reduce the travel schedule but was placed on a rotation in which she was expected to be "on call" twenty-four hours a day for a week at a time. She received calls from customers in the wee hours of the morning and was still expected to be in the office by 8 a.m. – and stay there until 8 or 9 at night.

When Louis Gerstner took the helm of IBM in 1993, the downsizing and restructuring began with a feverish pace. IBM's stability was challenged when the mainframe market began to lose ground to networks and micro-computers, its stock price tumbled, and Gerstner began rounds of layoffs, downsizings, and early retirement initiatives. Workloads for those remaining kept increasing, but Catherine never objected. "I used to pride myself on thinking, I'm not going to complain. I can take it all on. I can do anything." She spent the days in meetings and handled her email at night on the computer IBM supplied to make it easy for her to work from home. She remarked, "It was like you didn't have a home life."

Descriptions of grueling work hours like these are not uncommon, though the causes and motivations vary. For a person like Catherine, the norms of IBM were critically important. She was breaking through gender bias and trying to establish herself as a team player at IBM. Most of her colleagues were experiencing similar work schedules and everyone was expected to carry their share of the growing workload. Knocking off at 5 p.m. in such an environment may be hazardous to one's chances for promotion and job security, but it can also be seen as loafing or free-riding by colleagues. They may feel a worker who doesn't put in those long hours is just shifting the extra work to them.

During the 1980s in Japan, when their work hours were among the highest in the world, I interviewed Japanese managers to learn more about why they stayed at the office until 9 or 10 p.m. and what they were doing. The lights in the Tokyo skyscrapers in almost every office were on late into the evening, even though most of them faced an hour or more commute on the train to get home. Their responses clearly illustrated the power of corporate norms. They said they would not leave before their coworkers, even though they had already finished what they had planned to accomplish

---

[43] Fraser, J. A. (2001). *White-collar sweatshop: The deterioration of work and its rewards in corporate America.* New York: W. W. Norton and Company.

that day. Leaving earlier was a sign that they were not committed to their coworkers or their company.

Growing emphasis on teamwork in modern management approaches, especially for so-called high-performance organizations, makes its own contribution to norms that include longer working hours. The Japanese were often working in teams, and the concept and value of the team have taken on considerable importance in popular management techniques.[44] Self-managed teams, empowered teams, virtual teams, and quality teams are all examples of this trend. Group dynamics in these settings can lead to longer working hours, simply because workers do not want to let their teammates down or leave the impression that they are not contributing their fair share to the project.

Corporate norms for longer work hours also emerge because businesses have growing needs for round-the-clock service, thus round-the-clock work from the employees. The globalization of commerce accounts for part of this. Business customers may be in any time zone, and they may need to reach their technical support, marketing consultant, or independent supplier at any time of day or night. I recently attended a presentation by a software development firm in Maryland whose technical lead was located in India. For her to participate in the discussion by audio conference and answer questions from the audience, she had to be in her office at midnight. Consumers also expect company personnel to be available outside the usual 9 to 5 workday, especially because the consumers themselves may be working longer hours and are not able to take care of their personal business except during off hours.

From a business perspective, employee work time is a complex factor in production. For example, a CEO whose orders require additional production of widgets would weigh the pros and cons of adding new workers to the production team or have the existing workers do more overtime. Many are choosing the overtime option, partly for economic reasons. Although overtime rates may be higher for production workers, the company does not need to invest in the cost of recruitment, training, and the additional benefits that a new worker would entail. Health insurance premiums, for example, are computed on the basis of the number of workers in the company, not on the overall size of the payroll. Also, many workers may want the additional pay and choose to work overtime. For the professional and managerial staff though, those extra hours do not generally lead to additional

---

[44] Katzenbach, J. R., & Smith, D. K. (1993). *The wisdom of teams: Creating the high performance organization*. Boston, MA: Harvard Business School Press.

overtime pay, at least not in the short run. Corporate norms that demand long working hours for this class of employees are very advantageous to the bottom line.

CARROTS AND STICKS: THE ROLE OF WAGE INEQUALITY

The unusual situation in the United States, in which the people in higher educational and income brackets are experiencing longer working hours, is related to another important ingredient involving rewards and punishments. In the United States, the distribution of income has shown disturbing patterns over the past three decades that have had a dramatic effect on worker's choices about working hours in different income brackets.

From the 1940s to the 1970s, both income and productivity figures in the United States grew steadily. Income differences between the bands from lowest to highest paid workers were high, but they all grew at about the same rate. For example, in 1970, the lowest paid one fifth of the population earned an aggregate share of 4.1 percent of the total income, whereas the share of the highest paid one fifth was 16.6 percent. In the late 1960s, the average income for the highest paid 20 percent of the population was a little over eleven times higher than the average income for the lowest 20 percent.

Average household income rose in all the bands, particularly after 1970, because so many women came into the workforce, often full time, and created a vast number of two-income families. The bands, themselves, however, began to diverge and move even farther away from one another (see Figure 3.1). The highest paid workers started racing ahead, albeit with fits and starts, and by the end of the twentieth century the highest paid one fifth was earning 13.7 times as much as the lowest paid one fifth. Between 1967 and 2000, the top 5 percent of earners were especially in that fast lane. Their average annual income in adjusted dollars almost doubled, whereas the lowest paid earners increased their average income by 42.5 percent.

Income inequality is not as large in European countries, and this helps explain why Americans are working longer hours compared to Europeans. Linda A. Bell of Haverford College and Richard B. Freeman of the National Bureau of Economic Research investigated the relationship between hours worked and earnings in the United States and Germany. They were especially interested in the way Germans and Americans answered the following question:

"Think of the number of hours you work and the money that you make in your main job, including regular overtime. If you had only one of three choices, which would you prefer?

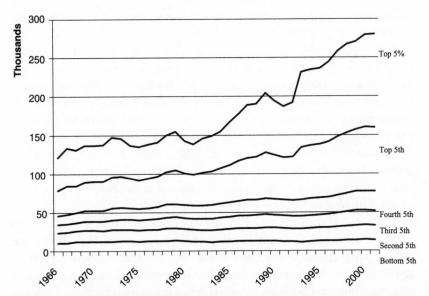

Figure 3.1. Income Inequalities: Mean income by each fifth and top 5% of families in the United States, 1966–2001.
From tabular data retrieved April 22, 2003, from U.S. Census Bureau Web site. (http://www.census.gov/hhes/income/histinc/f03.html)

■ Work longer hours and earn more money;
■ Work the same number of hours and earn less money;
■ Work fewer hours and earn less money?"[45]

In 1989, only 13.5 percent of the German workers said they would prefer to work longer hours for more pay, whereas 32.7 percent of the Americans chose that option. The difference between the two was smaller in 1997 (21 percent for Germans, 32 percent for Americans), mostly attributed to a somewhat stronger desire for more pay in Germany. Still, about one third of American workers were willing to sacrifice more leisure time to get more income.

Why should Americans be more eager to choose more work for more pay? Bell and Freeman proposed the inequality-hours hypothesis, which suggests that workers in the United States are making quite rational decisions based on their chances for future growth in income. The distribution of pay is

---

[45] Bell, L. A., & Freeman, R. B. (2000). The incentive for working hard: Explaining hours worked differences in the U.S. and Germany. Working Paper 8051, National Bureau of Economic Research. Retrieved December 27, 2001, from http://papers.nber.org/papers/W8051.pdf

more unequal in the United States than it is in Germany, so the rewards for working more can be much larger.

They present the example of Hans and Hank, hypothetical workers in Germany and the United States. Hans works for a German company where pay differences among workers are small, job security is high, and unemployment safety nets are in place. Hank's company has highly unequal pay among workers, limited unemployment benefits, and not much job security. Hans might not be promoted if he doesn't work long and hard, but his living standard would not change very much. Hank, however, faces severe consequences if he loses his job, but also faster and larger pay increases if he stays on the corporate fast track. The carrot that motivates Hank to work longer hours is much larger, and so is the stick.

If you look at the early 1990s in the graph, you see the "stick" side of the equation clearly. During that recession, the average annual income of those highest paid workers shows a very sizable dip, one that is much larger than the drops in the lower income bands. For the workers in those high-paying categories, growing accustomed to generous raises each year, the stick can be quite dramatic, especially if they had assumed job security and had taken on significant financial responsibilities to match their incomes. Their plight may not seem terribly sympathetic in the context of the graph showing the other bands, but many of you reading this were *in* the top bands. If you were one of those fast-laners who lost a job and took a sizable pay cut in that period, the memory of that painful "stick" would be vivid.

Lonnie Golden at Penn State and Deborah Figart of Richard Stockton College study the longer work hours in the United States, and their analysis suggests the trends in the United States are here to stay, at least for the foreseeable future.[46] The Internet along with communications and computer technologies in general played critical roles in these trends by changing the overall business climate and leading to a workplace environment in which longer working hours became the almost inevitable conclusion for some segments of the population. They also play another role as facilitator and enabler of the longer working hours. As businesses continue to find ways to remain competitive and respond to market pressures, they will operate on a 24 by 7 basis. Workers will have to synchronize their own activities with the demands at work, giving up time for leisure and family in the process. This synchronization process is where netcentric technologies come in, as the enabler.

---

[46] Golden, L., & Figart, D. (2000). Doing something about long hours. *Challenge, 43*(6), 15–37. Retrieved December 27, 2001, from Academic Search Elite database.

Netcentric Technologies and the Anytime/ Anywhere Workplace

"Nine to five," "quitting time," "lunch hour," "workweek," and "vacation" have taken on very different meanings for an Internet-enabled workforce. The expressions seem almost antiquated in light of the way netcentric technologies have made it possible to engage in work at any time of day or night, any place on the planet. The technologies allow us to slip some work into almost any time slot, regardless of when it is, where we may be located at the time, or what activities are competing with a demand for work. With a cell phone, PDA, or connected laptop, workers can synchronize their activities at the beach, at home, in the car, or on the train, with dozens of emails and phone calls, mixing work and nonwork in unprecedented ways.

TAKING BACK THE COMMUTE

The commute to work is one of the main time slots now available for productive work, thanks to netcentric technologies. According to the U.S. Department of Transportation, commute time averages between twenty and twenty-five minutes each way in the United States, though people in densely populated areas may spend far more time in traffic-congested highways. A special report on Washington, DC, for example, where average commutes extend beyond thirty minutes each way, found that Washingtonians spend more than seventy-six hours per year idling in traffic at a cost (in pay and fuel) of $1,025 per eligible driver.[47]

Those commuting hours are increasingly being used to extend work rather than to listen to news or music, or to sleep on the train. Drivers return calls on their cell phones, or check their email on PDAs on the train or while stopped in traffic. For many people, the ability to work during the commute is a great benefit, but concerns about the dangers of distracted drivers on cell phones have led to considerable legislation across the United States. Some states prohibit them entirely, whereas others allow hands-free use of the devices.

The commute is a dreadful experience for many people, especially when it is fraught with unpredictable congestion and delays. Being able to take advantage of that "nonwork" time to get some work done has been an

---

[47] Sipress, A. (2000). One day's commute has many stories: Crashes, impatience, guilt and even gunfire. *The Washington Post*, February 4. Retrieved December 27, 2001, from *The Washington Post* Web site: http://www.washingtonpost.com/wp-srv/local/daily/feb00/traffic4.htm

advantage for many, because it hardly qualifies as leisure anyway. Although some people use the time productively for relaxing nonwork – listening to music or chatting with fellow carpoolers, for example – many others appreciate the opportunity to connect to the office.

TAKING OVER EVENINGS, WEEKENDS, AND VACATIONS

The former line that separated the "workweek" from the nonwork evening and weekend, however, is also becoming fuzzier. When people come home from work, they may spend more hours at their computer checking email or working on projects, sometimes long into the evening hours. Time slots that used to be reserved for family activities – even it was only watching TV together – have been taken over or blended with work. Netcentric technologies made it possible to work in the physical vicinity of the family with most of the capabilities of the actual office so workers can switch back and forth from work to nonwork in new ways.

The evening, for example, can be fragmented into many work and nonwork time slots for people who have home computers and high-speed connections. The worker may sit at his or her home office desk to compose email messages, and then respond to his or her daughter's request to help with homework for a few minutes. While waiting for the water to boil for the pasta, the cook might return a few phone calls or download today's sales figures from the corporate server. Weekends and vacations can be fragmented in the same way as evenings. Many workers carry their laptops on vacation and set up as soon as they check in, plugging into the hotel's dataport and checking connections. Some carry them out to the pool and continue working while the children learn to dive.

FILLING THE LITTLE TIME SLOTS

The use of netcentric technologies to fill very small time slots has also helped workers synchronize the demands of the workplace. Many of these slots are part of a typical workday, though they might occur at any time of day or night. They are not just affecting how long we work and whether we fill what were typically nonwork spans with productive work. They also influence how we use time and how much work we can do with that time. Many moments at work have been downtime, in the sense that workers could use them as brief respites for rest, socializing, or just gazing about. The technologies make it possible to fill them with more work.

For example, I was with a friend who manages a large IT unit waiting for an elevator in a crowded building. We were on our way to a meeting, and he pulled out his cell phone. Without putting it to his ear, he pressed a few buttons and tapped out a text message on the tiny keyboard, all in under thirty seconds. He said, "Just wanted to let them know we'd be late without having to talk to them – that would take too long."

One way in which businesses have tried to take advantage of every time slot available to improve the productivity of its workers is through the use of online strategies for technical support. Businesses have generally considered tech support to be a bottomless cost center, one that invites cost reductions. However, customer attitudes toward tech support are very critical to loyalty and satisfaction. Businesses have tried to direct customers to automated phone messages to get the help they need, or send them to their Web sites. The biggest cost burden occurs when a customer demands to speak to live tech support, especially because the personnel who respond in person to telephone inquiries can deal with just one customer at a time. The tech support staff member will ask many questions, try to diagnose the problem based on what the customer says, and then test out various hypotheses to troubleshoot the problem. Often, those hypotheses involve time-consuming recommendations to "reboot your computer," or "unplug the cable modem for 60 seconds," and try again. The tech support person remains on the line while the customer does the troubleshooting, leaving a considerable amount of dead time in which the staff member does nothing but wait, read technical manuals, play solitaire, or converse in a friendly manner with the customer.

This dead time is a target for reengineering through netcentric technologies, and one method is to use online chat rather than a telephone call. A tech support person using text-based chat windows can handle many customers at once, switching from one to the other with a click of the mouse. Compared to the traditional tech support phone call, the online chat system is far more productive, mostly because much of the dead time is removed. Forrester Research estimated the costs of the various channels through which tech support could be provided, and concluded that a typical phone call costs the company about $33. Through the channel of online chat, however, the costs drop to $7.80. In 1998, less than 1 percent of firms actually used the online chat system, but Forrester predicts their use will grow extremely quickly.[48]

This new use of what was previously nonwork time, even though it was "on the clock," represents the kind of multitasking that the technologies

---

[48] Placing desktop support on-line (I): The technology base. (February 2001). *Computer Finance*, 13–21. Retrieved January 13, 2002, from Business Source Premier database.

facilitate to increase productivity. The tech support intensity of work is raised considerably with several chat windows open at the same time, and the person must learn to juggle several troubleshooting problems at the same time.

The ability to fill these various time slots with work has both productive and nonproductive consequences. People constantly try to adjust the level of stimulation and cognitive demands in their environment, finding ways to raise them when they perceive them to be too low, or reducing them when it gets too high. We seek out something to do when we are bored, but retreat from overload. Over a whole day, the optimal level of stimulation changes; we don't want high levels of stimulation when we are trying to get to sleep, for example. But a commute often represents a period in which opportunities to achieve an optimal level are few, so the cell phone or PDA helps reach that level. Sending a quick text message on the cell phone while waiting for an elevator is another welcome chance to fill a time slot that didn't reach an optimal level.

The downside to the netcentric technologies in this context, however, is that demands on a worker's attention and cognitive information processing can grow far above what the worker would choose. Hundreds of emails, phone calls, instant messages, and multitasked chat sessions can lead to overload, increases in job stress, and reduced productivity. For some, AOL's "You've got mail!" announcement is a welcome stimulant. For an increasing number of workers, however, it is overload.

WORK STRESS AND THE FAMILY

As working hours were increasing in the United States, the characteristics of families were also changing. One of the most important trends was the entry of women into the workforce. They entered because they had more opportunities, but also because they needed to supplement family incomes. At the same time, the number of children per family was declining, so the size of families was shrinking. Annual birthrates declined from about 98 births per 1,000 married women in the 1970s to 80 births per 1,000 in the late 1990s. We also saw a change in the composition of a "family." The household with 2 parents, 1 income earner, and 2.5 children declined, and other kinds of families became more common. These included the family in which both parents work, the single-parent household, and the household with two income earners but no children.

What happens to families when one or both of the income earners are working longer hours, job demands are intensifying, and workers feel more stressed out by the workplace? Quite simply, there will be less time to spend with the spouse and the children in "nonwork." However, it is too simple to say that work stress by itself causes problems in the family, and many well-designed studies have obtained inconsistent findings.[49] Recall that the rewards for working long hours can be quite high, so a family with one or more workers putting in many hours may reap significant economic benefits. Also, some people may find less "nonwork" time a desirable state of affairs. For example, women whose involvement in exciting and challenging employment requires them to spend less time cleaning house and caring for children may not necessarily think it a bad bargain.

Research on work stress and family life reveals that the relationship is a complex one that depends on how people handle the stress, whether it spills over into the family, and especially on whether people perceive they are overwhelmed by role conflict and overload. When the demands of work compete with family responsibilities and the worker has to make difficult choices about how to allocate time, spillover is most likely.

Diane Hughes and her colleagues, for example, examined the complex relationships between stress and work and marital tensions at home.[50] Their sample included married upper-middle-class professionals who worked at a pharmaceutical company, most of whom were college educated. The researchers asked each individual in the sample to report in detail on characteristics of their jobs, including questions about how often they worked on weekends or evenings, how much control they had over their working hours, how secure they thought their position was with the company, and how much skill the job required. They also answered questions about work–family interference. These questions were intended to assess how much family responsibilities interfered with the worker's ability to get the job done, and also how much work interfered with family responsibilities, such as spending time with the spouse or helping with household chores. Marital tensions and companionship were assessed through questions about how frequently the partners argued about various topics, such as finances or choices about how to spend leisure time.

For these married couples, the level of marital tension was related to work stress. The more a worker reported stress at work – especially if it involved job insecurity or increased pressure without much support from the

---

[49] Perry-Jenkins, M., Repetti, R. L., & Crouter, A. C. (2000). Work and family in the 1990s [Electronic version]. *Journal of Marriage and Family, 62*(4), 981–999.

[50] Hughes, D., & Galinsky, E. (1992). The effects of job characteristics on marital quality: Specifying linking mechanisms [Electronic version]. *Journal of Marriage and Family, 54*(1), 31–43.

supervisors – the higher was the level of marital tension at home. The relationship, however, was a complicated one that demonstrated the importance of work–family inteference. Work stress had far more impact on marital tensions for those people with the most interference and the most role conflict. For people who were able to avoid the role conflicts, heightened work stress had fewer negative effects on the marriage.

Greater interference between work and family responsibilities creates role overload and conflict, leading to feelings of being overwhelmed by so many commitments. This feeling of overload appears to be critical to the way work stress affects children in the families, as well. Ann Crouter and her colleagues at Pennsylvania State University studied dual-earner couples with adolescent children and found a pattern in which people who reported higher stress levels due to overload at work were more likely to have more conflict with their adolescent offspring.[51] In this study, all members of the family were asked to complete questionnaires, and the answers from the adolescents whose parents were overloaded suggested that conflict was not the only negative impact. They also reported lower feelings of self-worth and more sadness.

The picture that emerges is that some people whose jobs are intensely demanding are more likely than others to transfer stress to the family. We don't yet know precisely why some people are more vulnerable to the strains of work overload, but some of the reasons are clear. Job insecurity, lack of control over working hours, and insufficient support from other family members are examples of the variables that can lead to a person feeling overwhelmed by competing responsibilities at home and work.

WORK STRESS AND HEALTH

Over the past few decades, workers have reported rising levels of stress at work, sometimes dramatically so. For example, a survey conducted by Northwestern National Life Insurance Company found that the proportion of workers who reported feeling highly stressed on the job more than doubled from 1985 to 1990, and the number of workers reporting stress-related illnesses also doubled.[52]

---

[51] Crouter, A. C., Bumpus, M. F., Maguire, M. C., & McHale, S. M. (1999). Linking parents' work pressure and adolescents' well-being: Insights into dynamics in dual-earner families. *Developmental Psychology, 35*(6), 1453–1461.

[52] Northwestern National Life Insurance Company. (1992). *Employee burnout: Causes and cures.* Minneapolis, MN: Author.

Stress in the workplace can lead to significant health consequences, but the relationship between work and health is also a complicated one. On the one hand, people who hold full-time employment do not decline as rapidly – healthwise – as those who do not work full time.[53] Also, people who work report a higher quality of life than those who don't. Work is closely tied to feelings of worth and self-esteem. However, too much of a good thing can have negative effects, especially when work turns to overload and stress.

Research on the relationship between work stress and health has been ongoing for many decades, and many subtle effects have been found. People who feel they must work too many hours on too many tasks certainly report more stress, and they also have poorer health habits and more health complaints. In another study, men who reported higher levels of work pressure and job demands were more likely to seek medical attention and show signs of disease. They were also more likely to die in the ten year period following the original study.[54]

Just as with family life, the role that work stress plays in health is complicated and not easy to pin down. Longer working hours alone may not be the key ingredient, though it is certainly one of them. Role conflict and overload, lack of control, job insecurity, and other factors that increase the level of psychosocial distress, appear to be equally or even more important. For example, dozens of studies have found a link between job strain, defined as a combination of high psychological job demands and low control over the timing or nature of the work, and the risk of cardiovascular disease.[55] The element of control appears to be especially important in the link. People who work hard and long by their own choice are not as likely to experience cardiovascular problems.

COPING STRATEGIES

The new workplace, with its increasing job demands and anytime/anywhere netcentric access, may contribute to just the kinds of conditions that make work stress more likely to affect health and create problems in family life.

[53] Ross, C. E., & Mirowsky, J. (1995). Does employment affect health? *Journal of Health and Social Behavior, 36*(3), 230–244. Retrieved January 27, 2002, from Academic Search Elite database.
[54] House, J. S., Strecher, V., Meltzner, H. L., & Robbins, C. A. (1986). Occupational stress and health among men and women in the Tecumseh Community health study. *Journal of Health and Social Behavior, 27*, 62–77.
[55] Landsbergis, P. A., Schnall, P. L., Belkic, K. L., Baker, D., Schwartz, J., & Pickering, T. G. (2001). Work stressors and cardiovascular disease. *Work, 17*, 191–208.

For example, role conflicts and overload can be greater when the workplace expands beyond the office and the line between work and nonwork becomes unclear. When the home computer sounds an alarm each time an email or instant message arrives, or the cell phone rings during the last quarter of a child's soccer game, workers are confronted with troubling choices about how to spend time. They also lose control over the timing of work. Feelings of being overcommitted, overwhelmed, and unable to meet their responsibilities – either to their jobs or to their families – will mount.

People can be enormously resilient and clever about finding ways to cope, to reduce the effects of higher workloads and job strain on their families, their health, and their own well-being. Some people, for example, choose to withdraw from social and any other kind of activity after a particularly trying day. This strategy may work well as long as the high-overload periods are not constant and long term. As I mentioned earlier, the optimum level of stimulation changes over the day. If much of the work day is filled with a level that is above the optimum and the worker is unable to control it, the worker is likely to seek a much lower level during whatever nonwork hours are available. The husband who just wants to passively watch the news when he returns home from work, rather than engage in activities with the family, is seeking a lower level of stimulation.

For most people, demands at work are not constant, and some researchers have examined whether changes in the work overload affect the day-to-day variations in the quality of family life. Rena Repetti at the University of Pennsylvania investigated the changes in a study of air traffic controllers and their spouses.[56] The workloads of air traffic controllers depend on various factors such as the weather, visibility, and the overall volume of air traffic. She collected data on these factors and also surveyed the controllers and their spouses on their behavior in the evening, measuring the level of social withdrawal, expressions of anger, and amount of support the spouse offered. Repetti found that social withdrawal was the most common response to a tough work day. The air traffic controllers were recovering a balance in the level of stimulation and work intensity by seeking solitude and emotional withdrawal. Support from the spouse was critical to this recovery behavior.

Families in which both parents work and both are experiencing higher job demands and longer working hours have another set of problems. One

[56] Repetti, R. L. (1989). Effects of daily workload on subsequent behavior during marital interaction: The roles of social withdrawal and spouse support [Electronic version]. *Journal of Personality and Social Psychology, 57*(4), 651–659.

strategy is to find ways to synchronize working hours so that the workdays do not overlap as much. This provides more "coverage" for childcare as the parents take turns during a typical work day or week. Alternative working arrangements – such as telecommuting and flex-time – help parents who want to use this approach.

Another strategy that has been growing dramatically is the outsourcing of family responsibilities. When women entered the workforce in larger numbers, the first responsibility that had to be outsourced was childcare. The percentage of women with children under the age of six who were employed outside the home was about 15 percent in the 1950s, but by the end of the century, that figure skyrocketed to 65 percent. The role of childcare has been outsourced to day-care centers, relatives, au pairs, and sometimes the children themselves. Older children become responsible for younger ones, and "latchkey" kids must fend for themselves when they come home from school to an empty house.

Other family responsibilities have been outsourced, as well, particularly by workers in the higher income categories who can afford restaurants, precooked meals, maids, tutors for children, care for elderly parents, delivery services, shopping helpers, or handymen. The Maid Brigade, whose motto is "So you have the time of your life" is a franchise that began in 1979 and now has more than 250 locations in the United States, Canada, Ireland, and Singapore. Working women make up the largest percentage of its clientele, and they go online to schedule a housecleaning visit. The niche of a business like this is the high-income family whose job demands leave them little time for nonwork, especially to spend with their children. This category of service business is booming, according to the *Franchise Times*, and companies were reporting 15 to 25 percent growth rates during the 1990s.[57]

Online shopping is another approach working people are using to deal with rising working hours. Retail e-commerce sales have been climbing steadily since they first were introduced in the mid-1990s. According to the U.S. Department of Commerce, e-commerce sales increased 8.3 percent from the third quarter of 2000 to the same period in 2001, while total retail sales increased only 1.8 percent during that period. Retail e-commerce sales still only account for a tiny fraction of the total (1–2 percent), but the demographics of those who do shop online tell their own story. Nearly one third of U.S. adults shop online, and those shoppers tend to be people with high income and higher levels of education. Women have taken over the

[57] Ehrenreich, B. (2000). Maid to order. *Harper's Magazine, 300*(1799), 59–63.

lead in the profile. Sixty percent of online shoppers in 2001 were women, compared to just 39 percent in 1999.[58]

On an organizational level, many corporations began offering "work–life balance" programs and benefits. These vary considerably, but their common goal is to help their workers deal with the stresses and strains of a high performance, highly demanding workplace in which few barriers exist between work and nonwork. Some companies have implemented corporate childcare facilities and state-of-the-art day care centers with Web cameras that allow parents to watch their children at play. Others offer flextime, more paid leave, exercise rooms at work, stress management classes, reductions in travel time away from home, and even concierge services.

Some of the benefits have been well received, especially those that increase the workers' control over his or her own time. This finding should not be surprising given the research I've just described about the importance of control and how lack of it leads to job strain and health problems. However, other "balance" benefits have been met with skepticism. Single workers, for example, object to company work–life benefits that are so heavily oriented toward married people with children. If married workers were to take all the family leave allotted them for various reasons, the single workers would have to carry the additional workload. Also, many workers question the company's real commitment to work–life balance and hesitate to take advantage of the benefits for fear of losing their place on the fast track. A man, for example, might be very reluctant to take months off after his wife has a baby, even though the company's policy permits it. The man might be justifiably concerned. A CEO confided to management consultant Ken Lizotte that even though he considered himself a liberal person and totally favored allowing women in his company to take a few months off after giving birth to a new baby, he had trouble accepting the idea of a man, the newborn's father, doing the same thing.[59]

Realistically, the netcentric workplace – accessible anytime and anyplace – is not going away. Instead, it is likely to expand further into more geographic and chronological corners of our nonwork lives, with more media richness and intense demands for attention. The typed instant message that appears on the cell phone during the family trip to the zoo may evolve into a color video showing the boss's talking head. Wearable

---

[58] Brown, J., Green, H., & Zellner, W. (2001). Shoppers are beating a path to the web [Electronic version]. *Business Week, 3763*, 41.

[59] Lizotte, K. (2001). Are balance benefits for real? *Journal of Business Strategy, 22*, 32. Retrieved December 19, 2001, from Business Source Premier Database.

technologies will expand access to email or videoconferences, even to the morning jog.

The changes that technology and the Internet have brought to the workplace through their effects on the overall business climate, job security, and the pace of business are also not going away. As consumers, we will not want to give up the "terrific deal" that gives us customized products at affordable prices when we want them. As a result, the global and highly competitive business climate is not likely to subside, and the impact on workers will grow. Whether the wage inequalities that make rewards for clinging to the new workplace's fast lane will remain so high and the punishments for slowing down so severe is an open question.

The individual caught up in a cycle of work–life imbalance has limited choices because so much of the context is beyond the person's control and due to forces that have considerable momentum. The many strategies I described – from outsourcing home responsibilities to work–life balance benefits – can help, though some of them may have other kinds of costs to weigh. It is clear, however, that workers in the fast lane have more difficult decisions to make about how they spend the time of their lives.

4 Business Communication

Annoyed that he rarely saw many cars in the company parking lot at 8 a.m. or at 5 p.m., the CEO of a Kansas City-based company fired off an email to the 400+ managers. [60] "We are getting less than forty hours of work from a large number of our KC-based employees. The parking lot is sparsely used at 8 a.m. Likewise at 5 p.m. As managers – you either do not know what your employees are doing; or you do not care." "In either case," he continued, "you have a problem and you will fix it or I will replace you. NEVER in my career have I allowed a team which worked for me to think they had a 40-hour job. I have allowed you to create a culture which is permitting this. NO LONGER."

He went on to list six possible punishments, including layoffs. He promised that "Hell will freeze over" before he would endorse additional benefits. His metric for compliance was to be the number of cars in the lot. It should be substantially full at 7:30 a.m. and 6:30 p.m. on weekdays, and half full on Saturdays. "You have two weeks. Tick Tock." The intemperate message did not stop at the inboxes of the managers, of course. The email was quickly aired publicly on a Yahoo financial bulletin board, so anyone with Internet access could read it. Investors did, and they reacted so negatively that the stock dropped almost 30 percent in a few days. [61]

The network is an amplifier and this case is an example of how business communications have been affected, sometimes dramatically. Ironically, this company and this CEO were both very tech-savvy. The company made software for the health care industry, and the CEO was very attuned

---

[60] Electronic invective backfires. (2001). *Workforce, 80*(6), 20. Retrieved March 11, 2003, from Business Source Premier Database.

[61] Reese, J. (2001). Email quagmire [Electronic version]. *Public Relations Tactics*, May 2001, 6.

to how significant technology had become in business. In an interview a year earlier he was featured for his genius in a PBS series, and he said, "There was a transformation going on, that the role of, if you will, the computer in our society was quickly going to shift, where the computer would become much more of just a layer of technology . . ."[62] Even business people who understand technology and the Internet do not necessarily use them wisely, nor do they grasp how they have changed the nature and reach of communications.

Courses in business communication at colleges and universities have traditionally focused on letter writing, memos, proposals, and business presentations. The Internet's influence, however, along with the transformations that the net triggered, rendered many of those syllabi obsolete almost before the student graduated. Now the art and science of business communications require us to adapt our styles to a variety of new forms and learn many new skills. As you will see in this chapter, netcentric innovations have had both subtle and dramatic effects on almost every aspect of communications. To understand why videoconferencing is not the same as a face-to-face meeting, why email is not just a faster version of snail mail, or why instant messaging plays a different role than a quick telephone call, we begin with a review of the communication process.

From Sender to Recipient and Back

Regardless of what medium is used to communicate, the communication process can be broken down into several components beginning with the sender's motivation to share something with one or more recipients. It might be information, a question, an idea, an emotion, or perhaps a joke. The sender must transform the content to be shared into a message, encoding it using a variety of strategies and often more than one. The encoding process may take advantage of spoken or typed words, graphic images, facial expressions, postures, pitch of the voice, or gesture.

The third phase in the communication process is the transmission of the message itself, and again, the sender has many choices. If the recipient is standing in front of the sender, the transmission will probably involve spoken words, gestures, posture, facial expression, and tone of voice, though it may also include a blackboard or scribbled diagrams on the back of an

---

[62] Slivers of Genius, Transcript of an interview with Neal Patterson. (2000). Retrieved March 11, 2003, from the Small Business School PBS Series Web site: http://www.smallbusinessschool.org

envelope. If the recipient is not present, the sender might choose the phone, a letter, a memo, an instant message, an email, or any number of communication media that depend on technology. The fourth event is the receipt of the message by the recipient, and the fifth is the processing of that message by the recipient. The recipient can then provide feedback or response to the sender to confirm that he or she received a message at the minimum, thereby closing the communication loop for this single event.

This simple model masks the many complexities and uncertainties that affect any communication process. The challenge for effective business communications in the workplace lies partly in how well we can navigate the many different communication choices we face and how we deal with all those complexities. Netcentric innovations have made some components of the communication process easier and faster, but they have also added surprising twists to the ways in which we communicate. Certainly they added many new choices – email, instant messaging, videoconferencing, for example. They have also altered the meaning and characteristics of many of the old choices.

Consider, for example, the coworker who chooses to send a message to his or her boss about a problem with the company's accounting reports. Should he or she use a paper memo? Before email, the paper memo might have been the logical choice. In the context of widespread corporate email, however, the choice to use a paper memo carries a different kind of signal. Perhaps the worker wants hard-copy documentation for the communication event, or maybe he or she is concerned that system administrators or managers are monitoring the email. The coworker might also realize, wisely, that any email can be forwarded very quickly to large numbers of people – even to the bulletin boards on the Web, like that message from the CEO at Cerner. That can happen to a paper memo also, but the amplification power of the network just makes it much easier.

Many of the uncertainties about communication are not new, but like so many other features of the workplace, they have been amplified and changed by netcentric technologies. For instance, just because a message was sent does not mean the recipient received it. Snail mail goes astray, and people may or may not read memos dropped on their desks. Even in the face-to-face setting, message reception, or at least message processing, may fall through the cracks. If you are speaking at a conference, for example, some of your audience may be paying less than full attention to your remarks. Even though the message was sent and apparently received, it did not make it to this next step of the communication process, in which the recipient decodes the message. For email, the concern about message reception is a valid one. Email systems have become more reliable, but many people still send a follow-up email if they haven't received any response within twenty-four hours, just to check to see whether it was received in the first place. Also, the sheer increase in email volume combined with the rise in spam has led to some very full email inboxes. Your recipient may simply not notice your email amidst the deluge.

The Range of New Choices

The Internet and netcentric technologies have vastly increased the speed of communication, but how have they affected communication *effectiveness*? They have certainly provided many more choices. And because netcentric technologies are still a "work in progress," the landscape of communication choices can be overwhelming – even absurd. Hypothetically, a worker might compose a voice mail greeting that gives callers every possible opportunity and choice to communicate with her:

> "This is Kay. I'll be out of the office from September 3 through September 7, but you can reach me via email at Kay_T@paradigmdesign.com. That's K A Y underscore T T as in Thomas @ P A R A D I G M D E S I G N dot C O M, no space between paradigm and design. I am also available through instant messenger using the nickname of KT67008 if I am online. You can also call me on my cell phone at (300) 555-1212. My fax number is (300) 555 1101. If you need to reach me immediately, page my beeper at (409) 555-8888. The company Web site at www.paradigmdesign.com lists corporate addresses for mail if you need to send materials to the office. Please leave a brief message at the beep, or press 0 to reach the receptionist."

According to research reports, the majority of attempts to contact a business person via the telephone meet with failure, so perhaps it is not completely absurd for someone to compose a message like Kay's so the caller is given some hope of success, if a different communication choice is made. Given the common failure to reach people by phone, it is not surprising that so many flocked to the asynchronous environment of email in which conversations can be spread over time and interactions can take place within whatever time slots each participant had available. Though choppy and fragmented, the medium presented fewer frustrations compared to voice-mail tag.

The vast array of choices have led some researchers to develop hierarchies of "connectedness," presumably to establish how far along a person is toward becoming one of the digerati class – the early adopters of technological innovation who are truly connected. Surveys that attempt to assess the degree to which people are connected sometimes use a simple quantitative approach, in which the number of different technology-based communication tools a person uses is the measure of "connectedness." For example, the Wired/Merrill Lynch Digital Citizen Survey[63] polled 1,444 Americans to examine their views on technology and society. The survey analysts divided the respondents into four categories:

Superconnected: These are people who exchange email at least three days a week and use a laptop, a cell phone, a beeper, and a home computer.

Connected: These are people who exchange email at least three days a week and use three of the four other technologies.

Semiconnected: These are people who use at least one but not more than four of the other technologies.

Unconnected: These are people who do not use any of the technologies.

Only 2 percent of the sample fell into the superconnected category, but Kay's greeting indicates that she would definitely be in that group. The Internet's hourglass architecture makes these connectedness strategies and communication innovations possible, but that does not necessarily mean that they contribute to workplace productivity, nor do they necessarily make communication more effective. A variety of efforts are underway to converge many of these communication media, and help reduce the fragmentation. At least then, a caller would not need to write down several different contact addresses. For example, systems are growing that enable people to provide callers a single phone number that can be routed to whichever phone they happen to be answering at the time. Also, convergence among text messaging, email, and phone calls is in progress, which would make it possible for Kay to pick up her email by phone and listen to a machine-read version of it.

The range of new communication channels make the selection and use of an appropriate channel more complicated. They vary on many levels, and their differences affect the effectiveness of communications in different contexts.[64]

[63] Wired/Merrill Lynch Forum Digital Citizen Survey. (1997). Retrieved December 3, 2001, from http://hotwired.lycos.com/special/citizen/survey/survey.html

[64] Daft, R., & Lengel, R. (1986). Organization information requirements, media richness and structural design. *Management Science, 32*, 554–571.

Describing the Communication Channels

The sender must choose among a growing list of communication channels. That list now includes the face-to-face meeting, a cell phone call, a call to the individual's office number, a voice mail message, a formal business letter, an interoffice memo, a fax, email, instant message, videoconference, a notice on the Intranet, or a handwritten note. These choices are growing more difficult, and it is not uncommon for people to change their minds a time or two before they send the message. A message that the sender thinks might best be transmitted by phone, for example, might not work well at all using voice mail. It is not so surprising that many people hang up before leaving a message on voice mail, and they are not just telemarketers.

The channels vary in many ways, but one key difference lies in their *media richness*. Some channels, such as email, letters, and memos, are leaner than others in terms of the breadth and depth of the communication cues that can be transmitted. The term "low bandwidth" has been borrowed from technology jargon to describe these channels, because they restrict the sender's use of certain kinds of signals, especially the nonverbal variety. High-bandwidth channels, in contrast, offer the sender different means to communicate a message, along with nuances of tone, urgency, or other kinds of meaning. They also allow natural language and immediate feedback from the recipient, giving the sender a chance to modify his or her use of the channels in midstream.

The lower bandwidth channels include letters, fax, and email. Letters are particularly low because of the time delay in transmission and in receiving a response. Instant messages have less bandwidth in terms of the amount of text one can transmit at a time, though the opportunity for instant response adds another kind of richness to the communication event. Voice mail has greater media richness because tone of voice can be transmitted along with the words. Telephone conversations offer additional bandwidth because the recipient can respond immediately and the sender receives feedback. Face-to-face communication has the highest bandwidth, because the channels include everything from gestures, facial expressions, and voice, to olfactory and touch cues. The interactive videoconference would fall between telephone and face-to-face communication in terms of media richness.

According to media richness theory, email falls somewhere between the telephone and the letter in terms of the availability of multiple channels of communication. It lacks voice, but it provides faster delivery and response compared to a letter. However, communication channels do not just vary along a continuum of media richness, and different channels have various advantages and disadvantages. Email as a medium, for example, should be viewed in a larger context that takes into account certain value that the medium offers.[65] In particular, email offers the convenience of multiple addressing, external recording, and computer processing. It is very easy to address an email to many people at once, especially through distribution lists or mailing lists. It is recorded digitally, so email exchanges can be reviewed later (for better or worse, as we will see later in this book). They also add a new kind of value that did not exist before: the ability to process the exchanges by computer. For instance, email systems allow you to search and sort your messages in innumerable ways. You can sort the messages by date, by sender, or by subject, and you can sift through the text in the hundreds of messages in your inbox to find specific phrases. If you know you received a message with the phone number of a good marketing consultant, but can't recall who sent it, you can search all your messages for the words "marketing consultant" or "marketing" or "consultant." This power is unavailable for face-to-face or telephone conversations. It is rarely available for letters, unless a corporation takes the time to scan every letter using optical character recognition technology and convert them into searchable electronic documents.

CHOOSING A CHANNEL FOR ITS RICHNESS

Why do people in the workplace choose one channel over another when they communicate? Research on the selection of particular channels in different situations shows that media richness is a key ingredient. Linda Trevino, Jane Webster, and Eric Stein conducted a field study of media choices, attitudes, and use in a variety of work organizations and found that people made choices for quite a variety of reasons.[66] Their sample included low and middle managers from a professional association, a university, and several corporations. They divided the sample into four groups, and sent each one a questionnaire in which they were asked to think about the last time they chose one of the following to communicate: letter, fax, email, or face-to-face meeting. These channels cover the range of low to high media richness.

---

[65] Sproull, L., & Kiesler, S. (1991). *Connections: New ways of working in the network.* Cambridge, MA: MIT Press.

[66] Trevino, L. K., Webster, J., & Stein, E. W. (2000). Making connections: Complementary influences on communication media choices, attitudes, and use. *Organization Science: A Journal of the Institute of Management Sciences, 11*(2), 163–183.

The participants confirmed that their perception of media richness for the four channels differed, with letters having the lowest and face-to-face meetings having the highest. One important reason they chose to use a channel with more or less richness had to do with the contents of the message itself. For example, the respondents were asked to rate the equivocality of the message they chose to send through the medium in terms of its emotional content, its openness to multiple interpretations, and other characteristics. Some messages are straightforward, factual in content, and not easily misinterpreted, but others can be interpreted differently depending on many factors – the personality of the person who is receiving the message, the cultural context, the time of day, or perhaps the company's financial position. The respondents who were recalling their use of one of the lower bandwidth channels tended to describe the content as less equivocal.

This finding should not be too surprising. It makes sense to use the leaner channels for straightforward messages, where misinterpretation is less likely when only text is used to transmit. However, the workplace is filled with examples of how email – presumably a low-bandwidth medium – is used to transmit and discuss sensitive issues that would definitely rate at the top in terms of "equivocality." A worker who receives an equivocal message on such a low-bandwidth medium from a boss might puzzle for days about its meaning. In one case, the boss typed a brief "Thanks, I own you" after the worker stayed late to complete a project. The worker shared the message with colleagues and debate over the real meaning erupted. One coworker insisted it was a typo and the boss meant, "I owe you." Others were sure it was a Freudian slip that suggested a deep-seated lust for power. The boss claimed it was just a joke.

The research findings confirm that business people judge the equivocality of the message content and use that judgment to help them decide what channel to use, but the link between these two is not as clear for the new media, especially email. Clearly there are other factors involved in the decision. Though most people might not use email as egregiously as the Cerner CEO did in the example at the beginning of this chapter, many are not clear about when to use it, or how it affects the workplace.

CHOOSING A CHANNEL FOR ITS COST AND CONVENIENCE

Trevino and her colleagues uncovered other factors that were linked to the selection of a particular channel for a particular communication, some of which spring from practical constraints. For example, people tend to use the leaner media, particularly email, when their colleagues are more distant and there is little funding for travel. Even if the message would warrant a richer medium, the costs to bring the players together for a face-to-face meeting would be prohibitive.

Another factor associated with the choice of medium involved the number of recipients, a finding that is especially interesting in light of the Cerner incident. When a sender needs to reach a larger number of people, email becomes an attractive choice. It is cheap, easy to send, and quickly delivered to as many recipients as the sender likes. For the CEO, these factors probably outweighed any concern for the psychological impact of using such a harsh tone on a low-bandwidth medium, if in his pique he even took the time to weigh the pros and cons of different communication channels. The participants in Trevino's study were influenced in their choice by the size of the audience, but this criterion can be very misleading for media such as email. The recipients who actually receive the transmission may far outnumber the original distribution list because of forwarding. It is certainly possible to make photocopies of a letter or fax and distribute them to others who were not the intended recipients. It is just far easier with email.

CHOOSING A CHANNEL FOR ITS SYMBOLISM

Media symbolism plays a role in an individual's choice of communication channels in the workplace, as well, and people choose particular channels based on the impression they believe it will make. Trevino and her colleagues asked the participants this question, replacing the word "medium" with the particular channel assigned to each participant (fax, email, letter, face-to-face meeting):

> "Think beyond the content of the message itself to other reasons for sending this message [*by the medium*]." For example, "Sending this message via [*the medium*]:
>
> ■ conveyed my desire for teamwork, participation, involvement, or cooperation;
> ■ transmitted my sense of the urgency or immediacy of the message;
> ■ communicated that the message was low priority or not very important;
> ■ conveyed that the message was formal, official, or legitimate."

The medium is part of the message, and people tend to choose one or another based on the medium's symbolism. The researchers also asked the participants to reflect on what their coworkers would think about what their choice of channel meant. For example, would coworkers perceive the choice as signaling a desire for teamwork, a sense of urgency, or a need for formality? Again, the results demonstrated that the choice of channel was made with some attention to how others would perceive the choice.

The role of a medium's symbolism is linked to the organization itself and the corporate culture. It should come as no surprise to a new Microsoft employee that he or she is expected to use email extensively, though after damaging corporate email was resurrected to haunt the company in the government's antitrust suit, the medium's organizational symbolism may have cooled somewhat. In *Business @ the Speed of Thought*, Bill Gates writes, "Electronic collaboration is not a substitute for face-to-face meetings. It's a way to ensure that more work gets done ahead of time so that meetings in person will be more productive. Meeting time is so precious that you want to be sure you're dealing with facts and good recommendations based on solid analysis, not just anecdotal evidence. You want to be sure that meetings produce actionable decisions, that you don't just sit around speculating and talking about philosophical stuff."[67]

The social influence theory emphasizes that the choice of a channel is heavily influenced by the organization and its norms and by the symbolism particular channels carry within that organization. Some organizations depend heavily on face-to-face meetings and ask traveling workers to join via conference phone even if they must use a phone from an airplane. Others seem eerily quiet, as workers email or instant message one another from the next cubicle or office rather than step around the corner. Nevertheless, within any organization there is considerable variety and employees choose their channels for diverse reasons. One of my colleagues, working in a highly email-oriented environment, rarely used the medium to send email although he read it regularly. He delivered even the most innocuous and nonequivocal messages in a manila envelope under the door, with every opening taped so tightly closed that I was never able to open them without scissors. As we will discuss later in this chapter, cultural factors play an important role, and some cultures place higher value on face-to-face meetings than others do. Finally, the new media may be stubbornly resisting a clear-cut fit into traditional models of communication simply because they are new, and people are still learning how and when to use them. Textbooks on business communications have been prescribing strategies for writing letters, memos, and other kinds of communiques for many years, and norms for these media have developed over decades – even centuries. Email and other new media, however, have fewer norms and their use is more idiosyncratic in the workplace.

[67] Gates, W. H. (1999). *Business @ the speed of thought*. New York: Warner Books.

Attitudes about New Media

In the first decade of the twenty-first century, with the Internet's widespread introduction into the workplace barely a decade old, people have vastly different experiences with electronic communication media. Some have been using email for years within their organization and workgroups, whereas others have never used it. New employees just entering the work-force from college may be quite familiar with new communication media, having used them routinely to communicate with study group members, friends, family, professors, and online acquaintances. Other new media, such as videoconferencing or simple text messages transmitted via cell phone, are less widely used but have already made significant penetration in some corporations.

The diversity in experience partly explains why people at work carry different attitudes about the media and make different choices about when and how to use them. John R. Carlson at the University of Utah and Robert W. Zmud at the University of Oklahoma believe that experience is the key ingredient, and people's attitudes and choices change as they become more familiar not just with the medium itself but with the message topics and organizational context, and also with the styles of their communication partners. They proposed the *channel expansion theory*, which emphasizes the important role that knowledge-building experiences with the new media play in developing and changing the attitudes people hold about the media. In particular, people change their thinking about how rich the media can be.[68]

Carlson and Zmud sent out two versions of a set of surveys to faculty, staff, and administrative email users at a large southeastern university to assess the importance of four types of knowledge-building experiences. One version asked the respondents to think about a communication partner or a message topic with which they had more experience, and the other asked them to think about a partner or topic with which they had little experience. All respondents were asked to agree or disagree with statements such as, "I am very experienced using email," "I feel close to my communication partner," and "I feel that I am well-versed in the concepts associated with the topic." They were also asked about their attitudes toward email's richness as a medium. The results of the study confirmed that perceptions about a channel do indeed expand to become richer when we have certain types of experiences. The more comfortable people felt with email, and

---

[68] Carlson, J. R., & Zmud, R. W. (1999). Channel expansion theory and the experiential nature of media richness perceptions. *Academy of Management Journal, 42*(2), 153–171.

the more experience people had with a particular communication partner, the richer they thought the medium was. Also, the respondents held more positive views of email's richness when they were knowledgeable about the topic, though this variable was not quite as important as the others. It was interesting that one variable that was not important was the actual number of messages exchanged between the respondent and the communication partner. It appears that the experiences that affect our perceptions of the new media don't necessarily have to be numerous. They just have to add to our knowledge about it in some way.

Email: A Case Study

The words Samuel Morse transmitted as he officially inaugurated the telegraph in a public demonstration in 1844 were, "What hath God wrought." The choice indicated that Morse was either cognizant he was making history or aware of the need for a press-worthy phrase to promote his invention.[69] From there, the inaugural messages sent via new communications media went downhill, at least in terms of their memorability and grandeur. Alexander Graham Bell's first message on the telephone was, "Mr. Watson, come here. I need you." Though Roy Tomlinson is credited with sending the first email message, he can't recall what it was. "Most likely, the first message was QWERTYIOP or something similar."

EMAIL'S INFORMAL ROOTS

Two of the key figures in the Internet's early development were J. C. R. Licklider and Albert Verazza. In one of their papers, they attempted to explain email's immense popularity among ARPANET researchers, even though it was not one of the applications originally planned for the network:

> "One of the advantages of the message systems over letter mail was that, in an ARPANET message, one could write tersely and type imperfectly, even to an older person in a superior position and even to a person one did not know very well, and the recipient took no offense. . . . Among the advantages of the network message services over the telephone were the fact that one could proceed immediately to the point without having to engage in small talk first, that the message services produced a preservable record, and that the sender and receiver did not have to be available at the same time."[70]

[69] Standage, T. (1998). *The Victorian Internet.* New York: Berkeley Books.
[70] Licklider, J. C. R., & Verazza, A. (1978). Cited in Campbell, T. (1998). First email message. *Pre-Text Magazine*, Mar/Apr, 1998. Retrieved December 5, 2001, from Pre-Text Web site: http://www.pretext.com/mar98/features/story2.htm

   The history of email underscores its importance as an informal communication tool, one that filled a cavernous hole in the tools that were available
at the time. It clearly filled a need for asynchronous, direct – even abrupt –
communications that bypassed the time-consuming formality and delays
of letters, hierarchies, and organizational boundaries. It is from these roots
that modern email derives its informal quality. Even if email users have no
idea who Licklider or Verazza were, and even if they don't recognize the
term "ARPANET," they find that email fills many of the same communication needs. It gave its early users a chance to converse asynchronously with
anyone in their sphere of communication, regardless of position or status,
and it still does that today.

EMAIL'S EVOLVING NORMS

From its informal roots, email has emerged as a powerful and very
widespread medium for business communication. The nature of the way
it evolved has often caused confusion about its role, and the norms for its
use are far from stable. Though modern business communication courses
include email and sometimes other forms of the new media in the curriculum, there are few "templates" for the perfect business email the way
there are for business letters. This is a key reason researchers are having
difficulty pinning down why people choose certain channels or develop
particular attitudes about business communication practices using email or
other electronic forms.

   Compare, for example, the standard forms for business letters. The formatting rules for such letters are prescribed rather rigidly, with the letterhead at the top, followed by the date, which is followed by the inside address. The address itself follows a standard format, with the recipient's name
appearing with a title. The next line begins with "Dear," followed by the
person's first name or title plus last name. The rules for deciding whether
to use "Dear Mary" or "Dear Ms. Arcas" in the salutation are a bit looser,
though guidebooks generally recommend that the sender only use the first
name if the recipient is known to the sender and they are already on a first
name basis. The use of "Ms." rather than "Mrs." or "Miss" spread in the
1970s, partly to avoid titles that carried implications about marital status.
"Sincerely" and "Cordially" are standard complimentary closings, followed
by the space for the signature and the sender's typed name and title. Rules
also exist for identifying enclosures and copies to other parties. Business
memos also have prescribed rules for formatting, with familiar lines beginning with "Date:", "To:", "From:", and "Subject:".

   Email, however, has far fewer prescribed standards in the workplace. For
example, people begin the body of their email messages with a variety of

Hello again

Hi there!

Hi from Pete

David,

Hi David,

Good morning David,

Howdy David,

Dear David Crystal,

Annwyl David Crystal (Annwyl is Welsh for Dear)

Dear Professor Crystal,

Estimado profesor Crystal,

Figure 4.1. Email Salutations to David Crystal, author of *Language and the Internet*.

salutations. As you can see in Figure 4.1, "Dear" is in evidence, though it is often confined to email from a sender the recipient does not know. As a communication medium, email represents a mixture of speech and writing, and the formatting styles appear to reflect this. People often use ellipses or other kinds of punctuation to suggest a pause that might separate phrases if they were speaking, and they use very varied paragraph and indentation styles.

One reason for this heterogeneity is that people use email in the workplace in many different ways, and the styles shift depending on the intended use, the capabilities of the sender, and the recipient. People have become extraordinarily adept at mixing and matching styles and formats, attempting to establish the right tone at the right time while still taking advantage of email's speed, convenience, and low cost. Trying to nail down and prescribe a standardized "business email style" may be difficult and nonproductive.

Informality, and the instability of standardized norms, has led to considerable variety in the way people use the medium, especially the language and formatting styles they choose. Linguist David Crystal, author of the *Cambridge Encyclopedia of the English Language*, discusses the enormous variation in the language of email in his *Language and the Internet*.[71] For openings, for example, he found that two thirds of his own email sample contained a salutation, but unlike paper-based letters there was enormous variety.

[71] Crystal, D. (2001). *Language and the Internet*. Cambridge, UK: Cambridge University Press.

As you can see, the salutations cover the gamut from the highly informal to the highly formal, and they play a key role in establishing the tone of the message, whether formal or informal, personal or professional, respectful or lighthearted. Physical cues and formatting generally perform these functions for paper documents. A letter, printed on paper with heavy cotton content, beginning "Dear Professor Crystal" and ending with a hand-signed signature block, sets a tone of formality. The language within it would be predictably formal. In contrast, a hand-written note on a sheet of notebook paper sent through intraoffice mail would be predictably informal. In terms of physical cues and formatting, email is far more homogeneous, and unable to signal this kind of tone easily. An email from your son has the same look and feel – physically speaking – as an email from your boss.

SETTING THE TONE IN EMAIL

In the absence of physical cues, the subject line and salutation help set the tone for the email. In the workplace, once the author has selected email as the channel, he or she must then make deliberate choices about what tone would be appropriate and how to convey it. Because of the various uses of email, both formal and informal, and the lack of standards such as those that exist for letters and memos, the job of tone-setting is especially difficult and can easily go awry. The tone the author believes was set may not be what the recipient interprets. The author may think he or she is being casually friendly with a salutation such as Hi, Dave, but the recipient may take it as a disrespectful affront.

On a show about email for which I was a guest, Sam Donaldson told the story of how the tone of one of his emails had been grossly misinterpreted. He had sent an email to one of his staff who did a great deal of writing for his shows. The message concerned the script for an upcoming segment, and in the email he remarked in jest – or what he was sure would be taken as jest – "Of course, everyone knows that I do most of the writing." Her reply was apologetic and cool; she apparently assumed he was not joking and was seriously deluding himself about who did the writing. He was clearly upset about the misinterpretation and could not understand how someone he knew so well could think he wasn't kidding around.

Surprisingly little research has been done to investigate the ingredients of tone in workplace email. However, we do know that the lack of nonverbal cues makes them particularly susceptible to misinterpretation, and that their use as "written speech" adds to their unpredictability. Research dealing with the way people attempt to create an impression online shows that

most people are awkward when the only tools they have to create an impression are the keyboard and mouse. And oddly, we often forget how much
difficulty we ourselves have making the impression we want to make with
that keyboard when we form impressions of others via electronic communication. For example, Rodney Fuller's research on impression formation
demonstrated that people who communicate entirely through email and
have never met their colleagues in person tend to overestimate the partner's
coolness and rationality and underestimate the person's emotional and feeling side.[72] In an earlier book, *The Psychology of the Internet*, I examined in
much greater depth the psychological aspects of the online environment
and how that environment affects behavior. One of the key features involves the nuances of tone that so easily get lost or distorted in the lower
bandwidth communication media.[73]

With the exception of the emerging virtual teams in which the participants are located in distant parts of the globe, much workplace email
is transmitted between people who do know one another and have met
face-to-face. Often, they are close colleagues. The tone of an electronic exchange is thus interpreted in a larger context that includes everything else
the coworker knows about you. This is perhaps why Sam Donaldson was so
surprised and dismayed that his email was misinterpreted. The event suggested that the impression he thought he had created at the workplace, and
the context in which he assumed his email would be interpreted, was not
entirely accurate. Without the nonverbal cues, irony and humor often go
awry when transmitted via email, even between long-time coworkers.

Modern business communication texts are expansive about how to organize a message and establish tone in a variety of contexts when writing
letters, memos, or holding face-to-face interviews. For example, in the sixth
edition of *Business Communications Today*, Courtland L. Bovée and John V.
Thrill describe the direct organizational plan in detail, recommending it
for messages dealing with routine content, good news, and goodwill. These
are messages that are not particularly sensitive, and they should begin with
the main idea and most important information in the first paragraph. The
remainder of the message provides necessary details. Messages carrying bad
news, or messages that are supposed to persuade the reader who is either

---

[72] Fuller, R. (1996). Human-computer-human interaction: How computers affect human communication. In D. L. Day, & D. K. Kovacs (Eds). *Computers, communication
and mental models.* London: Taylor & Francis.
[73] Wallace, P. (1999). *The psychology of the Internet.* New York: Cambridge University
Press.

uninterested or unwilling, are better suited to the indirect approach. Bad news, for example, should begin with a neutral statement as a transition to the reasons for the bad news. The bad news can then be either stated clearly or only implied, and the sender should follow it with something positive, such as, "You'll certainly find an opening in which your skills and aspirations match the job requirements exactly."

Such precise instructions about how to handle tone in email are generally lacking, or brimming with caveats. When a communication medium is used for so many purposes, and when its use in a variety of workplace contexts is growing so rapidly, it is difficult to develop a handbook of email style. Instead, guides, magazine articles, and textbooks often propose a list of do's and don'ts, and tips that mix technical issues, courtesy, legal issues, and common sense. In business, however, more formal uses of email are growing rapidly, almost as a replacement for the much slower snail mail.

FORMAL USES OF EMAIL

Although vast quantities of email fall into the informal "written speech" category, email is increasingly being used for situations in which the sender might have chosen a more formal business letter or memo to strike the right tone, or for legal reasons. The sender chooses email because of that medium's characteristics but then constructs the email in a way that mimics the more formal paper-based communication medium. For example, the controller of a company may send out an "email memo" to everyone in the organization to advise them of an upcoming policy change about reimbursement for travel. This email might follow the standard memo formatting as much as possible, given the constraints of the medium. Nevertheless, the format would be quite recognizable as a memo. The tone is clearly official, informative, and binding with respect to corporate policies.

Many emails also resemble the letter format, beginning with "Dear" and ending with a standard complimentary closing. David Crystal's list of salutations, for example, included "Dear Professor" and "Dear Dr. Crystal," in addition to "Hi there." These letter formats are often used to distribute information to a large community (Dear Colleague letter), relying on a recognizable and formal style. Most of the letter-formatted emails I receive have a serious tone and are distributed widely to the organization.

Another use for email is simply to introduce a more formal document, such as a business letter or project proposal, transmitted electronically. Email systems often limit the kind of formatting the sender can do, and email systems may not display the sender's message the way it was originally formatted anyway. For example, one email guide reminded senders to put a carriage return after every seventy characters or so, similar to the way we typed letters on typewriters before word-wrap became the norm. The reason for this advice is that some older email systems may truncate lines in awkward places and display the email with odd line breaks.

```
If you are able to attend the meeting on January
31, 2001, please contact
our travel agency for additional details about
expense reporting. We
will be happy to assist you.
```

The use of email to transmit formatted documents is becoming widespread, though it may seem somewhat odd. I often receive informal emails whose only purpose is to introduce the attachment, which is a letter:

```
Pat, here is that letter I promised you. Hard copy
should arrive tomorrow. -Don
```

The email contains an attachment that follows the standard business letter format, again, as much as possible. Although the sender may include a digitized version of the letterhead on the electronically transmitted letter, these documents may exclude the signature. The point is to speed up communication between people who are working together but still adhere to formal business letter standards. Emails are also used to introduce proposals, presentations, and other kinds of documents which the sender prefers to transmit as attachments, with formatting intact. This is especially important for documents that contain tables, charts, or other graphics.

An important limitation on formal email is that the infrastructure to establish it as a formal and binding communication tool is not yet established, as I discussed briefly in a previous chapter. The electronic infrastructure must provide assurance in several areas: *acceptance, security, integrity,* and *authentication.*[74] *Acceptance* means that a document transmitted electronically must be accepted by courts of law, just as its hard-copy version would be accepted. *Security* must also be ensured – whatever digital documents exist should be secured so they won't be lost, stolen, or compromised.

---

[74] Minihan, J. (2001). Electronic signature technologies: A tutorial. *Information Management Journal, 35*(4), 4–8.

In traditional business, the original signed document might be stored in a locked cabinet and transported by means of a commercial express mail carrier. Although many would debate the security afforded by those traditional strategies, they are what businesses now rely upon. A digital version of a document might lose a few packets of data during transmission, and its storage could be compromised by faults in the storage medium. Hard disks crash, and material stored on digital media such as CD-ROMs do not last indefinitely. Some estimate the life span of a CD-ROM, for example, is five years, partly because the technology used to create them, write to them, and read them changes so quickly. Even if the CD-ROM is still stored safely in the filing cabinet, is there software and hardware available to read it? (I have hundreds of 5 ¼ inch floppy disks in my basement, but no floppy drive that can read them now.)

The third component of assurance is *integrity*, which means that the document that is received must be exactly the same as the one that was sent. Not only must the transmission be reliable, but also the recipient must be assured that nothing was altered between sender and receiver. Finally, the document must be *authenticated* as actually coming from the sender. The recipient must be assured that the transmission was initiated by the sender, and the sender can't repudiate it. We generally rely on signatures for this, but we also use the tape recorder. Stock brokers, for example, typically tape conversations to document requests for stock purchases or sales.

Our traditional mechanisms to establish these levels of assurance are hardly foolproof, but the electronic environment will need rigorous strategies to provide this kind of assurance, especially because people in business will need confidence that their electronic exchanges and transactions are at least as reliable as their paper-based ones. Don, for example, felt he had to follow up the electronic transmission of his letter with a hard copy sent by mail.

EMAIL AS EVIDENCE

Although assurance is still a work in progress for electronically transmitted documents in many legal contexts, email has certainly been turning up in court rooms. Prosecutors are using email as evidence in numerous high-profile corporate cases, and corporate policies on its use are getting increasingly stringent. One of the more noteworthy cases involved Henry Blodget, a Merrill Lynch analyst whose publicly stated praise for certain companies enticed investors to buy the stock. When his private emails were released, however, they showed very different opinions. For example, he called one stock that he publicly encouraged investors to buy a "piece of crap" in his private email.[75] According to one report, the New York state attorney general convinced Merrill Lynch to settle for $100 million for allowing one of its analysts to so egregiously mislead investors.[76] Soon after, Merrill Lynch developed a required workshop for its employees that focused on how to use email appropriately.[77]

Even when people are fully aware of the characteristics of email and have seen it used in numerous court cases, they may still get into considerable trouble. They mix styles and use a level of informality that could offend recipients in a business context, or at least be misinterpreted. They say things with this "written speech" that they do not want forwarded, even when they know, intellectually, how easy it is to forward email and how often it happens. They also know, or should know by now, that email is not private. It is archived, and deleting it from your own machine doesn't delete it from the server, or from the many backup tapes. Nor does it delete it from the recipient's hard drive.

One reason for this disconnect is that email is composed alone, in private, without the cues that help guide and constrain any social interaction or remind people of the potential legal consequences. You can't see your recipient's facial expression, hear the person's voice, or notice his or her posture or dress. The trappings of email, such as the encrypted password, lead workers to think it is private. The delete key leads workers to think email is really deleted.

Studies of computer-mediated communication demonstrate that people are vulnerable to *disinhibition* when they communicate electronically, partly because of the characteristics I just described. The physical distance from the recipient, along with the privacy in which the sender composes the message, appears to make it more likely that the sender will step over boundaries and say things they would not say in a letter or in person, for example. They may use language, phrases, and a tone that they would not use in person. For the worker and the corporation, this disinhibition is difficult to stop, but it can be disastrous.

For protection, corporations are requiring workshops such as the one Merrill Lynch developed, and they are taking other measures as well. Some

[75] Lavelle, M., Barnett, M., Benjamin, M., Clark, K., Grose, T. K., Newman, R. J., Perry, J., Pethokoukis, J. M., Sherrid, P., Schmitt, C. H., & Streisand, B. (2002). Rogues of the year. *U.S. News & World Report, 133*(25), 32+. Retrieved March 12, 2003, from Business Source Premier Database.

[76] Brown, E. (2002). To shred and protect. *Forbes, 170*(11), 114+. Retrieved March 12, 2003, from Business Source Premier Database.

[77] Varchaver, N., & Bonamici, K. (2003). The perils of email. *Fortune* (Asia), *147*(3), 96+. Retrieved March 12, 2003, from Business Source Premier Database.

companies are limiting email storage, and some are establishing formal policies that wipe out all email from servers and backup tapes after thirty to ninety days. These measures may help a little, but email is essentially a self-replicating organism. In any case, many situations may require the company to retain old emails and turn them over if a court demands them. Arthur Andersen, for example, was convicted partly because they destroyed Enron-related emails.

THE AUDIENCE FOR EMAIL

Several common netiquette tips attempt to deal with the issue of audience, a key variable in developing effective business communications. When business students study the use of letters, memos, presentations, or marketing tactics, they learn a great deal about how to analyze the audience and tailor the message to fit. They learn how to predict how their audience will react to certain kinds of appeals or persuasive messages and how to be sensitive to cultural issues, status, gender, age, and formality levels. On email, however, it is more difficult to tailor a message because the audience is never entirely obvious. Who will read your message besides the person or people you send it to? We know that the company owns the mail system and has the right to read anything you write, though most managers probably do not exercise this privilege routinely. We also know that forwarding messages with or without the sender's permission is common practice in many organizations.

People forward messages for a variety of reasons, many of them perfectly innocuous. They may simply want to share the sender's views with another coworker, or they may just be trying to save time and avoid retyping when the message contains factual information that needs wider distribution. They may want to bring a new employee up to speed about an online discussion of a workplace issue and use an aggregated composite of email exchanges as a discussion transcript for the new person's benefit.

In some contexts, however, people forward messages for far less noble or productivity-related reasons. They may want a supervisor to see your untactful response or send documented evidence that you are an incompetent, lazy employee who wastes company time. More than a few people save email going back years and can locate exchanges a decade or more old. Although many people in the workplace are now more knowledgeable about email's lack of privacy, they may not have been then. Their early messages may be retrieved from the archives and forwarded around.

Because of growing concerns about forwarding, some companies mandate a statement at the end of every email their employees send that reads:

This message contains information which may be confidential and privileged. Unless you are the addressee (or authorized to receive for the addressee), you may not use, copy, or disclose to anyone the message or any information contained in the message. If you have received the message in error, please advise the sender by "reply" email, and delete the message. Thank you very much.

The message may or may not prevent forwarding without permission, but it certainly reinforces the sender's wishes about the practice.

Email is also vulnerable to misdelivery from human error and inattention, and netiquette tips often address this. For example, they advise senders to be careful about replying to the sender rather than all the recipients of the message. This is a common mistake on email, and results in innumerable, trivial messages sent to large distribution groups unnecessarily. It also can result in a barrage of follow-up responses reminding the offender to confine replies to the sender. It is especially common on RSVPs. When a sender invites dozens of people to a conference or meeting, at least a few will reply to the whole group, "I'll be there!"

Misdeliveries are also common because the recipient's address appears on the To: line, and it may be obscure or not even visible in some circumstances. A sender can compose an entire email, click send, and then learn later that the message was misdelivered. The SEND key is very easy to click, and clicking on it often does nothing but send immediately, with no chance to recheck the recipient's address or change your mind about sending. Some email systems ask for a confirmation or perform a spell check, but many do not.

Philip Roth describes one of the most ghastly misdeliveries in his novel, *The Human Stain*. Delphine Roux, a lonely classics professor at a small university, composes a personal "in search of" ad to send to the New York Review of Books by email. She accidentally sends it to the distribution list for her colleagues instead. Her distress is so great that she demolishes her own office and pretends that an enemy broke in, compromised her computer, and sent out the forged message under her email account to humiliate her. Such email misdeliveries are not just grist for novels. For example, Laura Lowery, a Washington, DC, public relations executive, misdirected a racy message, meant for her boyfriend, to the distribution list of her colleagues at work – including her supervisor.[78]

Another reason email presents a special challenge in the workplace is precisely because it is such a convenient communication medium in so many

[78] Kleiner, C. (1999). Online buffs hit and miss on manners. *U.S. News & World Report, 126*(11), 60.

contexts. At work, one can easily send an email to a boyfriend called "Tiger," and one would expect the tone, language, formatting, and approach to be different from what one would use to address a colleague, boss, customer, or business associate. We are using the same communication medium in contexts that have very different norms associated with them. Given the homogenous nature of email in terms of the way it appears on the screen and the physical acts required to compose and send messages, it is not surprising people would mix up the norms rather easily.

The cues that signal appropriate styles of communication in a face-to-face contact are very salient and easy to spot. In a face-to-face meeting in a conference room with leather chairs, and in which everyone is in business attire, one is not likely to forget business communication norms. Shouting, name-calling, or off-color jokes are inappropriate. Winking [;)] or sticking your tongue out [:P] would also seem out of place. When we use email, however, the cues that signal the context for communication are much less salient. When we compose email, regardless of the recipient, the physical cues that might trigger a switch from what is appropriate in a business context to what is perfectly OK for friends and family are very sparse. In fact, the only cue may be the obscure email address on the To: line, which is not a very powerful means of reminding people of the context.

EMAIL MARKETING AND SPAM

Email marketing exploded in the 1990s, and inboxes everywhere filled up with ads for get rich quick schemes, hair loss treatments, invitations to gambling casinos, vitamins, pornography, vacation getaways, and just about everything else. The fact that marketers could send messages to thousands or millions of prospective customers for free was too enticing to ignore. This approach is much less expensive than direct mail, and even a miniscule return response on a mailing of a million emails, sent out at virtually no cost, makes direct email a very profitable and worthwhile marketing strategy. After many complaints and some lawsuits, many businesses now politely ask you to check a box if you want to receive messages about their new products and sales. This approach is called *opt in*, since you must proactively choose to receive the commercial messages. Most companies, however, much prefer the *opt out* approach, in which they check the box for you and insist that you uncheck it to decline the deluge of email marketing. Most people leave check marks in place probably because they don't have time to read all the fine print on a Web site. This means that few opt in and most do not opt out. The result is a vast quantity of commercial email.

Companies that use opt in or opt out are at least giving the consumer a choice about receiving email, but spammers do not give people any choice. They use programs to comb through Web sites, chat rooms, discussion boards, and organization directories to capture and record email addresses and then add them to voluminous lists that can be sold to those who want to send out unsolicited commercial email to millions of people. To avoid detection, spammers often choose a variety of crafty methods to prevent the recipients from finding out who they are or where they are located. They also use various strategies to determine whether you read the spam. A popular trick is to include a "remove me from the list" function that users can click, presumably to avoid receiving mail from them in the future. However, people who click on that button typically just confirm to the spammer that they have reached a valid email address, which can be confidently spammed again.

Tracking down a spammer for violations of privacy can be incredibly difficult. Robin Peek tells the story of one such attempt:

> "I recently received email from Infowinner.info and Dotcomdiscounts.info, two different companies that I had never heard of. So I decided to track them down and read their privacy statements. I found that both had not only identically written privacy statements, but identical addresses and telephone numbers. And furthermore, each stated that 'by entering into any sweepstakes offered by [either company], you are essentially opted in.' And that 'our subscribers are fully aware about the use of their personal information prior to choosing to subscribe to any of our sites.' Ah, but here's the rub: I don't enter sweepstakes. And when I went back to Infowinner.info the next day, the site was gone."[79]

The rush to obtain valid email addresses has so much momentum because email marketing is cost-effective. Many "free" products are available for employees to download, and their only price is contact information. A recent product, for example, promises to keep your email address book up-to-date by sending out automatic update requests to all the people in your contact list. When your email partners receive this automated request, they can update your address book, then choose to join this network of address updating. The result, as more people join in, would be a pyramid scheme that will provide the software vendor an incredibly rich harvest of valid, business-related email addresses. Bill Machrone, VP at Ziff Davis Media, sees this kind of software as a serious potential threat to privacy

[79] Peek, R. (2003). Spam jeopardizes email publishing. *Information Today*, March, 20. Retrieved March 12, 2003, from Business Source Premier Database.

and confidentiality, because you are essentially sending a complete list of your contacts to a third party, outside your company. Though the company promises not to do anything with the information without your permission, such promises have been broken in the past, especially after the company changes hands.[80]

As I described earlier in this chapter, email evolved as an informal communication tool for researchers, and commercial email was initially verboten. Times have changed, and now email marketing, solicited or unsolicited, has turned into a major problem in the workplace because it can be such a distraction to workers and a burden on system resources. Companies are racing to implement various spam filtering software along with their virus detection products that identify various components of potential spam and either delete it before it arrives in the employees' inboxes or change the subject line so it is easy to spot as SPAM. Some analysts predict that the only way to stop the flood is to meter the Internet, so the cost of commercial email falls to the sender, and not to the organization and the employee's time and productivity.

EMAIL HOAXES

A special variety of spam is the email hoax, widely distributed and redistributed over the net to those harvested email addresses. Their originators take advantage of the net's amplification power to spread pranks and schemes to millions, and they can cause serious disruptions and productivity losses in the workplace.

One type of hoax warns the recipient about a virus that does not exist. This variety sometimes includes specific instructions for the recipient to first determine whether they have the virus, and then follows with the steps needed to cleanse the infected computer. One hoax, for example, sent instructions in English, Czech, Italian, Danish, and many other languages to users around the world, warning them about a possible infection on their computer from a file that carried a little teddy bear as its icon. The file was actually a legitimate component of the Windows operating system. The message included the instructions to remove it, and also the admonition to distribute this helpful message to everyone in the recipient's address book so they could eliminate the file as well. In this case, the file was not necessary for normal system operation anyway, so those who fell for it did not damage their systems. However, they certainly lost time.

---

[80] Machrone, B. (2003). The Plaxo worm and the lovelorn. *PC Magazine, 22*(5), 57.

Other hoaxes are more nefarious, and thousands of people have been duped into damaging their own computers and then innocently passing the hoax along to everyone in their address book to spread the damage further. Some hoaxes carry stories that touch the heart or raise the hackles of the recipients, motivating them to drown a particular email box with get well greetings or outrage. The "sick child" hoax is especially popular and quite successful. Here is an excerpt from one that convinced many people to deluge each other's inboxes:

> "You guys . . . . . this isn't a chain letter, but a choice for all of us to save a little girl that's going to die of a serious and fatal form of cancer. Please send this to everyone you know . . . or don't know at that. This little girl has 6 months left to live her life, and as her last wish, she wanted to send a chain letter telling everyone to live their life to fullest, since she never will. She'll never make it to prom, graduate from high school, or get married and have a family of her own. By you sending this to as many people as possible, you can give her and her family a little hope, because with every name that this is sent to, the American Cancer Society will donate 3 cents per name to her treatment and recovery plan. One guy sent this to 500 people!!!! So, I know that we can send it to at least 5 or 6. Come on you guys . . . . and if you're too selfish to waste 10–15 minutes and scrolling this and forwarding it to EVERYONE, just think it could be you one day . . . . and it's not even your $money$, just your time. Please help this little girl out guys, I know you can do it!! I love you guys!"[81]

One type of Internet hoax that costs some people considerable sums is the "4-1-9" scam. The sender, claiming to be a representative of a foreign government, pleads that he has millions of dollars lying around for some reason, perhaps from an unclaimed estate or "overinvoiced" contracts. The sender wants to transfer the funds into a U.S. bank account to avoid problems in his own country, but can't set one up himself. If you will do this for him, you get to keep a large chunk of the transferred funds. If you bite, the sender might convince you to travel overseas to meet the parties and see official-looking documents with stamps, seals, and logos. As you get deeper into the scheme, a threat to the deal suddenly arises that jeopardizes its completion. Your new business partner begs you to pay "advance fees" of

---

[81] A Little Girl Dying, Hoaxbusters Web site. (n.d.). Retrieved March 14, 2003, from http://hoaxbusters.ciac.org/HoaxBustersHome.html

some kind to save the deal – taxes or attorney fees, for example. At that point, the partner vanishes along with your funds.[82]

In the workplace or outside of it, people fall for Internet hoaxes for many of the same reasons they fall for other kinds of scams. A key reason is simply our natural *truth bias* – people tend to believe most of what they see and hear. We take things at face value and don't immediately assume that people we deal with have ulterior motives. If we did not have this truth bias, the world would be quite a difficult place to live. Indeed, people who show a strong tendency toward suspiciousness are advised to seek professional help. The problem now is that the Internet has vastly increased the power that scammers have to reach into inboxes with innumerable schemes, mixing their messages with perfectly valid mail from new clients. The net's amplification power benefits scammers and hucksters just as much as reputable business people.

EVOLVING EMAIL ETIQUETTE TIPS

The early etiquette guidelines address a relatively basic set of issues, and many of them were geared toward helping senders avoid the most egregious email mistakes. Xerox PARC is credited with developing the first set of such guidelines in the 1970s, called the Electronic Mail Briefing Blurb. Their advice was succinct, but its authors clearly recognized that email as a communication medium had special properties and people who used it needed some help in learning how to use it without getting into trouble, offending their coworkers, or taxing the network's resources:

- "Wait a day or two before responding to an offensive Email.
- Reply only to the message sender, not everyone on the sender's original list of recipients.
- Don't send anything via Email that you wouldn't want to see in public."

Guidelines began appearing in the magazines and business journals in the early 1990s. In 1993, for example, when the Internet had only 20 million users, Philip Elmer-DeWitt and David S. Jackson offered their *Time* readers just five basic rules of online etiquette:[83]

---

[82] Public Awareness Advisory Regarding "4–1–9" or "Advance Fee Fraud" Schemes. (n.d.). Retrieved March 14, 2003, from the United States Secret Service Web site. http://www.secretservice.gov/alert419.shtml

[83] Elmer-DeWitt, P., & Jackson, D. S. (1993). First nation in cyberspace. *Time, 142*(24), 62–65.

- "Don't type in all CAPS (IT'S LIKE YELLING.)
- Keep it short.
- Indicate irony with a ;) (a wink, sideways).
- Don't Email unsolicited ads.
- Don't ask stupid questions."

Note that the "e" in email was capitalized – a common practice for new technologies. As email became more widespread in the workplace, however, and people acquired the knowledge-building experiences with it as described earlier, the "e" became lowercase. In addition, the guidelines began addressing more subtle aspects of the communication medium, and the tip list expanded. The recommendation to use emoticons – various facial expressions created mostly with punctuation marks – to indicate humor or irony was one of the early tips that was reevaluated. *Successful Meetings* in 1998 advised email users to be careful with their use, because many people may not even understand what they mean. A more important concern is the way they influence the impression the sender creates to the recipient. Emoticons received considerable attention in the media during the 1990s, partly because they demonstrated that people could use imaginative methods to transmit nuances of tone and nonverbal cues even when they had only the ASCII keyboard to work with. Emoticon dictionaries containing hundreds of keyboard-generated variations of smiley faces, frowns, winks, and arched eyebrows appeared. In practice, though, the use of emoticons appears to have been overestimated. One study of online discussion groups, for example, found that only 13.4 percent of the messages contained graphic accents.[84]

People began learning that humor and irony often transmit poorly, and many workplace netiquette guides warned their users about this. Sam Donaldson's misinterpreted ironic comment is a case in point, and management consultants advise people in the workplace to be very careful in their use of humor in electronic business communications.[85] Mary Munter of Dartmouth College and her colleagues offer business users some very practical

[84] Wittmer, D. F., & Katzman, S. L. (1997, March). Online smiles: Does gender make a difference in the use of graphic accents? *Journal of Computer-Mediated Communication, 2*(4). Retrieved May 2, 2003, from *Journal of Computer-Mediated Communication* Web site: http://www.ascusc.org/jcmc/vol2/issue4/witmer1.html

[85] Sloboda, B. (1999). 'Netiquette'-new rules and policies for the information age. *Management Quarterly, 40*(4), 9–35.

guidelines for using email in the workplace that include, "Use jokes and informal idioms with great caution, if at all."[86]

Both our knowledge-building experiences and court cases have contributed to very specific netiquette warnings about expectations about the privacy of electronic communications. Even the early Electronic Email Briefing Blurb advised about the public nature of email, but the nature of the medium, particularly when used in informal settings, continually leads people to treat it as private conversation. Courts have routinely confirmed that email managed by the company is the property of the company, not of the individual, and corporate executives can examine it at any time. (We take up the issue of workplace surveillance and monitoring in a later chapter.)

A final netiquette tip that has undergone major revision involves commercial email. Commercial messages were initially banned on the Internet's communication tools, if not through laws, then through the use of social pressure and group influence. The netiquette guides usually included admonitions about preserving the Internet's noncommercial nature. When commercial enterprises began using the Internet for direct marketing, by sending out unsolicited advertisements to thousands of Internet mail addresses, the response was loud and angry. But email marketing became such a valuable tool for businesses that it took off in the 1990s and the protests subsided somewhat. They are raging again, however, as I described earlier in this chapter, because this particular netcentric innovation has been so mishandled and abused by some. Once again, we see how the amplification power of the Internet can operate. The few commercial email messages that might be welcomed by employees are being drowned in the flood.

Business Communication across Cultures

Business people have always had to grapple with cultural differences in communication styles, and business courses routinely include a lecture or two to help newly minted MBAs improve their intercultural communication skills. Examples of major and minor blunders and misunderstandings abound. As a faculty member and business consultant in Japan in the 1980s, I found it very difficult to persuade Americans that the Japanese expression "It's difficult" in response to one of their proposals meant "No." To the Americans,

---

[86] Munter, M., Rogers, P. S., & Rymer, J. (2003). Business email: Guidelines for users [Electronic version]. *Business Communication Quarterly, 66*(1), 26–40.

that response to a proposal usually triggered a redoubling of the American effort to surmount the difficulty.

Edward T. Hall proposed sorting cultures and their various communication styles along the dimension of context.[87] This dimension reflects the degree to which the information contained in a message is conveyed by the context of a message, as opposed to the message itself. Cultures that were considered "high context," such as Japan or Taiwan, rely less on the words contained in verbal communications and far more on the communication's context. Nonverbal messages are critical, and the environment in which the communication occurs sets the stage for establishing meaning. The importance of adhering to various formalities is well understood among the society's members, and departures can lead to embarrassment.

The Japanese use the expression "stomach talk" to refer to the nonverbal communication needed to establish a trusting business association. (The stomach is considered the center of the life force.) Business associates depend on nonverbal messages to develop trust, come to a meeting of the minds, and establish a personal relationship from which business transactions and agreements can then spring. While I was in Japan, an experiment on electronic negotiations was underway in which participants physically located in the United States and Japan were attempting to conduct a simulated negotiation using a variety of electronic media. The Japanese thought the project was intriguing, but one remarked, "Of course, we'd never do it that way." It didn't support stomach talk.

Low-context cultures tend to extract the information from a communication from the words it contains and rely to a lesser extent on the communication's context. The United States and Germany are examples. Countries may lean toward one end or the other partly because the individuals within the country have more shared context. The words in a message do not have to explicitly relate every aspect of the situation because the individuals have a long history of shared values and knowledge. People in low-context cultures also tend to be more individualistic, whereas those in high-context cultures are more collectivist.

High-context cultures tend to rely more on personal relationships to establish the context for communication, and they also tend to prefer more indirect approaches in communication. The direct organization plan I described earlier, commonly taught in business school in low-context cultures, is often ineffective or misinterpreted in high-context cultures. The letter

---

[87] Hall, E. T. (1983). *The dance of life: The other dimension of time.* New York: Doubleday.

English   Semitic   Oriental   Romance   Russian

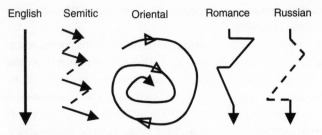

Figure 4.2. Styles of paragraph development. From Kaplan, R. (1966). Cultural thought patterns in inter-cultural education. *Language Learning, 16,* 1–20. Reprinted by permission from Blackwell Publishing.

below, for example, uses that direct plan. Pete Jones, an American, sends it to a member of the Chinese delegation who had stopped by his booth at an agricultural exhibit[88]:

> Dear Sir:
>
> Your name and address were referred to me by the Illinois Department of Agriculture – Far East Office. They stated that you had expressed an interest in our products and requested further information.
> I am therefore enclosing a brochure which itemizes our products and services. Please let me know your exact requirements. I will be happy to provide you with further details.
> Thank you for your participation at the Illinois Slide and Catalog Show. I look forward to your reply.
>
> Sincerely,
> Pete Jones
> Director of Sales
> Agri-Equipment Division
> Enclosure

Predictably, the letter drew no response. Robert Kaplan's diagram, above, is often used to illustrate the different cultural styles of communication.[89] The direct approach, typical for low-context cultures, is the straight line, and this is the one that Pete Jones used to communicate with the high-context Chinese.

The growth of email communication across the globe has, on the whole, been very advantageous given its low cost, speed, and convenience.

---

[88] Boiarsky, C. (1995). The relationship between cultural and rhetorical conventions: Engaging in international communication. *Technical Communication Quarterly, 4,* 245–259.

[89] Kaplan, R. (1966). Cultural thought patterns in intercultural education. *Language Learning, 16,* 1–20.

However, the roots of email as an informal communication medium in Western countries make it especially hazardous for intercultural communications, particularly when low context meets high context. Combining the direct approach with email informality could doom any relationship immediately.

Charles P. Campbell suggests that people from low-context cultures can learn to adapt their communications when they are dealing with high-context cultures, and his advice is especially useful for intercultural email.[90] The goal is not to try to mimic the communication style of the recipient in an unnatural and uncomfortable way but to blend the styles of both cultures in a way that is both audience centered and sincere. The sender should find a way in each communication to relate to the recipient in a personal way and to continually build on the recipient's perceptions of context. For example, an alternative opening paragraph for Pete Jones' letter could read:

> Dear Mr. Yen Zen-jiu: (*instead of Dear Sir*)
>
> I hope that you have had a safe journey home and that you have found your family in good health. The midwestern part of our country which you graciously visited continues to have wet weather, but I am thankful for the rain after our two years of drought.

Many business people in low-context cultures would have a difficult time composing a paragraph like that for email, yet it represents the kind of fleet-footed switching of styles so important to effective email communication.

Although email is the killer app of the Internet in the workplace, other technologies have emerged that have even fewer norms and present new kinds of challenges. Instant messaging is an example of a communication tool that leans further toward speech, compared to email, and is more immediate in the sense of feedback from the recipient.

Instant Messages in the Workplace

Business communication texts are only beginning to include instant messaging as a legitimate format, but the technology is emerging as an important one in some business contexts. It appears to be filling a role on the fringes of email and telephone conversations, in which short and quick text exchanges with immediate response work well.

---

[90] Campbell, C. P. (1998). Rhetorical ethos: A bridge between high-context and low-context cultures? In S. Niemeier, C. P. Campbell, & R. Dirven (Eds.), *The cultural context in business communication*. Amsterdam: John Benjamin Publishing Company.

Online chat gained many participants, along with a fairly notorious reputation, through Internet Relay Chat. This network of chat servers began in Finland in 1988, launched by Jarkko "WiZ" Oikarinen at the University of Oulu. Over the years, disputes among various groups led to fragmentation and the emergence of numerous smaller networks, such as EFNet, Undernet, and DALnet. They generally used the same protocol, but policies varied, and users who logged in to one network could only chat with users on the same network. The IRC world was the home for an extraordinary variety of people who used the networks for everything from discussions about rock bands to online dating and sex. IRC gained in respectability when it was used during the Gulf War to transmit live reports.[91]

The use of live, text-based chat as a business communication tool was almost nonexistent until the late 1990s, when some companies began using synchronous chat software on their intranets. They did not call it "chat," however. Michael Castelluccio, writing for *Strategic Finance*, argues that "chat" would have been an impossible sell in business, because it conjures up images of employees finding ways to waste time – not just at the water cooler, but at their desks. Instead, the term instant messaging (IM) became the buzzword, even though the technology is the same. The term suggests a more serious use that could be applied to traders on the floor gathering immediate business intelligence.[92] Now the initials are used as both noun and verb, as in "He IMed me."

One of the most important characteristics of IM is that the sender is not just sending a message into the ether, without knowing that you are at your desk to pick it up right away. Unless the sender asks for a confirmation (some email systems have this feature), he usually doesn't know whether it actually was received. Business correspondence on email can be somewhat unreliable, with servers going down, mistakes in addressing, and viruses corrupting entire inboxes. With IM, however, the sender can check to see if the recipient is online before sending anything. If so, the sender can expect a quick response.

The forms and formats for IM are constrained to short text messages, and informality tends to be even more common in IM than in email. Partly, the informality is due to the severe limitations of the medium. Because it is synchronous, people must make tradeoffs between editing their message to correct spelling, grammar, or tone and maintaining a reasonable pace and rhythm of interaction.

---

[91] Some examples of the logs from the chat sessions during the Gulf War are posted at http://www.ibiblio.org/pub/academic/communications/logs/Gulf-War/

[92] Castelluccio, M. (1999). Email in real time [Electronic version]. *Strategic Finance*, *81*(34), 34–38.

The public Internet supports instant messaging though chat networks themselves are somewhat fragmented, in the sense that users on one network may not be easily reachable by users on another. However, privately operated networks are emerging that do not rely on AOL, Microsoft, or other widely used servers, and that limit buddy lists to authenticated employees. Staff members in San Francisco can hold an IM conversation with their counterparts in Madrid, but not with their family members. The software that corporations install also has more features for monitoring and moderating online chats.

Although some believe that instant messaging is the next killer app for business communications, others think usage will quickly fall off after the initial enthusiasm. Being "online" for IM means that you can be interrupted at any moment, and the sender will expect a response. Though this may be an enormous advantage during times when certain messages must reach you immediately, it can also interfere with productive work.

A more likely scenario is that IM will become common in particular types of work and in specialized contexts, but will not be left on at all times for all employees. For example, many technical help desk managers prefer IM to the telephone. Technical support often involves long periods in which the recipient enters commands or tries different strategies suggested by the help desk staff member, and IM makes it possible for the support person to fill those gaps by supporting more than one person at a time. IM technical support is also useful for home workers with one phone line and no broadband since they do not need to disconnect from the Internet to place a call. IM has been especially valuable for some virtual teamwork with members distributed around the globe.

One reason that some employees are fond of IM is that for certain types of quick exchanges, it can be quite productive. For example, a sales agent may be writing up a contract but needs the new phone number for the office in New York. She knows the number is not yet on the intranet. She could choose email as her communication channel, but the recipient may not know it or may not be around to pick up the email. If she has IM, she can log in, see who is online, and pick the coworker who is most likely to know. She could send a quick message:

```
<jsthomas> Dana, do you have the new number for the NY
off?
```

She knows Dana is online and active, so a response should be forthcoming almost immediately:

```
<dtflores>212-555-5555
<jsthomas>thx!
```

This would be a breathtaking display of speedy business communication to obtain information, especially given the alternatives of email, phone, letter, fax, or face-to-face contact. It meant that J. S. Thomas could complete her sales contract immediately. IM is partly heralded as a productive communication tool that serves a specialized need because it can be so brief, and people do not generally expect adherence to the usual social norms, such as polite greetings, closings, or other civilities. On IM, the "direct approach" can be carried to its logical extreme to achieve some valuable time savings.

Extending Netiquette

Many of the principles of business communications have not changed, even though the communication media have. We continue to draw on our knowledge of human behavior and the impressions we create by that behavior in business settings. As we gain more of those knowledge-building experiences with the new media that emerged from the Internet and its netcentric innovations, we will improve and refine how we use them. The netiquette tips will change over time, and some of the advice may eventually seem as quaint and unnecessary as warning new employees not to talk with their mouths full at business dinners.

Now, however, during this turbulent and transitional period in which electronic communication media are multiplying along with the challenges they present, blunt and even superficial netiquette tips are still needed. Don't flame, don't include too many attachments, don't reply to all, don't use email to fire people, don't use bad grammar, and don't expect your email to be private. To really take best advantage of electronic business communication tools, however, and to avoid egregious misunderstandings and mistakes, we must do more than adhere to such simple rules. We will need to examine the properties of each of the tools and reflect on how those properties influence the communication event. Email, instant messaging, videoconferencing, Web-based meetings, groupware, and other innovations support different kinds of communication with characteristics that are not the same as the phone call or a face-to-face meeting. It will take experience to use them effectively, as people learn from their mistakes.

5 Leadership in the Internet Age

Joe Namath, the legendary quarterback for the New York Jets, once said, "To be a leader, you have to make people want to follow you, and nobody wants to follow someone who doesn't know where he is going."[93] In the Internet age, these two components of successful leadership are arguably more challenging than they were in the past. Knowing where to go and charting the course for an organization in a turbulent and fast-paced business environment are quite difficult. The Internet has brought about considerable instability and astounding opportunities for new investments in the competitive landscape of business. As we discussed in previous chapters, corporations are having great difficulty predicting who the next competitor will be, and changes in the value chain can occur almost overnight, thanks to the net. A corporation that found its sweet spot by adding value to one link in the chain may find, the next day, the link is bypassed with an innovation that spreads virally. The net has created a host of new ways in which business can be transacted and value added. It has also upended many traditional business models by making the value they added in the past far less important or necessary.

Namath's second component – persuading people to follow – is also more challenging. Today's workforce has many options and motivations, and they come from highly diverse backgrounds, culturally, ethnically, and – thanks to the virtual workplace – geographically. In a netcentric world, becoming a leader and then succeeding once you reach the top appear to require new kinds of knowledge, skills, and abilities, or KSAs as human resource professionals call them.

[93] Leader. (2003). *Journal of Business Strategy, 24*(2), 48. Retrieved March 22, 2003, from Business Source Premier Database.

Whether or not you agree with Namath's definition of the good leader, it is clear that leaders are confronting new challenges. In this chapter, we look at the elusive quality of leadership, beginning with a brief overview of the ways in which researchers have approached the topic over the years, and the new styles of leadership that have emerged in the netcentric era. Getting to the top and then staying there have never been more rewarding, nor have they been more difficult.

Leadership under the Microscope

To study a phenomenon, we should have a definition of it. But like so many elusive psychological variables there is no consensus about what the term "leadership" actually means. Here are some of the many definitions that have been offered:

> The ability to inspire confidence and support among the people who are needed to achieve organizational goals – *Andrew DuBrin*

> A process whereby an individual influences a group of individuals to achieve a common goal – *P. Northouse*

> The process of persuasion and example by which an individual (or leadership team) induces a group to take action that is in accord with the leader's purpose, or the shared purposes of all – *Warren Bennis*

> A function of knowing yourself, having a vision that is well communicated, building trust among colleagues, and taking effective action to realize your own leadership potential – *John W. Gardner*

These definitions all stress two main features of leadership. One feature involves the characteristics of the individual – a certain trait, ability, or innate potential. The second emphasizes the behaviors an individual uses in leadership settings. These two features and various combinations of them have been central to the major theories of leadership that have emerged in the twentieth century.

BE WHAT I AM: THE TRAITS OF SUCCESSFUL LEADERS

The *trait* approach to leadership proposes that individuals who become successful leaders possess some combination of traits that led to their success, such as the "ability to inspire confidence and support," as DuBrin put it. This line of thinking initially emerged from the "great man" theory, which proposed that history was shaped by the influence of a small number of extraordinary leaders, with equally remarkable personal qualities. It led to

many studies in which researchers tried to pin down the traits that successful leaders have in common to find that magical combination. Once
identified, the findings could be used to predict who would become future
great leaders. One would only need to measure how much of each trait the
candidates possessed.

Timothy A. Judge and his colleagues conducted a general review of the
many research studies that tried to link personality and leadership over the
years and found some consistencies with respect to the so-called "Big Five"
personality traits.[94] These are neuroticism, extraversion, openness to experience, agreeableness, and conscientiousness. Extraversion, which refers
to the tendency to be social, outgoing, assertive and active, and to display
energy and zeal, was the trait that showed the strongest relationship to measures of leadership. Successful leaders also tended to show somewhat higher
levels of conscientiousness and openness to experience and lower levels of
neuroticism manifested by anxiety, insecurity, or hostility. Although these
findings suggest that successful leaders share certain traits, the traits themselves are very general. Also, the higher correlations in all of those studies
mainly involved samples of students in experimental investigations of leadership, and the actual correlations for business and government leaders were
much weaker.

Another way researchers have tried to identify particular traits of successful leaders is to simply ask them what traits they possess that they believe
are most important. We often try to learn from someone we admire, hoping
to pick up a guidebook from them so that we can be as successful as they are.
For example, we might ask an octogenarian how he made it that far, and his
answer is touted as a formula for a long life. The man might say, "I only eat
cabbages from my garden and I smoke a pack of cigarettes a day." Though
probably true, his dietary and smoking habits may have little to do with his
longevity. To some extent, the trait theories failed because they confused
correlation with causation, just as we would be doing if we attributed the
man's longevity to the cigarettes and to the cabbage diet. Learning that a
successful leader possesses personality characteristics such as dominance or
conscientiousness does not mean that those traits are at the roots of his or
her success.

Despite the intuitive appeal of the trait approach, it has not been very
successful. Effective leaders vary a great deal, and researchers are not able

[94] Judge, T. A., Bono, J. E., Ilies, R., & Gerhardt, M. W. (2002). Personality and leadership: A qualitative and quantitative review. *Journal of Applied Psychology, 87*(4),
765–780.

to find any consistent magical combination that all of them possess outside, perhaps, of some very general tendencies. Some are gentle and soft spoken, but passionately committed to a goal and able to draw people to them through *referent power* – the power to lead by example. Others, such as Bill Gates, exercise *expert power*, gaining the support of their followers by virtue of their expert knowledge in the field. Commonalities among the many different successful leaders have been very difficult to find.

DO WHAT I DO: BEHAVIORAL APPROACH TO LEADERSHIP

Disenchanted with the inability of the trait approach to pinpoint the characteristics of effective leadership, researchers turned to examining what successful leaders do rather than who they are. The behavioral approach led to extensive studies to learn the habits and behavior patterns of the target group, emphasizing the process of leadership rather than the characteristics of the leader as a person. Stephen R. Covey's best-selling *Seven Habits of Highly Effective People* took advantage of this approach, and it became a leading handbook for business people on the way up. His list advocates behaviors such as taking a proactive stance, seeking to understand first and be understood second, and using win/win strategies in interpersonal leadership.

Several large studies were conducted using the behavioral approach, and one of the best known was conducted at Ohio State University during the 1950s. The researchers developed an enormous compendium of behaviors, more than 1,800 of them, that might be typical of leaders. Here are some examples:

> The leader ...
> knows about it when something goes wrong
> calls the group together to talk things over
> puts the welfare of the unit above the welfare of any one person
> tries out his or her own new ideas in the unit

Though there were many types of leader behaviors, the researchers found they could be grouped under two main headings. One type encompassed behaviors called "consideration," which generally meant behaviors that were employee-centered, supportive, and participative. The second type was called "initiating structure," and it covered the more task-oriented and directive behaviors. Efforts to determine whether leaders who emphasized one style over the other would be more effective were also not very successful. The next phase in thinking about leadership emphasized how leaders might manage their own behavior and how they could be flexible about their choice of style based on the situation.

DO WHAT I DO, WHEN AND WHERE I DO IT: CONTINGENCY APPROACHES

Military commanders can be effective leaders with very directive styles, especially in wartime. Leaders whose employees can easily jump ship to another company, as technical professionals could easily do during the last decade, need to nurture their employees' sense of commitment. For them, an employee-centered approach would probably work best. Appreciation of the different contexts of leadership, both between organizations, over time within the same organization, and even from moment to moment with the same group of followers, led to another way of looking at leadership success. The contingency approach proposed that effective leadership is not so much a set of personal characteristics, nor is it a collection of behaviors. To be successful, a leader should adapt to the context. The leader should consider the nature and motivation of the followers, the task at hand, and the ultimate goal before choosing a leadership style.

For example, one of the leader behaviors identified in the behavioral approach was the tendency to call the group together to discuss the issue in a participative way. However, calling the group together to discuss a trivial issue, or one that was so sensitive that the group could never agree on it, could be counterproductive and unnecessarily time consuming. The adaptable leader, using a contingency approach, would consider the context before inviting group participation. If the problem required different kinds of expertise to solve, or if everyone needed to be on board to implement the solution, the participative, employee-centered style would be more effective.

Contingency approaches are intuitively appealing and they led to many leadership development workshops. Up-and-coming business leaders were presented with different situations and asked to analyze the context. Once they grasped the nature of the employees and the task to be accomplished, they were guided toward a specific leadership style.

These approaches to leadership all emerged before the Internet era, the dot.com explosions (and implosions), the creative destruction of many traditional business models, and the Enron debacle. They were all fairly limited in their ability to come up with a unified conception of the "successful leader" in terms of personality characteristics, generalized behaviors, or behaviors in specific contexts. Their shortcomings became especially apparent in the 1990s, when many "new economy" entrepreneurs with their own ideas about how to lead a company joined the ranks of the more traditional business leaders.

Leadership Styles in the Internet Era

Emerging theories of leadership that accompany the Internet era downplay terms like "employee-centered" and "task-oriented." Instead, terms like "daring," "charismatic," "visionary," and "passionate" are more likely to be used to describe successful leaders. The biography of John Chambers, president and CEO of Cisco Systems is posted on Cisco's Web site:

> Chambers has been lauded by government leaders and countless publications worldwide for his visionary strategy, his ability to drive an entrepreneurial culture, and his warm-hearted, straight-talking approach. Widely recognized for his evangelistic style, Chambers is considered one of the most innovative and dynamic leaders in global business today.

Gopal Kanji and Patricia Moura e Sá at Sheffield Business School in the United Kingdom describe several new leadership styles that are drawing attention in the Internet era, though little research has been done yet to understand their effectiveness.[95] They point out that modern organizations are complex adaptive systems, confronted with unpredictable and very rapidly changing challenges. Traditional and static models of leadership have failed to predict which temperaments and behaviors will contribute to a successful leadership style, partly because the corporate environment has become so volatile. New notions of effective leadership are fuzzier, but they seem to encapsulate what it takes to survive and thrive in this transitional and turbulent period when instability and unpredictable change are the most salient characteristics of the business environment.

The *transformative leader*, for example, is one who becomes the charismatic focal point to draw the energies of everyone within the company and provides a role model of behavior. This is the leader, often filled with passion for a single goal, who can inspire followers to greatness by his or her own example. Transformational leaders are quoted in the press with the most daring and visionary remarks, though they may not play a major role in the actual management of the company. In one sense, they become a spiritual leader for the organization, able to unite the employees and commit them to a shared goal.

---

[95] Kanji, G. K., & Moura e Sá, P. (2001). Measuring leadership excellence [Electronic version]. *Total Quality Management, 12*(6), 701–718.

Another leader style that is emerging is the *transactional leader*, the individual who organizes a reward architecture and identifies unit goals to keep the employees on task, working on projects that effectively contribute to the mission. This person creates the underlying structures that reward and motivate people for performance in line with organizational goals. The two types, transformative and transactional, are complementary: The transformative leader provides the vision and encourages commitment, and the transactional leader, who is often the chief operating officer (COO) watches over the reward structures, contractual agreements, and strategic goals.

Systemic leadership is a radical concept that says, essentially, that leadership behaviors must lie in every employee for the company to succeed. It stresses the need for every individual within the organization to become a fully responsible autonomous agent who can exercise powers of judgment and make decisions that contribute to the organizational goals. In an age when very rapid decision making may be needed, the most effective "leadership" may be the kind in which the people in the organization, relying on shared values and frequent communication, can trust one another to make good decisions for the whole organization. The Chinese philosopher Lao-Tse, born in 604 BC, is often quoted in seminars that emphasize how a leader can be quite effective by taking a quieter, more supportive back-seat role, and by building leadership potential in the followers:

> The wicked leader is he who the people despise. The good leader is he who the people revere. A leader is best when people barely know he exists; when his work is done, his aim fulfilled, they will say, "We did it ourselves."

Interest in new kinds of leadership styles continues to evolve in the Internet age, especially as business cycles reassert themselves and we see the shakeout of leaders who can start businesses but not keep them going. Charisma, vision, risk taking, and innovation were key elements to leadership during the Internet's infancy, when the "angel" venture capitalists poured money into the start-up coffers of entrepreneurs with almost any new idea that capitalized on the Internet's hourglass architecture. Since the stock market tumble in 2000, many of the CEOs learned an important lesson about leadership. Charisma and innovation were no longer enough to sustain a company through the bad times when the outpouring of funds dried up. Instead of focusing on revenue and growth, which makes a company look like it is on target to become the next new economy giant, the CEOs learned they had to pay attention to the fundamentals just to stay afloat. One fundamental is, quite simply, profits. As long as the venture capitalists were providing the funding, the red ink could be ignored. When their funders went elsewhere, the CEOs had to adapt, perish, or turn over operational management to one of those transactional leaders.

One entrepreneur who exemplifies this switch in leadership behavior is Rick Sapio, head of Mutuals.com.[96] He started the Dallas-based company in 1994, whose revenues increased by more than 100 percent annually during its first six years. The company is an infomediary that provides fee-based analysis and advice to investors about mutual funds, mostly over the net. As I discussed in an earlier chapter, business models that provide unbiased filtering and analysis services to help people who are swamped with information via the Internet have popped up frequently.

Sapio has a sign over his door that reads "Profits equals revenues divided by expenses." The math may not be quite right, but the phrase dramatizes the CEO's intense interest in the bottom line, not just in the numerator. Sapio says, "We were not accountable to being a profitable company at the beginning and hence our energies weren't focused on looking at expenses. We were looking only at revenue." Now, thanks to the CEO's refocusing on fundamentals, the company has a 15 percent profit margin – not much compared to the dot.com heyday, but solid. He makes sure financial transactions are entered daily, and he meets with his executive team each day to go over the numbers. Expense vouchers are scrutinized and employees who overspend without getting prior approval pay from their own pockets. Sapio himself had to pay $6,000, because he thought the team would give him approval to get some leadership coaching, but failed to put in the request in advance.

New Challenges for Internet-Age Leaders

Leading an organization has always been an enormous challenge, but in the netcentric era, leadership is confronted with several new ones. Some are qualitatively different, whereas others are challenges that have grown immensely because of the Internet. As we discussed in the last chapter, the pressure on professional and managerial personnel is high and the desire to stay in the fast lane through mind-boggling work schedules intense. For the CEO and executive team, the Internet age has created many more transformations in their experience of the workplace. The rewards for those at the very top are enormous, but the expectations are equally high.

[96] Barker, E. (2002). *Cheap executive officer. Inc.*, *24*(4), 114–115. Retrieved June 25, 2002, from Academic Search Elite Database.

HIGH PAY, HIGH EXPECTATIONS

Charting a successful course for a company in the Internet era is arguably more difficult than it was in earlier periods, yet the expectations for leadership have not eased. Indeed, expectations have risen, and the CEO in particular bears a crushing burden. The recruitment and appointment of a new CEO for a major company, for example, often makes the national news as the media turn the new business leader into a superstar, and shareholders expect great things from a newly appointed CEO.

The top team is well paid for shouldering the burden, absurdly well paid, as so many might argue. The gap between the highest earning executives and the rank and file has turned into a yawning cavern, and nowhere is this more obvious than in the compensation offered to the CEO. In 2000, the twenty highest paid CEOs earned an average of $117.6 million each. The average compensation for CEOs of the 365 largest companies in the United States topped $13 million.[97] The change in the pay dispersion can be clearly understood from a comparison of multiples. In 1980, CEO compensation was about forty-two times the pay of the average worker in the company. By 2000, that multiple soared to more than 530. The rise of CEO compensation relative to the average worker slowed somewhat in 2001, partly because compensation included stocks and share prices dropped dramatically. Nevertheless, the rewards for reaching the fastest lane and staying there are incredibly high.

REACHING THE TOP IN THE TOURNAMENT

What is involved in reaching the top? The steps vary considerably, and some people become CEOs, especially in the innovation-oriented Internet era, because they invented the product and started the company. Another route, though, is described by *tournament theory*, a stressful game of winner take all that also helps explain why pay dispersions are growing wider.

The concept behind the corporate tournament is that managers must always be competing against one another to achieve that next promotion and make it to the next rung on the ladder. With each round, fewer competitors survive, but the winners stay on to compete in the next round for ever larger rewards. The final tournament winner becomes CEO. The losers are left behind and are generally expected to leave the organization, because their performance in this particular tournament would limit their career prospects. At a new organization, they can enter the tournament again and

---

[97] Lavelle, L., & Jespersen, F. F. (2001). Executive pay. *Business Week, 3728,* 76+. Retrieved June 25, 2002, from Academic Search Elite Database.

try to do better. The large pay dispersions support a fiercely competitive tournament style of managerial retention with huge rewards for the survivors, and especially for the final survivor. The tournament models can help ensure that only the brightest stars will remain; they also maintain very strong incentives for managers to continue to perform at every level. However, this pattern also increases turnover and reduces employee commitment to the organization. In addition, it can be detrimental to teamwork and social relations within the company.

LINKING PAY TO PERFORMANCE

Executive compensation is enormously complex and supplemented with various perks, house payments, travel, stock options, bonuses, and material goods, as well as with promises to reduce the risk of messing up, such as guaranteed severance packages or golden parachutes. The trend toward higher and higher compensation for the top management team has been going on for some time and has received considerable scrutiny. When shareholders were benefiting from the long economic boom in the 1990s, the criticism was muted. Many thought the astronomical compensation paid to CEOs, who were navigating the difficult waters of the Internet era and producing so much wealth, was warranted. Because many of the compensation packages were linked to company performance, the public was rather tolerant of the pay offered to the superstars, whose names were linked with visionary thinking and the new economy. However, when the downturn came and shareholders were severely burned, the public began to scrutinize those generous compensation packages with much greater care. In particular, analysts examined in great detail the relationship between CEO compensation and the actual performance of the company. If CEOs were being paid generously when their companies were delivering outstanding rewards to the shareholders, would they also share in the pain?

Unfortunately, the analysts often found that the CEOs were remarkably well protected from the downturn. For example, the CEO of Qwest Communications, which posted a $4 billion loss in 2001 and whose stock price tumbled 55 percent, fared extremely well. He received $1.5 million bonus, $24 million in cash, and many more millions in exercised options. As Qwest laid off workers and shareholders lost value in their investments, its CEO continued to be paid very handsomely.[98]

Business Week's executive scoreboard tallies the compensation of top executives and compares it to the company's performance and shareholders'

---

[98] CEOs: Why they're so unloved. (2002). *Business Week, 3779*, 118.

return, providing a stark numerical analysis of trends in management compensation.[99] After naming the highest paid executives in the United States, the analysis continues with computations that identify which CEOs gave shareholders the most for their money. They compute shareholder return and compare that to each executive's compensation. The scorecard lists executives such as George Perlegos of Atmel and Dane Miller of Biomet, whose comparatively modest salaries are juxtaposed against outstanding performance for their shareholders. The ones who gave shareholders the least return on the dollar, in terms of executive compensation, were nearly all in the high-tech Internet arena. Peter Karmanos of Compuware, for example, shows a salary plus long-term compensation of $93.9 million, but the shareholders all lost money during the period. In other words, the trend appears to link good performance by a CEO to higher compensation. The relationship between poor performance and compensation, however, is mixed, and many executives continue to take in lucrative compensation packages that grow year after year, regardless of what happens to the shareholders or the employees in the bad years.

The growing dispersion in pay within corporations is a very important trend, especially because the gigantic and very public compensation packages for the CEOs and the executive team are widely known. Why are some companies going down this path while others are not, or at least not so aggressively? Why are some industries – including the high-tech industries – so much more likely to reward their top execs with packages that are many hundreds of times larger than their average workers'? Is there any evidence that the Internet and its effects on the business climate are linked to greater pay dispersion? Are wide pay dispersions good for certain kinds of businesses, but not for others? Are some top execs really worth that much?

HIGH PAY, HIGH EXPECTATIONS, ESPECIALLY IN HIGH TECH

Businesses in the high-tech arena appear to be especially prone to wider pay dispersions. Matt Bloom and John G. Michel of the University of Notre Dame researched pay dispersion across different companies and industries and found that the context in which an organization is attempting to survive and thrive is a key element in whether high pay dispersions emerge, and whether they actually help the company succeed.[100] Depending on the

[99] Lavelle, L., Jespersen, F. F., & Arndt, M. (2002). Executive pay. *Business Week, 3778,* 80–87.

[100] Bloom, M., & Michel, J. G. (2002). The relationships among organizational context, pay dispersion, and among managerial turnover [Electronic version]. *Academy of Management Journal, 45*(1), 33–43.

context, there could be an optimal level of pay dispersion that balances the benefits of the tournament against the drawbacks of that kind of internal competition.

Bloom and Michel first assigned a score on pay dispersion to the corporations in their sample, based on the disparities in pay among the managers. Then they analyzed the context in which each corporation was operating, including measures such as opportunities for new investment, instability, and diversification. They selected these aspects of the environment because one might assume that high scores on any of them would require an extremely talented and high-performing leader, one who might be more easily identified in a tournament style of competition. For example, a company confronted with many choices for new investments based on its own R&D or plans for expansion would presumably depend very heavily on the insight and expertise of its CEO. An unstable environment would also need an especially canny CEO. When new competitors come out of the woodwork or barriers to entrance change suddenly, the environment for a business can be quite unstable. Their results confirmed most of their hypotheses – corporations that had the most investment opportunities and that were confronted with the most unpredictable and unstable environments were the ones with the highest pay dispersions. Not surprisingly, given the nature of tournament competitions, these firms were also the ones with highest rates of managerial turnover. To the winner belongs the spoils; to the loser, the pink slip.

This kind of business environment – unpredictable and unstable – characterizes the Internet era. Disintermediation and rapid changes in the value chain add to the unpredictability and instability. The role the Internet plays in creating opportunities for new investments is also a large one. Deciding whether to pursue one or another innovation – when there are so many of them – is a task that requires considerable insight and probably a good deal of luck as well. Obviously not all investment opportunities have something to do with the Internet itself, but the technology has contributed more than its fair share thanks to its hourglass architecture. And even those that appear to have little to do with the Internet, such as a plant opening in Asia, could depend on the technological advances. The availability of the e-supply chain is an important consideration in where to build plants.

THE CHANGING WORKFORCE: NEW KINDS OF DIVERSITY

Another challenge Internet era leaders face is the workforce itself. It has been becoming more diverse for some time in terms of ethnicity, and now it is also becoming more culturally diverse; more heterogeneous, in terms of age, religion, and values; and more global. With people working longer, for example, CEOs have a broad range of people in terms of age to mobilize. Aging baby boomers may work alongside people from the silent generation and right across the hall from Generation Xers. Recruiters seeking talent in pools of recent college grads are confronting what appears to be another group – the "millenials." These people were born after 1980, and their life experiences have been quite different from those of any previous generations.

The globalization of business was facilitated and to some degree triggered by the Internet. Combined with the speed and ease of communication that the Internet makes possible, globalization has created another kind of diversity in the workplace. Business communications is no longer hampered by slow delivery or bottlenecks due to geography, and the term work*place* has become somewhat anachronistic. People can work together regardless of their location, and that includes far more than telecommuters who work at home two or three days a week to avoid the hour commute on the beltway. We discuss global teams in a later chapter, but in this context, the CEO confronts a diverse workforce not just in terms of differences among people working in the same location. Those people share a geography, a time zone, local television news stations, schools for their children, pay scales, and rumors passed around the water cooler. Their skin color and religion may differ, but they have many things in common simply because they are in the same geographic location, subject to the same country's laws and cultural milieu. Adding global diversity into the mix means that people are working together who not only are diverse but also are living in another country, so they lack the binding threads of living in the same community. They don't share the same schools for their children, shopping centers, sports teams, or TV stations.

They also may not be on the same pay scales or personnel policies. For example, team members in Atlanta, Georgia, even though ethnically and culturally diverse, would all use the same performance appraisals and would be within the same pay scale. Though not necessarily equal, their rewards would at least be within range of one another. A teammate who joins the virtual team from another country, India, for instance, might be working with completely different personnel policies and pay scales. The people from India might see their pay scale as equitable, but the introduction of team members from Atlanta with similar skills but much higher pay is a new and destabilizing twist – made possible by collaborative technologies.

Multinational corporations with operations in several countries have been struggling with divergent personnel policies and pay scales for many years, but the new globalization of the workplace adds another dimension.[101] When communications were slow and geography was a barrier to teamwork, the different policies were not as noticeable, because within a geographic region they would be similar.

THE CHANGING EMPLOYMENT RELATIONSHIP

The link between innovation and business success makes human intellectual capital a corporation's most valuable asset. Yet holding on to this asset is not as simple as holding on to factories and bank accounts. As we will discuss in more depth in a later chapter, the relationship between the employer and employed has changed dramatically. Many of the rewards that a CEO once had to build organizational commitment and hold employees to the mission are weaker than they were. Competing rewards, such as recognition by one's professional peers in the same field, are not even under the CEO's control. In an era in which top human talent is in such demand, that talent has many options for work and can even choose not to work at all. One of the most important challenges for CEOs is to recruit and retain the very best people possible.

Almost every corporate Web site features its own position openings and tries to attract the kind of talent it needs. Google, for example, competes for high-tech workers in the San Francisco Bay area, with what it hopes will attract the right people. Their hyperlink to the open jobs listing reads "Cool Jobs at Google, Current Openings, Perks, Culture . . . " They also feature the reasons to work at Google, which include perks such as massage therapy and roller hockey.[102]

TECHNOLOGY SAVVY

Though computers and the technology professionals who tend them have been around for decades, most CEOs, particularly those from companies outside the high-tech arena, have not come from their ranks. Most come from positions in finance, marketing, and manufacturing, the areas considered most essential to the success of the business. As a result, many CEOs have had to play catch-up during the Internet era and a deepening sense of angst has weakened their confidence – even for those that survived the tournament. The phrases "get it" and "don't get it" have been used to separate the technology-savvy, Internet-aware CEOs from their stodgy counterparts

---

[101] Begley, T. M., & Boyd, D. P. (2003). The need for a corporate global mind-set [Electronic version]. *MIT Sloan Management Review, 44*(2), 25–32.

[102] Google Web site. (n.d.). Retrieved July 2, 2002, from www.google.com/jobs

in other companies who were in danger of falling victim to the Internet's waves of business transformation. Even Bill Gates "didn't get it" during the early years of the Internet. During its infancy, Microsoft ignored the global network, assuming it would remain a backwater for researchers and computer geeks. The company made a very rapid strategic turnaround, however, when they began to appreciate the net, embrace its power, and then influence its evolution.

The head of the technology unit, called "data processing" in the dark ages, was almost never part of the executive team. This unit mainly supported back-office accounting and payroll functions and was usually housed in the basement. But as technology became more and more central to a business's operations, more expensive, and then eventually became the enabler for brand new business models and innovations, the "computer manager" emerged in higher levels of the executive hierarchy. The "chief information officer" (CIO) began appearing in many companies, and this person's role was not just to oversee all the back-room computer operations. The CIO was also expected to be a part of the executive team, guiding the company's forays into technology-based business plans and helping them transform the business to adapt to the Internet era. Though rarely a candidate for the highest post in the tournament, the CIO was at least a part of the team.

The life span of the average CIO at a company, however, is brutally short – just eighteen months according to research by the META group. A CEO who came from finance can easily pick a good vice president for finance that the CEO will trust. They speak the same language, and the CEO can judge the quality of the VP's strategies, ideas, and advice. But the language, issues, and strategies that surround technology are all very different from other areas of business. CEOs who don't know an operating system from a Web site have to take the CIO's ideas on faith, and that is very unsettling for most CEOs. Especially as technology costs rise and returns on investment are elusive, the CEO may boot one CIO after another. Yet without the technology savvy needed to chart a business course through the Internet era, CEOs have little choice but to trust people they can't understand and who don't speak the same language. For their part, CIOs are learning to speak more like business leaders and now use vocabulary such as "core competency," "target markets," and "competitive advantage" more fluently than they had in the past. Nevertheless, the CEO without technology savvy is at a serious disadvantage for setting business strategy.

Another disadvantage for the technologically illiterate CEO is the inability to grasp the role the Internet plays in organizational forms and communication. Flatter corporate hierarchies have been emerging for some time, particularly as technology allowed downsizing among the ranks of the middle managers. When senior managers can do ad hoc queries themselves on user-friendly software to create meaningful graphs and charts of business activities, the value of the middle managers as information analysts dropped. Email and other collaborative technologies help make it possible for a senior manager to have a wider span of control, and more direct reports, because communication occurs more fluidly. However, email not only helped make the flatter hierarchies more successful but also made them considerably more permeable and more informal.

The CEO of a large organization who was accustomed to meeting with the ranks of employees only in carefully planned gatherings, or communicating with them through one-way memos and announcements, has had to learn new skills to deal with Internet communication. Employees now have much more power to send their message back up the hierarchy, and also throughout the company to all their coworkers. Discussions and debate can no longer be controlled or contained by a central office because, once they are out on the net, they are loose; replies can be instant, widespread, and impossible to control.

I recall a vivid example of how the "head office" unintentionally sparked one of these interactive email debates by subscribing everyone within a university system to a mailing list to distribute a promotional newsletter. The system office of the University System of Maryland, which includes University of Maryland, College Park, along with ten other degree-granting institutions in the state, is a small headquarters. To improve communications, people at the system office decided to send out a monthly electronic newsletter called USMemo. They subscribed all faculty and staff who had an email address in the directories to the listserv and sent out their debut message. They intended it to be like most newsletters – a one-way communique – but they failed to grasp how the Internet transforms communication. The storm that followed, in the form of replies to the listserv that also reached everyone's inbox, was instructive. Some expressed their anger that system officials would subscribe them to any listserv without their permission and send them what they categorized as unsolicited spam. Others took the opportunity to begin a debate about what role the system should play in university affairs. For a few days, the issue was publicly debated on the listserv, though I never saw any administrators from the system office participate.

THE OUTRAGE FACTOR AND A CRISIS OF TRUST
Many of the high-tech business leaders of the economic boom years during the 1990s were greatly admired for their vision, innovative approaches, and

nontraditional leadership styles. The giant compensation packages they received caused little grumbling as long as their companies were growing and stock prices rising. One HR executive pointed out that the only thing that could reign in the trend was the "outrage" factor – when the executive's deal is so far into the stratosphere that shareholders, employees, and the public become outraged. People have been tolerant of escalating compensation packages when the CEOs were producing fabulous, or at least outstanding, results. But as I discussed earlier, the compensation has not been closely tied to performance during the economic downturns, and outrage predictably increased. CEOs whose workforce and shareholders considered them grossly overpaid had to deal with a new challenge, but an even greater one lay just over the horizon.

In the midst of the economic downturn, another turning point occurred that made the challenges of leadership in the Internet era radically greater. In December 2001, the Houston-based conglomerate called Enron filed for bankruptcy protection, unleashing the largest corporate bankruptcy in history up to that time.

The Enron saga includes accusations of cooked books, accounting "irregularities," hasty shredding of critical documents, and intense scrutiny by the federal government, the press, and the public. Thousands of employees lost not only their jobs but also their retirement savings, which had been heavily loaded with Enron stock. Investors suffered badly as well. The stock price tumbled from over $84 to just a few pennies a share, wiping out billions in value.[103] Enron executives who were responsible for the debacle were condemned as the story unfolded, and the public learned they were touting the stock – and selling their own shares for enormous profits – even when they knew bankruptcy was imminent. Kenneth Lay, the company's CEO, claimed he knew nothing about it, yet according to a shareholder lawsuit, Lay and the other top executives cashed in over a billion dollars of their stock before the bankruptcy announcement.[104]

When the Enron news broke, the public and the Securities and Exchange Commission began to look at the company's auditor – Arthur Andersen. Why didn't they discover the irregularities and alert authorities that the company was in very deep trouble? Some Andersen employees, as it turned out, appeared to be neck-deep in the accounting contortions themselves,

---

[103] Goett, P. (2002). Houston, we have a problem [Electronic version]. *Journal of Business Strategy, 23*(1), 2.

[104] Newman, P. C. (2002). The mind boggles. *Maclean's, 115*(23), 21. Retrieved July 4, 2002, from Academic Search Elite Database.

and were shredding documents that were supposed to be maintained. Employees at Andersen, indicted by the Justice Department on obstruction of justice charges, were found guilty on June 15, 2002. Interestingly, a key piece of evidence against Andersen was an email that was widely distributed, reminding staff to comply with the company's document retention and destruction policies. The government argued that this was a coded message to destroy, rather than retain, Enron documents.

Enron's catastrophic demise was particularly unsettling because Enron was one of the poster children of the glorious new economy, extolled for its innovative strategies and brilliant growth rates. The company had earned award after award for its success and was listed on *Fortune's 100 Best Companies to Work For*, the *All-Star List of Global Most Admired Companies*, and *The 100 Fastest Growing Companies*. Business researchers had been pointing to Enron for years as an example of nimble strategy and effective leadership in a fast-paced business climate. Researcher James O'Toole, for example, wrote an especially prophetic article that highlighted how Enron's leadership created an environment in which highly creative people could think for themselves to take a backwater Texas-based gas pipeline company into the Internet era:

> "Enron management transformed the company by consciously creating the opportunity for many leaders at all levels of the organization to take risks, create new businesses, and share in the fruits of their success. . . . Enron's CEO Kenneth Lay . . . established an environment in which they could think creatively, speak up, try new things – and motivate the existing corps of managers . . ."[105]

Ironically, Enron leadership also took great pains to project the company as an ethical and responsible corporate citizen. Its Code of Conduct stated that "business is to be conducted in compliance . . . with the highest professional and ethical standards." Its values, set forth in the annual report to shareholders, include respect, communication, excellence, and integrity – "We work with customers and prospects openly, honestly, and sincerely." Curtis C. Verschoor, accountancy professor at DePaul University, argues that Enron appeared to the outside world as a dependable, highly ethical, honorable, and responsible corporate citizen. The company's leadership did all the right things to generate trust and confidence from the public, the

---

[105] O'Toole, J. (2001). When leadership is an organizational trait. In W. Bennis, G. M. Spreitzer, & T. G. Cummings (Eds.), *The future of leadership: Today's top leadership thinkers speak to tomorrow's leaders*. San Francisco: Jossey-Bass.

energy regulators, investors, and employees. But the core values that the leadership actually practiced were quite different from those they listed in their annual report. They included deception, arrogance, concealment, and self-interest.[106]

The public's trust in corporate leadership was shaken by the Enron and Andersen calamities. Had they been isolated occurrences, the public's trust in corporate accountability and integrity might have quickly recovered. Unfortunately, within just a few months during the first half of 2002, more scandals came to light:

- Dennis Kozlowski, CEO of Tyco International, is charged with evading more than $1 million in taxes on paintings he bought in New York.
- Email among Merrill Lynch stock analysts show that even as they tout certain high-tech stocks to their clients, they call them "crap" to one another.
- Insider trading scandals reach new heights when Sam Waksal, former CEO of the biotechnology firm Imclone, is accused of warning his relatives and his friend Martha Stewart that the company's promising new cancer drug was denied approval by the FDA. Stewart sold her stock before the news became public and landed in the center of an insider trading investigation.
- Global Crossing executives are sued by Judicial Watch for "pumping and dumping" stock before the company's bankruptcy announcement.
- Telecom giant WorldCom admits an accounting fraud in which their profits had been inflated by almost $4 billion since 2001. More than 17,000 people are laid off after the news announcement, and the stock plummeted to below a dime. One commentator remarked that a minute of telephone time from MCI, WorldCom's subsidiary, is more expensive than a share of its stock.
- Just days after the WorldCom scandal burst into the news, Xerox announces its own accounting mistake involving improperly recorded revenues. It overstated its profits by up to $3 billion in the past five years.

These revelations have done more than just erode the public image of corporate executives by catching a few with their hands in the till. They have ushered in what could be a very long period of distrust, and not just distrust in the corporate leaders who may be bilking their own employees and destroying their retirement savings. The scandals also point to deeply

---

[106] Verschoor, C. C. (2002). Were Enron's ethical missteps a major cause of its downfall [Electronic version]? *Strategic Finance*, February, 22–25.

unethical behavior in the structures that are supposed to serve as checks and balances, to ensure the public receives accurate, truthful, and unbiased information about the internal state of a company. The accounting firms who audit the corporate books are suspect, as are the Wall Street analysts who advise investors about whether to buy, hold, or sell a stock. Indeed, many analysts were advising investors to buy WorldCom stock until just weeks before they went bankrupt, and then they only changed their advice to "hold."

ETHICAL LEADERSHIP

The challenge for the CEO and leadership team in this climate of distrust only begins with a new commitment to the highest ethical standards. The CEO will also have to find ways to deal with outrage and help restore trust from employees, shareholders, and the public. Even a CEO who never stole a dime will need to convince stakeholders that the management team is not a den of thieves and is not concealing anything from them.

Constance Bagley of the Harvard Business School points out that the growing emphasis on ethical leadership behavior is very welcome, but that few leaders have any training or practical guidance in how to evaluate the ethics of their decisions.[107] She proposes a simple decision tree to help leaders decide whether to pursue a particular action. First, they should ask if the action is legal, and if not, it should be rejected immediately. If it is legal, they should then ask whether it will maximize shareholder value. If so, the leader should then evaluate the ethics of the action. The leader must weigh the possible value to the shareholders against any potential negative effects on other stakeholders – customers, employees, suppliers, the environment, or the community. This evaluation can be extremely complex, but it should shed light on ethical issues that might have been ignored when only the maximization of shareholder value is used as the criterion for action.

Another branch in the decision tree involves actions that do not maximize shareholder value. The leaders should then consider whether a decision to take no action would be ethical. Would the company's stakeholders be harmed by inaction, and would that harm outweigh the cost to the shareholders? For example, a CEO opening a new office in a developing country might not be legally required to install the same workplace safety measures that are required in the home office. But to proceed ethically, the CEO should weigh the cost to the employees of not installing them. Bagley

---

[107] Bagley, C. E. (2003). The ethical leader's decision tree [Electronic version]. *Harvard Business Review, 81*(2), 18–19.

proposes that cases in which inaction would be unethical, even though they will not contribute to shareholder value, should be carried out but disclosed to the shareholders.

Ethical leadership will always be a balancing act in which costs and harm must be weighed against benefits and value. In the Internet era, however, the evaluation of these costs and benefits may be especially difficult, partly because so many of the innovations have had, and will continue to have, unforeseen effects. It is not very obvious how a particular action might harm or benefit stakeholders in many cases involving new technologies, and small errors in this evaluation process could turn into extremely large ones because of the amplification power of the network. For example, how should a leader evaluate the costs and benefits of a netcentric innovation that may lead to disintermediation? Is the potential loss of thousands of jobs in the community part of the natural process of creative destruction? Will the community be better off down the line because of the shakeout? Or should the leader reject the innovation on ethical grounds because it causes too much harm to stakeholders? In a highly competitive business climate, that rejection would be highly unlikely. Although the ethical decision tree doesn't answer questions like these, it at least helps focus attention on ethics and the broader consequences of business decisions.

Leaders of the Future

As older leaders retire, younger ones will emerge who have very different experiences. These younger leaders will have seen "new economy" companies skyrocket to success with new business models made possible by the Internet, and they will have seen many of them go bust almost as quickly. Some of them will have been part of this dynamic period of creative destruction and have worked at those companies. They may have accepted stock options as part of their compensation and will have seen those stocks become worthless. Others will have their own painful experiences with the pink slip and know what it means to lose a job.

These up-and-comers, which include more women and minorities, will be more diverse than the current crop of CEOs. Many will have benefited from leadership training programs and university courses that help people develop the skills they need to head complex, flatter organizations.[108]

---

[108] Doh, J. P. (2003). Can leadership be taught? Perspectives from management educators. *Academic of Management Learning and Education, 2*(1), 54–67. Retrieved March 22, 2003, from Business Source Premier Database.

They will also have grown up with the new communication tools and will have used email, instant messenger, the Web, and collaborative technologies most of their lives. They won't consider these technologies "innovations" any longer; they will consider them necessary and routine elements of living and working – just as we no longer think of a refrigerator as a "technological innovation."

The new leaders will be more accustomed to the rapid pace of change than their predecessors and will find ways to chart courses in much faster moving water. They will need to rely heavily on the Internet and the skills of their knowledge workers to gather business intelligence quickly and develop solid business strategies.

The lessons of the corporate scandals are quite likely to lead to more regulation and oversight by government and strengthened demands for transparency in corporate accounting practices. For the leadership, however, new rules and regulations will not be enough to reassure employees and the public that the company and its top executives are playing fair with them. They will be less effective if they cannot regain trust, even if they themselves were not responsible for losing it in the first place. They will have to be like Caesar's wife – not just honest and ethical, but obviously so. The escalating gap between the CEO's compensation and that of the average employee is likely to be reduced, partly because CEOs must do everything possible to reassure stakeholders that they will not put self-interest and greed above their commitment to making the company a success for all involved.

Being a CEO in the age of the Internet will be more about trust than about technology, but CEOs will learn to use the Internet to rebuild that trust, for employees, shareholders, customers, and the public.

6 Knowledge Management

Although the term "knowledge management" has been around for some time, most people in the workplace – including the managers – don't have a clear idea of what it is. Is it another management fad that will fade away like so many of its predecessors? Is it is a fundamentally new way of looking at an organization's assets, one that encompasses a very slippery but critically important resource? More than a few people are convinced it is the consultant's latest sales pitch, laden with more puffed up jargon than most of its predecessors. Others suspect it is a way for software vendors to sell complicated and expensive products that have intriguing names but little or no track record.

The confusion is understandable because knowledge is so difficult to define, let alone capture and manage. Dictionaries define it by drawing on terms that are equally difficult to define, such as *knowing, understanding, awareness, cognition,* or *having information.* For example, some of Webster's many definitions of knowledge include "the fact or condition of knowing something with familiarity gained through experience or association," and "the range of one's information or understanding," and "the circumstance or condition of apprehending truth or fact through reasoning."

Nevertheless, the rise of the "knowledge worker" was accompanied by a gnawing sense that there is some asset adrift in the workplace or inside the worker's head, something important that managers and organizations should harness – or at least deal with more systematically. This elusive asset was unlike others, such as employee time spent at work or the equipment on the factory floor. Yet in the midst of the knowledge society, in which knowledge workers were beginning to be more numerous than any other type of worker, many began to think organizations were mishandling and even ignoring the most critical asset they had. They became especially concerned during periods when many people would be retiring at the same time, or when workers walked out the door to accept a better offer from a competitor, taking their knowledge with them.

Understanding how to identify, capture, share, and manage this asset, however, has been far more challenging than most people supposed. And finding better and more efficient ways to create new knowledge has been even more difficult. In this chapter, we first take a close look at where knowledge management came from. Then we examine what knowledge means in the workplace, what kinds of knowledge might be important to manage, and how some organizations are faring in their knowledge management projects.

The Origins of Knowledge Management

In the 1980s and 1990s, computers were becoming standard equipment in the workplace – not just for the number crunchers in payroll and accounting but also for most knowledge workers. Initially, the computers were dumb terminals linked only to the mainframe. The functions they performed were constrained by the mainframe's software, which focused mainly on back-office operations. Corporate email and word processing were added to this mix, expanding the capabilities for communication and storage of digitized information, but storage space was limited and the software cumbersome to use.

When the microcomputer entered the picture, workers were offered the opportunity to save as much digitized information as they wanted. They had their own personal hard drive to fill up, and they could store unlimited quantities of information on reusable and inexpensive floppy disks. They could save documents, reports, letters, what-if spreadsheets, and any number of drafts of all their creations.

The limitless shelf space for digitized information changed habits in the workplace considerably. People didn't need to throw away documents when their filing cabinets overflowed and they naturally saved them. Each workstation became a growing repository of information that was created or modified by the worker who used it. Initially, the repository was only easily accessible by that particular worker. However, when local area networks were implemented, employees could share information on the servers. With each passing year, storage capabilities increased, as did the range of documents that could be stored in digitized format. Scanners allowed people to store images, and sound cards made it possible to store and play sounds. Movies could also be stored electronically as digital video.

When the Internet took hold, and particularly the World Wide Web, the sheer volume of information available to a worker skyrocketed again.

People could not only share digitized information with people in their work-group who were on the same local area network; now, they could share with any person or organization on the planet who had an Internet con-nection.

A major force that drove the keen interest in knowledge manage-ment was, quite simply, this growing volume of digitized information that could – potentially at least – be accessed and reused. With intranets and the Internet, the information could also be easily shared and transmitted around the globe. Computers and the Internet did not "create" knowledge management, but they certainly drew attention to the fact that at least some of the knowledge that resided in people's heads might be documented, shared, and harnessed as an organizational asset and resource.

Laurence Prusak, founder of the Institute for Knowledge Management at IBM, cites additional reasons for the rising interest in knowledge man-agement, particularly for knowledge that can be transmitted via the In-ternet and technology.[109] A key one is globalization, the pace of which dramatically increased. The number of global players, global distribution channels, and globally available products has grown tremendously. Orga-nizations had, in the past, relied on closer quarters in the physical sense to support the transmission of knowledge from one worker to another, though the strategy was more an accidental byproduct than an intention. People who passed each other in the hallway or ate at the same cafeteria would share knowledge naturally in conversation. Even coworkers located at dif-ferent branch offices would travel to corporate training sites or meetings to share knowledge, but globalization has made in-person knowledge sharing far more difficult.

Interest in knowledge management, then, arose partly because a ham-mer was invented and people noticed a growing mound of nails on which it might be productively used. The hammer was information technology, especially the net and netcentric technologies. The nails encompassed the digitized information that was growing by leaps and bounds. The nails – at least some of them – seemed like they might be particularly valuable, but the nail pile was very disorderly, astonishingly large, and not easily tackled or sorted out by technology alone. Compounding the problem was the fact that the kind of knowledge a corporation would want to harness would not just be located in digitized files. Also, much of that digitized information is not "knowledge" at all, regardless of how one might define the term. Much of it is garbage.

---

[109] Prusak, L. (2001). Where did knowledge management come from [Electronic version]? *IBM Systems Journal, 40*(4), 1002–1007.

If you take a look at the organization of your own computer workspace, you will see what I mean. Would a successor who took over your job after you left be able to figure out your electronic filing system, and be able to tap into your knowledge about how to do what you've been doing for years? Or would the successor have to start from scratch to acquire the same knowledge, with little more than an hour of conversation with you on the phone as an orientation? You probably have important information stored in email archives, in various directories on your hard drive, on backup CD-ROMs, on floppy disks, on zip drives, on the server, and possibly on your own Web site, in addition to your desk drawers and metal cabinets. You have many versions of the same document, and it might be difficult to tell which one is the final – if indeed any of them are. If you are like most people, you don't use any kind of consistent naming convention for many of your electronic files, even if you have a very well-organized paper filing cabinet. You might just name your files something that seems appropriate at the time you save them.

Your coworkers are likely to be just as casual as you are in the way they manage their digitized information. From the organizational perspective, then, this potentially valuable goldmine of "knowledge" is not so easy to identify, let alone manage. And, of course, much of the knowledge that is really valuable to an organization is not digitized at all.

The realization that knowledge is more complicated and elusive compared to raw data led people who became interested in managing knowledge down two paths. One path led toward the development of technology-based approaches to capture, sort, organize, and disseminate knowledge – in the form of digitized information of some kind – to the people who needed it. The other path led to approaches in which technology might not be used at all. These stressed the value of intellectual capital, and how to encourage people to create and share knowledge. This second path leaned more toward the psychological and sociological aspects of the workplace rather than the technical solutions for capturing and disseminating knowledge. As we see later in this chapter, there are some critical human issues that emerge in knowledge management projects, some of which have caused the projects to fail completely.

What Is Knowledge?

Throughout the last decade, people involved in knowledge management have struggled with the question of what knowledge is, and with what knowledge is worth the time and trouble to manage in an organizational setting. For example, what is the difference between information and knowledge? Is knowledge management just an inflated version of information management?

DATA → INFORMATION → KNOWLEDGE

One useful way to distinguish knowledge from data and information is to see them as a continuum in which the material becomes richer, more valuable, more laden with meaning, and more important within a particular context. Data refers to the raw numbers that make up, for example, the transactions for the week within a company. As more meaning is added, the data can be manipulated and summarized, and then turned into information that reveals trends and patterns. The transactions can be summarized according to region in a bar graph so the sales manager can see which items are selling where. Adding more meaning and context, the sales manager might draw from a depth of experience and combine the graph with business intelligence from sales people in each of those regions who know what the competitors are doing locally. The manager's insights, drawn from experience, graphical information, and business intelligence, may point to a relationship between certain kinds of competitor activities and the sales of particular items. This enrichment and enhancement of the information about sales by region turns the material into something that not only has meaning within the context but also is actionable if the person puts it all together and is willing and able to act on it. The sales manager might use this knowledge to launch marketing campaigns designed to counteract the competitor's strategy, tailored by region.

There are no unambiguous dividing lines between data and information, or between information and knowledge. At each level, however, more meaning is added, though that meaning might not be apparent to everyone when it reaches its highest levels.

TACIT AND EXPLICIT KNOWLEDGE

One reason knowledge in the workplace has been so difficult to come to grips with is that the term is used so broadly and vaguely to refer to so many different things. An office worker may have knowledge of the demographic characteristics of the country, or an insurance agent may possess knowledge about how to process a claim for an auto accident. Knowledge to a scientist involved in genetic research might encompass an easy familiarity with the basic principles of genetics, a broad grasp of all the latest findings in the field by other scientists, and the insights the scientist applies to generate new knowledge.

We can categorize different types of knowledge in several ways, but a useful way to do it in the age of the Internet is to distinguish between *explicit* knowledge and *tacit* knowledge. Explicit knowledge is formal and systematic, and it can be documented and shared with others. It is not necessarily simple at all, and because it can be shared doesn't mean that everyone will grasp it by reading the documentation. For example, knowledge of a programming language is explicit knowledge, but it can take a great deal of time to acquire this knowledge, and not everyone is able to do it.

Tacit knowledge refers to the far more elusive kinds of knowledge that are difficult to document and share, partly because the "knower" is not sure exactly how to describe what he or she knows. A talented craftsperson, for example, would have a great deal of tacit knowledge about building custom cabinets, but much of it would be difficult to document. When the craftsperson chooses certain types of wood, shapes the pieces using heat or pressure, sands and smoothes the surfaces, and assembles the pieces, he or she is drawing on years of experience of what has worked in the past. He or she may not be able to tell you exactly what combinations will work, or write down checklists for ensuring success.

Ikujiro Nonaka, of the School of Knowledge Science at the Japan Advanced Institute of Science and Technology, has focused on this distinction, particularly because it shows a key difference in the way Japanese and American workers view knowledge.[110] Nonaka believes that Americans think about knowledge too narrowly, emphasizing "information" in the data → information → knowledge continuum described earlier. Explicit knowledge is critical, but an organization risks a great deal if it has no measures in place to nurture and tap the tacit knowledge that resides inside people's heads, and which they have difficulty describing or communicating.

An example of how an organization was able to tap into tacit knowledge to achieve quite a remarkable competitive advantage involved the bread-making machine.[111] Cooking is both an art and a science, and bread making is a niche in the culinary domain in which tacit knowledge seems to be particularly important. When Matsushita engineers were trying to develop a home bread-making machine, they were able to get the basics. They turned out bread, but the crust was always overcooked and the inside was almost raw. Engineering analyses, including x-rays, were unable to resolve the problem.

[110] Nonaka, I. (2001). Making the most of your company's knowledge: A strategic framework. *Long Range Planning, 34*(4), 421–440.
[111] Nonaka, I. (1991). The knowledge-creating company. In *Harvard Business Review on Knowledge Management*. Boston, MA: Harvard Business School Publishing.

Ikuko Tanaka, one of Matsushita's software developers, decided to harness the tacit knowledge they were obviously missing by training with one of the best bakers in the world, at the Osaka International Hotel. She watched his style, and even he could not explain how or why he was kneading the dough a certain way. She went back to the drawing board to design some special mechanical ribs that would twist and stretch the dough very much the way the baker had done. The result was a new bread-making machine that set records for sales.

Creating Information and Explicit Knowledge for the Organization: Pre-Internet

When interest in knowledge management first began, organizations were beginning to enjoy some of the more sophisticated uses of computers and technology. The Internet was still an infant and the World Wide Web didn't exist, but the emerging capabilities in information technology were already making their mark. In the workplace, online tools for reporting and summarizing became extremely popular. To see a summary of sales by region, the managers no longer had to wait for the monthly report. They could pull up the tables and graphs themselves from the corporate servers.

People were also learning that they could easily manipulate the raw transactional data their mainframes churned out using PC-based software, to add their own spin in terms of meaning and interpretation. A download of transactions could keep someone skilled with spreadsheets, charting tools, and statistical analysis software productively engaged for a long time, adding the meaning and context that turned raw data into information, and then into knowledge. They could ask questions, such as, "Is there any relationship between widget sales volume and salesperson salaries by region?" or "Are women or men more effective at telemarketing for different products?" They could build what-if scenarios with spreadsheet software to evaluate a variety of strategic choices, from starting up a new business to building a plant overseas. The tools gave them the opportunity to enter various estimates for variables such as start-up expenditures, monthly sales, average salary per manufacturing worker, and many others. Using their experience combined with the instant calculations, they could evaluate many different hypotheses and business scenarios.

Growing telecommunications capabilities and networks were also part of the context during this early period in the 1980s. You may recall how the corporate policy manual was often distributed before everyone's computer was networked. A notebook with divider tabs was sent to each department containing critical information about how to do things within the organization. It explained how to fill out an expense voucher and what the per diem limits were. It might have had tabs for recruitment and hiring, employee benefits, grievance procedures, the organizational chart, and a directory of important telephone numbers. The information changed all the time of course, so "change pages" were distributed to the departments for the secretaries to insert. Secretaries may or may not have kept up with the change pages, and individuals always made copies of portions of the manual to keep on their desk. Over time, there were probably no two manuals throughout the organization that were exactly alike. Once the network was available, many corporations put documents like the policy manual on a server so anyone could look at them, and everyone would see the latest information. The savings in time and printing costs were quite substantial.

The networks were also pressed into service to encourage people to share more of their tacit knowledge, so newcomers would not have to reinvent wheels. For example, team members were asked to document their brainstorming sessions and share the lessons they learned from their projects. The results could be posted on the network servers so other teams could learn from the early mistakes. Expert systems were also being developed to capture tacit knowledge in a more systematic way. The software created could be implemented on the network and accessed by people who were less experienced but working on similar problems. For example, the health professions have had some excellent success with expert systems such as MYCIN, a system that helps health care workers analyze symptoms of infectious diseases, and VIBES, a program that helps diagnose and give advice about visual impairments.

These two major technology breakthroughs – the development of analytical and reporting tools and the networking of desktops within corporations – drew attention to new possibilities for creating, harvesting, and managing knowledge for the organization. The mounds of organizational data were growing, and they were grist for the mill of organizational knowledge. Also, people within an organization know many things, things they did not necessarily gain from raw data but from experience and insight. When the Internet and especially the World Wide Web entered the picture, the possibilities for managing all kinds of knowledge and information expanded considerably.

Post-Internet Knowledge Management

By the mid-1990s, the Internet had begun to reach workplaces, and corporations around the globe added their own Web sites to the worldwide network. One early consequence was that the data available to anyone in the workplace multiplied exponentially. The sheer size and phenomenal growth rate of the Web is a part of this trend, but data that had formerly been stored locally are also now available through the net. For example, I can go to www.census.gov and download hundreds of electronic files containing raw census data to analyze in any way I choose. The Bureau of Labor Statistics has made it especially easy for users to download tables and files of employment information for further analysis. Even the very powerful search engines are unable to keep up with this immense content.

For marketers and behavioral scientists, consider how much more raw data we now have about *what* people are doing when they explore the vast World Wide Web. An Internet Service Provider such as America Online can potentially record every login and each mouse click of every person who uses their network. Suppose AOL has 20 million-plus users, and each one logs in every day for about two hours. During the surfing time, suppose each user clicks the mouse an average of five times a minute. Multiplying this out comes to 540 billion mouse clicks a month. That's quite a lot of raw data, and embedded within it are personal preferences, buying patterns, demographic profiles, and subject interests. It's also a great deal of storage space, and AOL executives have said they have to delete all this routinely – it is just too much.

The Web also offered a remarkably efficient means of distributing information – and potentially knowledge – across the globe, quickly and easily. As long as the text, images, and tables were presented in standard HTML (HyperText Markup Language), browsers could read and display the material on any desktop. The tags used in the language allowed all those freely available browsers to quickly interpret various format commands, such as boldface, line break, or heading. A more sophisticated type of markup language, called XML (extensible markup language), is further standardizing the way documents are defined, marked up, categorized, and understood. This markup language also relies on tags, but they are used to define and standardize metadata about the document, its structure and content, for example, in addition to text formatting. Tags can also be customized for particular industries, such as libraries or medicine, so that applications that access the documents can parse them in more meaningful ways that consider the context.

Compared to what corporations were doing just a few years earlier, these standardized approaches to representing and sharing information were a huge step forward. Those organizations had networks and could post updated information for all to see, but it was in proprietary formats that required special software and licenses on each desktop computer, and this client software was typically installed by the corporate IT department.

The earlier networks created much better intraorganizational communication, but the organizations were islands of technology that used their own software. Even branches of the same company might be using different proprietary software – perhaps because the systems were purchased and installed at different times, by different IT departments. This meant the corporate branch employees in New York couldn't see the same information as people could in the Philadelphia branch, let alone the London branch.

When the Web first appeared, its standardized approach and superior usability gave it the momentum that propelled it to such explosive growth. Once people installed their free browser software, they could surf to any Web site open to the public and put up their own documents. At first, it was extremely valuable just to be able to see the text, even if it was not formatted with boldface, italics, headings, or columns. But people soon learned HTML to make documents look more appealing and readable. With XML, organizations and entire industries are gaining even more capability to exchange information that has been isolated in proprietary formats.

The growing capabilities of information technology and the Internet were the converging forces that made knowledge management such an intriguing subject. First, computerization began generating enormous quantities of raw data and then gave people sophisticated abilities to create information from that data. While the early networks facilitated intraorganizational dissemination of information, the Web made worldwide dissemination possible. The irony is that the sheer volume of data and information that emerged as a result of these forces created information overload rather than knowledge. This drew more attention to the need for better ways to manage it, learn from it, and create new meaning. People intuitively suspected they were awash with important and valuable raw material, but they were frustrated because they didn't know how to harness it all or pick out the wheat from the chaff. They needed just-in-time knowledge, which involves getting the right information to the right person at just the right time.

Knowledge Discovery and Data Mining

The growing volume of data sparked considerable interest in ways to discover and extract more meaningful information and knowledge from it. Researchers and practitioners proposed hypotheses based on their knowledge and experience and could use some of the data to confirm or reject them. But the data were so voluminous and arrived so quickly that new approaches were needed, ones that could explore the data and discover knowledge even when – especially when – no researcher had formed an *a priori* hypothesis. These approaches are called *data mining*. The metaphor conjures up the act of prospecting, for gold or silver perhaps, and the patience needed to come upon valuable nuggets amidst mounds of worthless gravel and rock. Data mining relies more on artificial intelligence, mathematical algorithms, and computer power than on human hands, but the goal is not that different: to extract interesting relationships, trends and behavior patterns from billions of data elements and use them to predict new outcomes.

Data mining grew out of traditional statistical approaches, but the field has amassed a very powerful set of software tools that can be used to explore extremely large data sets to uncover interesting but hidden relationships. The software programs turn up all kinds of relationships, many purely by accident, so the term "interesting" is extremely important in the data mining world. Suppose, for example, an exploration of the data left by last month's Web site visitors turns up a moderate relationship between the time spent on the home page by visitors and the temperature in southern Europe. Without human guidance, the software programs could not identify this as uninteresting, compared to, for example, a relationship between time spent on the home page and number of previous visits. Even so, data miners are reluctant to use too much guidance because they are looking for hidden relationships, and sometimes the most surprising can be the most valuable.

Fortune 500 companies have used data mining techniques very effectively to learn more about their customers and their preferences, buying patterns, and loyalties. The techniques are also being used in areas such as higher education, on data about the behavior patterns of transfer students, for example.[112] Researchers in Australia are using the techniques to explore legal databases, an especially difficult task because so much legal information is unstructured.[113] As they become more refined, data mining techniques promise to make contributions to the process of knowledge discovery in many different areas.

---

[112] Luan, J. (2002). Data mining and its applications in higher education. *New Directions for Institutional Research, 113*, 17–36. Retrieved March 24, 2003, from Business Source Premier Database.

[113] Ivkovic, S., Yearwood, J., & Stranieri, A. (2002). Discovering interesting association rules from legal databases. *Information & Communication Technology Law, 11*(1), 35–47. Retrieved March 24, 2003, from Business Source Premier Database.

Knowledge Management Practices and Projects

The elusive definitions and varied approaches to knowledge management led to quite a variety of projects in the workplace. Some of them are enormously successful, whereas others were disasters, but they all had in common some attempt to capture, create, disseminate, or manage knowledge – however that term might be defined. Because the workplace is fundamentally pragmatic rather than theoretical, it can be easier to understand how organizations are approaching knowledge management from descriptions of the actual projects and practices that have been launched under its umbrella.

The information technology research organization called Gartner Group describes five categories that loosely group knowledge management practices into related initiatives.[114] The first involves attempts to improve the management of vast quantities of electronic information and also improve access to it in the workplace.

IMPROVING INFORMATION MANAGEMENT AND ACCESS

Seeing how much space – both electronic and physical – is used to store documents, and how much time employees spend searching for information, would lead any prudent organization to pursue some improvements. Structured and integrated databases with powerful search engines and analytical tools have contributed a great deal in this arena, but the unstructured information and knowledge stored in filing cabinets, email, bookcases, and brains has been more of a challenge. One of the earliest attempts to harness at least some of this knowledge was the corporate intranet. This is the organization's internal Web site designed to collect all kinds of documents, such as the policy manual, telephone directories, and job listings, and make them available so everyone in the organization can see an updated version from wherever they happen to be. The intranet has also become a gateway to discussion boards, knowledge repositories, team-based Web sites, various collaborative technologies, and the corporation's transactional systems.

To improve the usefulness of intranets and allow employees to customize their workspaces, many corporations moved up to corporate *portals*. These are a more powerful version of the intranet that give employees the opportunity to customize what they see so it is more relevant to their own work. Rather than the generic corporate home page, a marketing manager

---

[114] Caldwell, F., & Harris, K. (2002). Management update: The 2002 knowledge management hype cycle. *InSide Gartner*, 23 January 2002. Retrieved July 14, 2002, from Gartner Research Services intraWeb.

might decide that her opening screen in the morning should be a kind of dashboard with real-time data of interest to her. It could contain the latest figures from the current advertising campaign, along with graphs and links to all the competitors. Portals have also made progress toward the single "sign on." Most corporations have built over time a number of separate systems with their own security for applications such as email, personnel, sales, or discussion boards. With a portal, a person can log in once and not have to log in over and over again to all these different systems.

Document management is another well-developed knowledge management practice that improves access to the less structured kind of information. This approach takes paper records, scans them as digital images, and indexes them so they become searchable electronically, at least by the indexes that were created for them. For example, a medical record might be scanned and indexes created for patient name, social security number, diagnosis, and other key words. Some systems add character recognition so the text within the document can be converted to readable characters rather than just images, and thus also searchable. This has been especially useful for businesses in which some or even most of the information that people need to retrieve is on paper or microfiche, not in electronic form. Medical records, court records, patents, transcripts, and real estate transactions are all examples. Although some of these are now available in electronic form, historical records are not.

MANAGING KNOWLEDGE ABOUT PROCESSES

A key competitive advantage for an organization grows from whatever knowledge it has about *how to do* what it does well. A winery succeeds because it can grow the best grapes, turn them into excellent wines, and market them effectively. To do that well, the winery employees and the organization as a whole must have a storehouse of knowledge about processes that work under different weather and soil conditions, knowledge that should be harnessed, shared, passed on, and improved upon over time. Process knowledge projects have focused on how this kind of knowledge might be managed, particularly through best practice programs and knowledge bases.

Best practice programs usually attempt to document experiences on projects that go well and capture the factors that led to success so they can be repeated. Banc One (now Bank One), for example, used the best practice approach to convert the banks it was acquiring over to its own system in a very systematic way. They had documented all the procedures and flowcharts that the new employees needed to learn about how to set up loans, process commercial transactions, open accounts, sell stocks, and perform the many tasks they would be doing under the new system. People who had set up other branches in the Banc One way served as trainers for the new employees, so they combined documentation with people to transfer knowledge. Each new branch was also assigned a sister bank that served as a "template." The sister had already done the conversion and was chosen because it was nearby and had a similar set of customers. The new bank employees could visit the sister to absorb more detailed knowledge from people who were actually using the procedures. The experiences of the sister could also help the new bank's managers predict problem areas and help the new bank avoid them. For example, if employees at the sister bank were resistant about adopting centralized procedures for processing, the new bank's managers could pay special attention to that area. Bank One also set up a master "template," in the form of a model bank located near its headquarters, so managers could implement new ideas there under close supervision before propagating them out to their branches.[115]

Knowledge bases also are designed to contain a large repository of process information for a corporation so the knowledge can be harnessed and transferred. For example, a software vendor may develop a knowledge base containing all the problems customers have reported and the techniques the technical support personnel have used to solve them. Combined with document management, a knowledge base can be a very rich source of information. Consider, for example, a medical knowledge base in which records of all kinds can be searched for certain combinations of symptoms. A health care worker would be able to search this knowledge base and find a much greater range of possible causes than even the most experienced professionals could ever keep in their own heads.

HARNESSING ORGANIZATIONAL KNOWLEDGE IN THE WORKPLACE

A diverse set of practices and projects have been launched that attempt to enhance organizational knowledge by encouraging workers to teach each other, share what they know, and build learning communities. Some organizations support communities of practice, for example, by creating specialized Web sites for people in the same professional area to communicate freely with one another. A large corporation might support a lively Web-based community of their legal professionals located all over the world to share knowledge about intellectual property, international law, employment law, or contract disputes. By bringing together people who have the same professional interests and providing them with collaborative tools to

---

[115] Szulanski, G., & Winter, S. (2002). Getting it right the second time [Electronic version]. *Harvard Business Review, 80*(1), 62–69.

engage in discussions and debates, an organization can prevent the isolation that can afflict geographically dispersed professionals.

Many organizations have implemented collaborative technologies to support the knowledge workplace, and these are very useful for collocated groups as well as for geographically dispersed teams. We examine how virtual teams work in a later chapter, but from a knowledge management perspective, these technologies can be used to support many kinds of groups who need to share knowledge.

Another type of knowledge workplace project that has benefited a number of companies is called "expert location." From the standpoint of the organization, the goal is to ensure the company knows what it knows, or at least knows who in the company might know something. When a team is put together to create a product, for example, they are not likely to have all the expertise they need to do the best job on the product. However, there may be someone somewhere in the corporation who has that expertise, and the expert location approach is designed to find that person. These projects usually collect and update resumes of people throughout the corporation, include various key words, and allow project teams to search the database in which they are maintained.

LEARNING FROM E-BUSINESS

As corporations began using the Web for e-business, that mound of data grew even faster and new possibilities for managing knowledge were opened. Organizations are communicating electronically with their customers, suppliers, and partners, so this source of information became an opportunity for knowledge management. In addition, the competitors were conducting e-business also, so some of their information became accessible for business intelligence gathering. This category of knowledge management projects covers that interface between the internal organization and the external environment.

The desire of companies to collect as much knowledge as they can about their own customers, and to nurture the relationship with those they want to keep, has always been strong. Knowledge management projects that focus on this desire have been popular, and the new technology-based tools such as data mining have been applied aggressively. Another variety of software has also emerged, called "customer relationship management" software (CRM). These products focus on the ways in which a corporation can attract and retain their customers (especially the most valuable customers) by analyzing and managing the relationships the corporation has with each one. Corporations have always tried to keep the customers they have happy, but thanks to e-business and the Internet, the information corporations can now use to make each customer happy and to maintain ties through targeted email is quite extensive.

Some of the information available for managing relationships with customers has always been available, such as the total amount you spend with a company each year, but now it can be combined with e-business information. Many Web sites, for example, offer registered customers a variety of targeted promotions based on their past behavior. They may offer the opportunity to sign up for special email-only deals, or subscribe to various customized newsletters. When you register at the Motley Fool, for example, which offers financial advice, you can sign up for any number of newsletters on investing, retirement, or other subjects; participate in financial discussion groups; track your portfolio; or create a mock portfolio for fun. The amount of information Motley Fool can collect about each person's financial life and interests is quite remarkable. Knowledge management projects involving customer relationships are designed to tap into that information, create knowledge from it, and turn it into competitive advantages.

NURTURING INTELLECTUAL CAPITAL

The least mature area of knowledge management is a loosely related assortment of projects in which corporations are attempting to nurture and manage intellectual capital, especially by finding ways to facilitate creativity, insight, and innovation, and document the elusive process of knowledge creation. These projects span a wide range and reach into many different nooks and crannies of the organization. Software vendors are developing very diverse products to assist with this kind of knowledge management, but technology may sometimes not be needed at all.

One group of efforts is designed to encourage creativity and help people think "out of the box" when they explore problem areas. Pressed for time, most people working in groups tend to latch onto the first clear definition of a problem and then want to adopt the first reasonable approach to solving it. They may not take time to explore different ways of formulating the problem, so that alternative solutions may become apparent. Consider the elevator problem, overheard by John Thomas of IBM.[116]

> A few years back, the tenants in a Manhattan office high-rise complained vigorously about the long wait for the elevators. Computer programmers were brought in to change the algorithms, but the complaints got worse. New, faster motors were installed at considerable expense, but the complaints

---

[116] The Slow Elevator, IBM Research Web site. (n.d.). Retrieved July 15, 2002, from http://www.research.ibm.com/knowsoc/stories_elevator.html

continued and many tenants threatened to move out. In desperation, the owner hired structural engineers to estimate the cost of installing additional elevator shafts. The cost of installation along with the reduced rentable space would be ruinous.

The managers, engineers, and computer programmers trying to tackle this problem had all formulated it the same way. The problem, in their minds, was that the elevators were too slow and the solution would be to speed them up. However, the cousin of the owner formulated it differently and suggested putting mirrors next to the elevators. The cousin's take on the problem was that the wait was reasonable, but the people waiting needed something amusing and productive to do. Once the mirrors were installed, the complaints stopped.

A variety of behavioral techniques are used to encourage people to expand the formulation phase and delay the search for solutions. One approach is the "Bohm Dialogue," which helps groups of people suspend their own judgments and biases while they collectively exchange questions and thoughts about the nature of a problem. The participants are expected to leave their competitive tendencies outside the door as they engage in conversation about a particular issue with other group members. Key components of this kind of dialog include suspension of decision making and silent spaces for reflection on what the last speaker just said.[117] Another group of projects emphasizes the use of metaphor to help people think creatively and develop new knowledge. For instance, when people are working on a particular problem within one domain, it often helps them expand their thinking by listening to and applying metaphors from a completely different problem domain. A group of people working on problems in transportation might become too narrow when they only think about trucks, trains, and ships. If they are exposed to metaphors that involve the human circulation system, or bird migration, the range of ideas they can apply to transportation is enlarged.

The Knowledge Management Hype Cycle

Innovative approaches that involve emerging technologies and promise to improve the workplace or provide competitive advantage to business usually go through cycles as they are evaluated, piloted, adopted, or discarded. They start out as innovations that appear to address some critical need that

---

[117] Bohm, D., Factor, D., & Garrett, P. (1991). Dialogue: A proposal. Retrieved July 15, 2002, from http://www.muc.de/~heuvel/dialogue/dialogue_proposal.html#5

has not received enough attention. Total quality management, for example, focused on quality, and management by objectives focused on goal setting. Initially, the approaches may attract considerable attention because they sound good on paper and the consultants who promote them may exaggerate their value. Expectations are raised very high – too high – and the technology that supports the innovation is immature and buggy. Employees, having seen these cycles before, may yawn at the latest one, groan, or just laugh. Many, however, resist spending more time on the current management fad and new technology, and "buy-in" is spotty at best. As pilot projects run over budget and fail to return the results that were anticipated or promised, disillusionment ensues. Eventually, if the ideas are worthwhile and the problem was really in the inflated expectations, the innovation is reconsidered. The bugs in the software are worked out, the expectations adjusted, and organizations adopt the valuable pieces of the approach that actually work. As the new approach becomes embedded in the workplace, its faddish name might be forgotten, but its contribution to productivity, if there was one, remains.

Gartner Group calls this the hype cycle,[118] and labels its five phases (1) innovation trigger phase, (2) peak of inflated expectations, (3) trough of disillusionment, (4) slope of enlightenment, and (5) plateau of productivity. It has been especially long for knowledge management innovations compared to other technology-based practices because it encompasses so much and our understanding of knowledge in the workplace is so unclear. As you can see from the range of projects I just described, many initiatives are now under its umbrella that were called something else in earlier years, or were not called anything at all other than "good ideas" for a productive workplace. Many business leaders began to think that knowledge management was little more than a term cooked up by consultants who needed a bright new symbol to attract customers after their last fad, business process reengineering perhaps, had faded.

The most mature knowledge management practices take advantage of well-developed technologies, such as carefully designed databases, document management systems, knowledge bases, collaborative technologies, and of course, the Internet and World Wide Web. In contrast, the least mature practices venture into terrain that is not well charted, in terms of either the strategies that can be used to manage knowledge or the technologies

---

[118] Linden, A. (2002). Gartner's 2002 hype cycle for emerging technologies. Gartner Research Services, Note number LE-16-7559., May 28, 2002. Retrieved July 15, 2002, from Gartner Research Services intraWeb.

that could support those efforts. After the dot.com bust in the late 1990s, few corporations were willing to risk major investments in such unproven approaches, regardless of the dynamic presentations by consultants and software vendors.

Social and Psychological Factors in Knowledge Management

Knowledge management has had an especially difficult path through the hype cycle because the pilot projects uncovered some important truths about human behavior in the workplace. Some of the most significant obstacles to the success of knowledge management projects turned out to be psychological and social, not technological. Sharing knowledge in the workplace, for example, sounds like a wonderful idea to top executives, but there are barriers to the human willingness to share that have little to do with the difficulty of learning new software.

One of the classic studies that unearthed psychological and social barriers to knowledge management projects involved the introduction of Lotus Notes into a consulting company. Notes is a type of groupware that can support many kinds of knowledge management efforts, from easily searchable knowledge bases to online collaborative work. Users can easily set up meetings, start discussion threads, and create databases to archive knowledge in specific subject areas that they want to share. Wanda Orlikowski of the Massachusetts Institute of Technology studied how the technology was introduced and why the project ran into problems.[119]

The Chief Information Officer of the consulting company was very impressed with the capabilities of the software, particularly for sharing expertise within the corporation. Many employees were eager to try it, but they were given little training. As a result, they tended to think of it as an extension of different kinds of software with which they were already familiar. Some thought it was another version of a spreadsheet that added new functionality such as word processing. Some viewed it as "big email" and others assumed it was "a database housed somewhere in the center of the universe." Clearly, the users did not have any mental models that properly matched groupware, nor were they able to see how it might offer new ways to increase their productivity.

---

[119] Orlikowski, W. J. (1992). Learning from notes: Organizational issues in groupware implementation. Center for Coordination Science Technical Report #134, MIT Sloan School Working Paper #3428–92. Retrieved July 15, 2002, from http://ccs.mit.edu/papers/CCSWP134.html

Social and psychological barriers prevented the project from becoming successful, even when employees glimpsed the power of the tool. Although the employees were expected to share their expertise, most were unwilling to do this because the compensation and promotion system did not reward sharing. As one employee put it, "I'm trying to develop an area of expertise that makes me stand out. If I shared that with you you'd get the credit not me. . . . It's really a cut-throat environment." When people are rewarded for possessing valuable and unique knowledge, as they often are in knowledge-intensive firms, they have little reason to share that knowledge with others. From their perspective, sharing only diminishes the value of what they possess. Though the top executives may see knowledge management and knowledge sharing as critical to the overall success of the firm, the individual workers do not always see it that way.

Knowledge "hoarding" is very predictable in an environment in which rewards are based on an individual's accomplishments and possession of unique knowledge. And it spans every level of the organization. I recall an incident that illustrates this point, in which I needed to print about fifty letters on letterhead. The networked office printer was out of paper, but the slot for the paper seemed obvious enough. I inserted the letterhead and ran back to my desktop to click print. When I tried to retrieve the letters I found they had printed on the wrong side of the paper. I put in another stack upside down, ran back to my desk, and clicked print again. This time, they printed on the correct side but upside down. The man who tended the machines walked by and put the paper in correctly for me. I thanked him profusely, but asked why there wasn't a little sign that told people what orientation should be used when loading the paper tray. He said there was one and pulled it out of the drawer. Then I asked why he kept it in the drawer instead of taping it to the printer. He smiled and said, "Job security."

Another psychological obstacle in knowledge management projects involves embarrassment. Most people don't like to admit they don't know something, and many are reluctant to ask for help or search out expertise when they need it. For example, one project was designed to improve the efficiency of copier repair people by giving them access to a knowledge base from the remote site where they were fixing a copier. In the pilot, the repair people were given a laptop and a modem, and they could call in to look up answers in a knowledge base when they were unable to fix a copier. Unfortunately, many of the repair people didn't want to use the laptop because they were supposed to be the experts, and it would be embarrassing to look things up from their customers' locations.

Embarrassment has also been a problem for people who try to offer their expertise to a knowledge base or knowledge management project. In technical settings, for example, a programmer might contribute a solution to a particular problem but then find four or five "critiques" appear the next morning. Other programmers wanted to point out flaws in the contributor's posting, or suggest better ways to achieve the same goal. In some cases, the "knowledge base" becomes a debate platform, with lots of one-upmanship but not very much genuine knowledge sharing.

The cost of knowledge management, in terms of time spent by each individual, has been yet another problem that derails projects early in their life cycle. Building a knowledge base in a particular domain takes time. People have been asked to enter their good ideas, best practices, lessons learned, or expert opinions at the end of the day or the end of a project, tacking on extra hours to each person's workday. From the perspective of the individual in the workplace, the cost of contributing their expertise outweighed any benefits they might have gained by finding useful knowledge in the database, particularly during the early stages of a knowledge management project when the pickings are sparse. A knowledge base needs a critical mass before it can be useful to a wide range of people. Before it reaches that mass, employees would quite rationally view the project as something that detracts from their own productivity – another management fad, perhaps. If they are not encouraged, rewarded, or provided with some kind of incentive, they will resist the effort it takes to build the knowledge base because of the personal cost to them.

The Future of Knowledge Management

Despite the rocky starts and problems with various knowledge management projects, most organizations and their leaders believe that knowledge is a critical asset and must be managed more effectively.[120] The long hype cycle is only partly due to the immaturity of the software and technologies. In fact, many of the most effective technological tools for creating and managing knowledge are neither particularly sophisticated nor expensive, and they are already present in most organizations. They include the Web certainly, but also the humble search engines and database backends. Complicated software tools do not necessarily lead to success and, in some cases, may even hinder it.

[120] Duffy, J. (2001). Knowledge management finally becomes mainstream. *Information Management Journal, 35*(4), 62–66.

The lengthy and frustrating implementation cycles have more to do with the social and psychological hurdles that must be overcome. Also, some of the structural factors that are deeply embedded within organizations – such as the reward systems – work directly against knowledge management programs because they are disincentives to sharing. Organizations and their leaders have difficult decisions to make regarding how to deal with these obstacles to knowledge management. Massive changes in the reward systems, for example, may contribute to more fluid knowledge sharing but could have damaging effects on productivity.

Regardless of what happens to the term "knowledge management," many of the practices and approaches under its umbrella that work well will survive and make strong contributions to organizations and their success. This term, though, drew needed attention to the fact that "knowledge," elusive as it may be, is the most important asset in the netcentric workplace.

7 Virtual Teams and Computer-Supported Cooperative Work

Amit wakes up each morning and immediately checks his email from his home in India. Overnight, his inbox filled up with messages, attachments, and sample software code from his coworkers in Boston, Massachusetts. They had reviewed the India team's work on a new Web site and sent comments and additional software code during their workday. The Bostonians went home, but Amit starts working with his colleagues in India on the project, reacting to the materials the Boston group sent. They have many questions, but they can't reach the Boston team until early evening. At 6 p.m., which is 8:30 a.m. Boston time, both groups get on the Web to look over the latest prototypes and start an audioconference with a speaker phone in each room. They run into a problem that someone in the UK office might be able to resolve, so they dial her office. Fortunately, it is mid-afternoon in the United Kingdom and they are in luck. She is at her desk and they patch her into the audioconference. Together, all the team members open up a Web site with a virtual whiteboard so they can make drawings and hold an audio discussion at the same time. By 8 p.m. India time, Amit and his colleagues are eager for dinner. The group closes down their whiteboard sessions, saving the images for reference on their local computers, and then each person says "good night" or "good morning," or "g'day," laughing about the oddities of working within a global virtual team.

Teamwork has become an increasingly important feature of the workplace, especially as new, flatter organizational forms have emerged. People with specialized expertise are needed to fluidly move from project to project, and managers need considerable flexibility to put together the best minds for each unique project. A single worker with knowledge of a particular area might be called on to participate in many different committees, project teams, task forces, or working groups. Some appointments become reasonably permanent, and others are short-lived, lasting only as long as the project continues.

Research on group behavior and teamwork has been going on for decades, and we know a great deal about what happens when people are asked to collectively perform a task, come up with a solution, or make a decision. The questions – and often the answers – have been quite intriguing and useful for understanding workplace dynamics. Consider what happens when a task force is appointed to improve some process in the workplace. Do they come up with a better solution than an individual would come up with? Do groups, in the form of search committees, make better hiring decisions than do individuals? How does the composition of the group affect its performance and cohesiveness? When people of different levels of the organization are placed on the same team, are they able to contribute equally? Or do higher ranking members dominate the decision making? How do the positive and negative relationships within the group affect its performance? Do team members need to like each other to do a good job as a team?

Technology Support for Teamwork

The majority of research on group work deals with how they operate when the members are collocated – working in the same room or within walking distance. They meet face-to-face to conduct their work, and all the elements of physical presence are part of the group's working environment. Most of the research also involved little technology other than blackboards, pencils, paper, and flip charts. Even though information technology was spreading rapidly throughout the organization and being deployed in several contexts, research on how groups might benefit from all of these new capabilities was sparse. Instead, researchers focused on the inner circle of Figure 7.1,

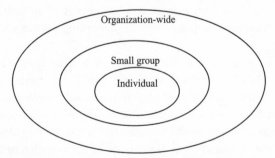

Figure 7.1. Applying new technology to different levels of an organization.

and found many ways to improve an individual's work, by improving the human–computer interface, for example. They also emphasized the organizational level, the outer circle, to understand how an entire organization adapts to new technologies.

The middle part of the circle, however, was receiving much less attention, even though so much work in an organization involves groups. Were there innovative ways to deploy emerging technologies to help people become more productive when they were working in small groups? Teamwork has always been a mixed blessing in organizations, sometimes resulting in better performance, sometimes worse. Social and psychological factors are critical, and it wasn't entirely obvious how technology could help, but there was great optimism and promise.

Efforts to understand how technology might best support group work got underway in disciplines such as business, psychology, communications, information sciences, and computer science. The field of *computer-supported cooperative work* (CSCW) emerged, and many interdisciplinary research projects were launched. Researchers began to analyze the impact of various technologies on cooperative groupwork, usually comparing the activities of computer-supported teams to the traditional face-to-face team, working in the same room without the advanced equipment. Researchers also started to actively design and test new technological tools for groups that attempted to take account of the way humans actually work together. The field drew people not only from the academic world but also from corporate research labs, software development companies, and government facilities.

Corporate networks and then the Internet added important new dimensions to studies of computer-supported cooperative work groups, because working "virtual teams" could now be quickly formed with members anywhere on the planet as long as they all had Internet access. Initially they used email primarily, but then began using far more sophisticated tools, such as Web-based whiteboards and desktop videoconferencing via the net. These new technologies promise to make geographic distance irrelevant for global teams. As you will see, it did not quite work out that way.

Expanding the Radius of Collaboration for Teamwork

In most organizations, small group work generally had been done by people who worked in proximity to one another. When appointing a task force, for example, a manager would preferentially choose people who worked in the same department, or invite people from other departments in the same geographic location, preferably the same building. Even a person who worked at a branch office on the other side of the same town might be passed over for the task force, simply because it would be rather inconvenient to come to meetings, and impromptu team get-togethers would be very hard to accomplish.

Studies of voluntary collaboration in the workplace also highlight a critical role for physical distance, one that put constraints on people's natural inclination to collaborate. The great majority of collaborative work within organizations occurs among people who work within fifty feet of one another. This *radius of collaboration* supports the kind of informal knowledge sharing and brainstorming at the proverbial water cooler that can be so instrumental in a group's effectiveness. People who run into one another at the office, or who have plenty of opportunities to sit at the same lunch room table, are far more likely to talk about their work and collaborate with one another. [121]

Office-space designers offer some strategies that can increase the radius, such as open-plan seating, easily accessible team rooms for impromptu meetings, or large common areas that link different buildings on a corporate campus. Some strategies can also intensify the collaboration within the radius, even if the radius itself isn't increased. "War rooms," in which workers are closely collocated for long periods to work intensely on a collaborative project, are one example. These are larger spaces equipped with "caves" for individualized work, and "commons" for group work, along with large computer screens, electronic white boards, videoconferencing capabilities, and many more technological aids. When individuals are part of a group and their work is tightly coupled and interdependent, this extreme collocation can be very effective. Control towers, for example, must support highly cooperative work that is also dependent on technology, so air traffic controllers work together in the same room, within easy visual and auditory contact. Many software development projects also use the war room approach for housing the team members, especially if the project involves highly sensitive or classified information.

Depending on the usual radius of collaboration for effective teamwork, however, has serious drawbacks from the standpoint of organizational flexibility and adaptability. Even midsized and smaller firms are under pressure from globalization to deal with customers and suppliers anywhere in the world. Their own staff are spread around the globe to be closer to the people

[121] Allen, T. J. (1977). *Managing the flow of technology: Technology transfer and the dissemination of technological information within the R&D organization.* Cambridge, MA: MIT Press.

they need to work with. If effective teamwork can occur in a virtual context, letting people participate as needed without congregating at a single location, a significant constraint on the company could be lifted.

Consider Dana, a software developer in Boston working for a Web development company with offices in Boston, San Francisco, Vancouver, Sydney, and Singapore. She has specialized knowledge of e-commerce payment gateways and shopping carts used to conduct online transactions. With computer and Internet-based cooperative technologies, she can contribute her expertise to several different teams trying to build Web sites for customers. She needn't travel, so the corporation saves large sums on the travel budget. She can participate for short or long periods, on more than one team at a time. She can also become a specialized resource, one that is not a full-fledged member of a team but who can be called upon when they start adding the "buy now" button to a customer's Web site.

From the company's perspective, the capability to create teams without regard to geography is liberating. Those expert databases that I discussed in the last chapter on knowledge management would be pointless if the experts had to shuttle around the world to participate in projects that needed them. When corporations can create virtual teams, they do not need to develop specialized expertise in every location as the firm grows and expands to different parts of the world.

From Dana's perspective, the value of virtual teamwork is equally high. She doesn't have to travel away from her home in Boston, or find live-in help to care for her children while she is away. When her children are sick, she can confidently stay home with them and continue her teamwork from her connected home office. She can even choose to become a telecommuter, staying home two or three days a week and avoiding the traffic.

From society's viewpoint, virtual teamwork also has many advantages. It may help to reduce traffic congestion, along with the costs of building roads, public transportation, and other services needed to support population density. If some percentage of the population did not have to drive to a population center to reach work each day, the parking lots would have spaces and pollution would go down.

On the surface, virtual teamwork has many advantages and some analysts predict that distributed work arrangements involving virtual teams will be the number one trend of this millenium's first decade.[122] Software vendors have been able to sell quite expensive "groupware" products to

---

[122] Kemske, F. (1998). HR 2008. *Workforce*, January, 47–60.

company executives, even when the products are buggy and unproven as means to support cooperative work. But do virtual teams work as well as collocated teams? Are they more effective in some kinds of projects, but much worse in others? To answer these question, let's first look at the characteristics of the team situation for each type of team, especially in the areas of communications and information access.

The Context of Teamwork

Although the process and the results of teamwork, such as the kinds of discussions conducted or the decisions reached, have always received attention, the context of the work has not. The context, however, is one of the most important differences between face-to-face and virtual teams.

FACE-TO-FACE CONTEXT

When people are in the same room trying to accomplish a task, make a decision, find a solution, or perform some activity, they are surrounded by a rich and complex assortment of sensory cues. They can see each person in the room, if not all at once, then simply by glancing around. Their facial expressions, postures, physical appearance, tone of voice, and speech tempo are all apparent to everyone in the room. Other sensory cues about the team members are also available, from body odor to a slap on the back. As I discussed in an earlier chapter, the face-to-face setting is high in media richness because information from every sensory channel can be exchanged from moment to moment. The face-to-face medium is conducive to quick clarifications in response to expressions of puzzlement. When anyone says something that the others don't comprehend, the feedback in the form of widened eyes or furrowed brows can instantly be used to initiate further clarification.

The social presence of each individual is also high. All those nonverbal cues that people use to form impressions of one another are quite salient in a face-to-face setting. Status cues can easily be seen, and behavioral patterns are perceived immediately. The high social presence also means that people are more publicly self-aware, in the sense that they know that others can perceive and judge all the cues they are emitting, whether verbal or nonverbal. Even the mere physical presence of other people is an important aspect of the environment. It increases attention to the task, or at least the drive to appear as though one is paying attention. The exposure increases familiarity with the idiosyncracies of each team member, and classic research in psychology demonstrates that familiarity usually leads to liking.

In the same room, people also have shared access to artifacts, such as a drawing on a whiteboard, documents lying on the table, a large computer screen, or a prototype of a new toaster they are designing. They can point to an artifact while they are speaking about it, hold it up, or move parts of it about to show how it works. When they speak, their words do not have to be completely descriptive, because they can use gestures to point or follow up with a clarification if the others show they didn't understand. Consider a meeting of a team composed of graphic designers, computer programmers, and a mathematician, who are working together to create math software based on an adventure game. They have sample graphics of the screen shots lying around on their circular table, and they also have a large computer screen on which the program is running.

Jose: Why did you put that here? (tapping the image of a "Submit" button on the paper printout on the table)

Mary: You mean this? (pointing to the screen, and touching the button with the mouse)

Daryn: Here, it works like this. (clicks the mouse button and the working prototype returns feedback)

Jose: OK but . . . (spreads hands to suggest button should be larger)

Not many words were exchanged in this portion of the meeting, but a large amount of information was exchanged because of collocation, not just of team members, but their artifacts. They could use gestures and words like "this" and "that" to achieve understanding rather quickly, moving fluidly from one kind of communication to another.

VIRTUAL TEAM CONTEXT

The virtual team's context is quite varied, but certainly very different from that of the face-to-face team. Virtual teams might use synchronous collaborative technologies, such as online chat systems, video- and/or audioconferencing, interactive whiteboards, or a combination of them. They might have team-based "awareness" capabilities that will let each of them know when a team member is or is not available for contact. Synchronous tools might also include group decision support systems (GDSS) that allow team members to brainstorm ideas, rearrange their ideas into coherent patterns and groupings on the screen, vote on various issues and tabulate the results immediately, or collectively rank order priorities. Asynchronous tools would also be employed, including collaboratively constructed Web sites containing project artifacts, asynchronous discussion boards, and that popular favorite – email. The team members are not collocated, but they have many other tools to help them work together.

Nevertheless, the main context for a virtual team member is not the conference room, but the separate office or cubicle, and the desktop. Instead of glancing around at other team members or artifacts, he or she spends most of the time facing the computer monitor with hands on the keyboard. Monitors have certainly grown in size, but they are still quite small in comparison to a room filled with coworkers, whiteboards, and projected computer images. For the virtual team member, much of the interactive teamwork occurs through this narrow porthole.

CONTEXT IN THE BACKGROUND

The immediate surroundings form part of the context for team members, but context is also established through some background effects, such as whether the members have worked together before or whether they anticipate long-term working relationships. These background variables affect the kinds of relationships that develop among team members and how cohesive the team becomes. They also affect the motivation level for team members to do their part.

These background factors give collocated teams another edge, at least in terms of trust and the development of relational ties. Because they come from the same area, and perhaps even the same building, they are more likely to have worked together in the past, and they also are more likely to anticipate working together in the future. They can communicate more easily in and out of formal meetings simply because they are nearby. It is much easier to poke one's head into a neighbor's cubicle to ask a quick question and get instant clarification to coordinate work. On the other end of the continuum is the brand new global virtual team, with members from different countries who have never met, never worked together before, and never expect to do so again. Meetings are mostly formally arranged, perhaps using a combination of videoconferencing, audioconferencing, or Web-based interactions. Between meetings, most communication is electronic, and often asynchronous.

Despite the potential handicaps in terms of context, the advantages of virtual teams are great and their numbers are growing. How are they faring compared to the collocated teams? Small groups who work together in the same room have their share of problems – especially having to do with group dynamics – that sometimes interfere with performance and prevent groups from doing as well on projects as they might. Virtual teamwork may actually offer certain kinds of improvements, at least under some circumstances. It is not necessarily the case that the face-to-face working group is always the "gold standard" for teamwork. Nevertheless, the reduction in media richness and social presence that accompanies virtual teamwork is not trivial. Let's next consider the group dynamics of face-to-face and virtual teams, particularly as it applies to the development of trust.

Group Dynamics in Virtual Teams

Groups, in principle, are expected to perform certain kinds of tasks better than individuals for a variety of reasons. Perhaps most important, a group consists of individuals, each of whom has special knowledge and experience he or she can bring to the table. All members should be able to look at a problem in their own ways, and offer creative insights and perspectives that a single individual, working alone, would not be able to do. A group can collectively divide up the responsibilities for a complex task, coordinate their activities, and move quickly toward the common goal. At least, that is the theory.

In practice, the social and psychological dynamics of working groups can dramatically affect the quality of their decision making and how productive they are. Sometimes, groups break down entirely, and members drift away or leave in a huff. Other times, groups turn out work that is flawed, and an individual might have done the job better at much lower cost. The factors that cause groups to do well or poorly are often related to the same contextual factors that distinguish face-to-face from virtual teams. The development of trust is one example.

DEVELOPING RELATIONSHIPS AND ESTABLISHING TRUST

A key ingredient for successful teamwork is trust. When work is divided and the project's success depends on each member making the right contribution at the right time, trust is essential. Members of a collocated team have many opportunities to develop trust in one another, both on the job and off. Sam's battery dies, and Monica, in a nearby office, gives him a jump-start. The school calls Monica at work – her son shows signs of chicken pox and should be picked up. Sam volunteers to finish Monica's statistical analysis of this month's sales transactions for the report, due in the morning. When Sam and Monica are assigned to the same team, they already trust one another.

Charles Handy, formerly of the London School of Business, argues that successful organizations in the information age require trust among their employees, and "trust needs touch."[123] Paradoxically, the more "virtual" an organization becomes, the more it will need to bring the people together for meetings, picnics, conferences, or other collocated events so they develop relationships with each other and establish the kind of trust that Sam and Monica have.

Research on trust within virtual teams tends to support Handy's point of view, though there may be ways to facilitate the development of trust in such contexts. Sirkka Jarvenpaa of The University of Texas at Austin and her colleague Dorothy E. Leidner of INSEAD explored the development of trust in global virtual teams consisting of students from around the world.[124] Three hundred and fifty graduate students from twenty-eight universities participated in the project, and each student was assigned to a small team, all of whose members resided in a different country. Motivation to participate and do well on the team project came from the course grade, but the researchers also promised a $600 reward for the highest performing team along with industry publicity.

The teams were each given voluntary and mandatory assignments, including the course project that involved developing a Web site to offer a new service to information systems practitioners. Team members communicated by email and also had access to a project Web site containing a central repository of information accessible to all teams. The researchers collected all email exchanges and also asked participants to complete a survey early in the project and again at the end. The survey was designed to measure the participants' trust levels and contained items such as, "If I had my way, I wouldn't let the other team members have any influence over issues that are important to the project" and "I can rely on those with whom I work in this group."

The teams varied dramatically on their levels of trust and the nature of their communications. For teams that ended the project with a low level of trust, communications were often unpredictable and uncertain, and few people took any individual initiative to get the team moving in some common direction. One team member writes, "What is happening to the rest of the team apart from James?" after a long period of silence from other team

---

[123] Handy, C. (1995). Trust and the virtual organization. *Harvard Business Review, 73*(3), 40–48. Retrieved March 3, 2003, from Business Source Premier Database.

[124] Jarvenpaa, S. L., & Leidner, D. E. (1999). Communications and trust in global virtual teams. *Organization Science, 10*(6), 791–815.

members. Another sends the message, "I am kind of confused . . . not sure I can be helpful." Participants in low-trust teams were not often forthcoming about their own reliability. One said, "I think (not a promise) that I'll be able to have the page (at least the skeleton of it) done early next week." That kind of remark does little to convince your team members that you are reliable and will carry your part of the workload.

Some groups did report a much higher level of trust, and their messages were often quite different. They were more likely to jump into the communications medium with enthusiasm, welcoming the other team members, telling something about themselves, and eagerly assigning roles or volunteering for responsibilities. They were also more likely to respond to one another more quickly, and with more substance. Although the high-trust groups were promptly reacting to one another's contributions and work products, the groups that failed to develop or maintain trust were not. One team member whose group started out with higher trust but lost it as the project went on lamented that he received little feedback about his own contributions from the others. He said he would "just use my own creativity as I haven't had any real comments."

Jarvenpaa and Leidner suggest that trust can be formed in these global virtual teams, but it is not equivalent to the strong relational ties that bind collocated groups. Instead, it is a kind of "swift trust" that is more task oriented and action based. This trust was fragile and temporal, and it was easily lost if technology problems arose, communication breakdowns occurred, or some members fell silent.

TRUST, COOPERATION, AND CONFLICT IN SOCIAL DILEMMAS

Studies of social dilemmas also demonstrate how difficult it is to establish trust in a virtual team. Social dilemmas are situations in which the interests of individual members of a group are at odds with the collective interests of that group. Some of them can be "beaten" if the individuals within the group choose to trust one another and cooperate, but a single defector can undermine the cooperation and push the group toward competitive behavior. Many dilemma scenarios, such as the "Prisoner's Dilemma," have been devised for experimental research, with varying payoff matrices that create different balances between individual and group rewards. They have been especially popular as a research device to study patterns of cooperation and conflict within small groups because they make it easier to quantify the elusive psychological variable of trust.

Elena Rocco of the Collaboratory for Research on Electronic Work at University of Michigan used a social dilemma to assess the level of cooperation and trust that groups could achieve when they were working face-to-face, compared to when they were working virtually, using electronic communication.[125] The dilemma involved investment in the market, and members of her six-person groups were each given thirteen tokens at the start of each of the twenty-eight rounds of the experiment. They could invest as much as they wanted and their payoff at the end of each round was a share of the group payoff, proportional to the investment they made. Individually, the more they invested the more they earned, but the payoff matrix held a trap. After a certain level, the bigger the total group investment the *lower* the group's payoff. This meant that groups who cooperated with one another, and voluntarily kept their investment levels in check, would earn the most. However, a single defector would run off with sizeable rewards if all the other members were cooperating, and then the trusting cooperators would lose out. After each round, participants received a report showing their past record of investments and payoffs, and also the total investment for the last round. The report did not show what each person had invested, so the identity of a defector – if there were one – would not be revealed. The group members got together to discuss the dilemma after the tenth, fifteenth, and twentieth rounds. Some groups met face-to-face during these communication periods, whereas others communicated electronically, but not anonymously.

The results showed striking differences in cooperation between the groups. After the first communication session (tenth round), the face-to-face groups figured out at once that they needed to cooperate, and they quickly developed stable investment patterns with no defectors. Initially, their cooperative strategy did not necessarily maximize the group's rewards, but some of the groups were able to achieve the maximum reward by the end of the study – all through cooperation.

The groups who communicated electronically, however, showed much more individualistic behavior and far less cooperation. During the communication period, most groups attempted to come to an agreement about how to cooperate with a collective strategy. After each agreement, there was a short period in which the participants attempted cooperation, but the agreements were quickly disregarded. Some people in each group chose opportunism; they defected by making a large investment, to the great

---

[125] Rocco, E. (1998). Trust breaks down in electronic contexts but can be repaired by some initial face-to-face contact. Conference proceedings on human factors in computing systems, 1998, 496–502. Retrieved May 7, 2003, from ACM Digital Library.

disadvantage of the members who were trying to stick to the agreement. After the initial defections, all members swung back to an individualistic choice. During the communication periods, their messages were dominated by aggressive expressions of blame, disappointment, and mistrust. The glaring failure of the electronically communicating groups to reach a cooperative strategy shows how difficult it is to develop trust without touch.

Most teams are neither completely virtual, as the experimental groups in this study were, nor completely face to face. Perhaps some advance face-to-face relationship building might make it easier for groups who later are limited to electronic communication to cooperate in the dilemma. Rocco added another condition using the same social dilemma, but this time, the groups who were to communicate electronically were allowed to meet face-to-face the day before the experiment. Their task during this preexperiment gathering was designed to elicit socialization and collaboration, so they might have some personal basis for trust the next day. Each group spent forty-five minutes building a tower out of paper, and they competed against the other groups who would also be in the dilemma experiment to make the best tower.

The groups who met face-to-face before the social dilemma experiment did considerably better than the ones who were communicating electronically and had never met before, though they still had some trouble establishing and sticking to an agreement. Cooperation increased initially after the communication period in the tenth round but then dropped off. Apparently, based on the analysis of the messages, the members of the groups intended to cooperate but were not clear about which system they had agreed upon. The virtual environment inhibited understanding, but some trust had already been established from their preexperiment gathering so they worked out the problems in the next communication period. By the end of the twenty-eight rounds, their cooperative performance was as high as the face-to-face groups.

CAN VIDEOCONFERENCING REPLACE TOUCH?

What is it about trust that is so quick to emerge with face-to-face encounters but so fragile and difficult to build when virtual teammates are using electronic communications? If trust really requires touch, and teams require trust to perform effectively together, then corporations must rethink their deployment of widespread virtual teaming. They may need to increase their travel budgets, to make sure group members at least get a chance to meet one another before the project kicks off.

Current technologies, however, support channels with higher media richness and more social presence than just the text-based communications those noncooperating and defecting groups were using. Perhaps some of the benefits of face-to-face meetings can be achieved through higher bandwidth. In a follow-up study to Ellen Rocco's, Nathan Bos and colleagues, also at the Collaboratory for Research on Electronic Work at University of Michigan, attempted to determine whether videoconferencing or audioconferencing could better support the development of trust for virtual teams.[126] They organized forty-five teams of three people each and assigned each team to one of four communication media: face-to-face, videoconferencing, audioconferencing, and text-based chat. Each team worked on the "Daytrader" game, another social dilemma in which players get thirty tokens at the beginning of each round of the game and must decide whether to invest individually or with the group. Individual investments received a guaranteed reward of double the investment – not bad, given economic volatility. Funds targeted for group investment are lumped together for the team, and the amount is *tripled*. The proceeds are then divided equally among the three team members. The dilemma involves the same risk of defection that plagues all social dilemmas. Acting collectively, the group can maximize its rewards. Defectors, though, can reap even more rewards if they deceive the other members of the group and act individually, at the expense of the other team members. The total payoff for the group at the end of each round and also at the end of the thirty-round game is the quantitative measure of cooperation. Groups engaged in the discussions and strategic planning after every five rounds using whichever communication medium they were assigned.

Not surprisingly, the face-to-face groups achieved a high level of cooperation early in the game, and the teams using text-based chat achieved very little throughout all thirty rounds. The groups using videoconferencing achieved a high level of cooperation but were slower to reach it compared to the face-to-face groups. Nevertheless, this finding bodes well for this higher bandwidth medium as an alternative to face-to-face meetings for virtual teams. It appears that one important ingredient of touch is "face time," which can occur over the net.

The audioconferencing groups were also able to achieve higher levels of cooperation compared to text-based chat groups, but their patterns of cooperation were very unstable. After each audioconference, their cooperation

---

[126] Bos, N., Gergle, D., Olson, J. S., & Olson, G. M. (2001). Being there versus seeing there: Trust via video. Proceedings of CHI 2001: Short Papers. New York: ACM Press. Retrieved September 1, 2002, from ACM Digital Library.

levels would go way up initially and the parties would at first stick to whatever agreements had been reached. Then, however, defections would begin. The cycle repeated itself after each communication period. Audio alone may simply not offer enough media richness to transmit whatever cues are needed to establish trust.

The researchers had also offered a ninety-token bonus every fifth round to the player in the team that made the most money in the previous five rounds, and most of the players showed an end-of-game dropoff in cooperation. This looked like the "defector's sprint" at the end. Players wanted to win the individual bonus, so they were willing to abandon cooperation and good will – particularly because no one could retaliate after the last round. This phenomenon was more pronounced in all the groups who were not meeting face-to-face, suggesting that whatever trust had developed was more like the task-oriented and fragile "swift" trust that appeared in the global virtual teams of students I discussed earlier. The relational ties that developed during face-to-face discussions were stronger and more able to withstand the temptation to defect at the end of the game. Thus, it seems some face time through videoconferencing is the best way for virtual teams to establish trust and facilitate cooperation, but it still falls short of touch.

Group Dynamics for Problem Solving and Decision Making

An important function of groups is to examine a problem, come up with ideas and alternatives for solving it, analyze and weigh the alternatives, and make a decision about the best course of action to take. Many people believe that groups will do a better, fairer, and more comprehensive job at this sequence compared to individuals. We rely on the twelve-person jury of peers to evaluate the evidence in a trial and decide the defendant's fate. We prefer to appoint a committee to deal with complex problems in the workplace and come up with a range of options. Committees with decision-making responsibilities abound in practically every organization because most people believe their solutions will be higher in quality. They certainly create more buy-in by employees.

Groups, however, have certain flaws for problem solving and decision making, and they may not always reach the best decision because of the effects of group dynamics. As everyone has observed, the person with the highest status often has the most influence, even if that person is not the most knowledgeable. Group discussion also can lead to *polarization* of attitudes and opinion. When an individual who leans toward a particular point of view on a topic begins discussing that topic with others who also lean in that direction, the group discussion tends to strengthen those preexisting attitudes. During the discussion, the members avoid bringing up points that would be more balanced. They tend to stop weighing the pros and cons of different points of view and instead keep reinforcing each other by making points to support their initial leanings.

Early studies on the *risky shift* phenomenon demonstrated how polarization operates in groups. Most people expected groups to be more conservative than individuals because, presumably, they would contain members with different viewpoints and the resulting decision would be more of a middle-road compromise. However, research demonstrated that in many circumstances, groups are willing to take more risks than individuals and go further out on a limb than the average viewpoint of the members. The process was first demonstrated in a study of the recommendations groups and individuals gave to the fictitious "Helen." Helen is a writer who was weighing the risks of dropping her lucrative career as an author of formula Westerns in favor of writing the great literary novel. When teams weighed the risks, their recommendations were less conservative than were those of individuals. They were, as groups, more willing to say, "Go for it!"[127]

The phenomenon of *groupthink* can also plague group problem solving and decision making, and it represents an extreme case of polarization. When a highly cohesive team becomes eager to seek concurrence and agreement, individuals are very reluctant to bring up counterarguments. The group is no longer able to scan the horizon for a wide variety of alternatives, nor can its members dispassionately appraise the pros and cons of any decision or alternate courses of action.

Are virtual teams susceptible to the same kinds of influences when they are trying to come up with alternatives and make decisions about them? In some cases, virtual teamwork actually improves group problem solving and decision making. In others, the reduced media richness and low social presence introduce elements that hamper groups even more. Let's first look at brainstorming.

GROUP BRAINSTORMING

In the 1950s, Alex Osborn published a book about stimulating creativity with the intriguing title *Applied Imagination*. One of his suggestions was

---

[127] Stoner, J. A. F. (1962). A comparison of individual and group decisions involving risk. Unpublished master's thesis, Massachusetts Institute of Technology, 1961. Cited by D. G. Marquis in Individual responsibility and group decisions involving risk. *Industrial Management Review, 3,* 8–23.

intended to increase the effectiveness of brainstorming through groups, by using a set of systematic rules. Individuals were brought together in a room and asked to think up as many ideas on a particular topic as they could, but never criticize or evaluate another person's contributions. They could improve on them or combine them, but not tear them down. The goal was to create a supportive group where even the most outlandish suggestions would be free to emerge, and thereby reduce the evaluation apprehension that people feel when they are offering innovative notions in a group setting.

Though the technique generated much enthusiasm, later research demonstrated it didn't work very well. Although a brainstorming group generated more ideas than a single individual working alone, it was not as effective as a "nominal" group working on the same topic. That is, six people working alone would come up with far more ideas than six people working together in the same room. The face-to-face context actually hindered the effective generation of original ideas for several reasons, one of which is called *production blocking*. First, only one person could speak at a time, and the others needed to listen. This meant that everyone in the room had less time for private thought on his or her own ideas. The waiting time created by the act of listening when others are speaking caused other kinds of problems, as well, including forgetfulness. A listener who had an idea in mind may forget about it while listening to someone else talk. Another reason face-to-face brainstorming may be less than effective is because of the *social loafing* phenomenon. When several people are working on the same task, each individual does not feel particularly accountable for doing his or her best. Some will loaf and let John do it, because they would get no individual credit for their work anyway.

The problems that hindered face-to-face brainstorming would be much reduced if the team used some technology – groupware in particular. This kind of software allows members to work independently and simultaneously, typing ideas on a keyboard, but they could also see what everyone else was typing as the entries scrolled by. The approach should decrease the amount of production blocking common in face-to-face brainstorming. Izak Benbasat of the University of British Columbia and John Lim of the National University of Singapore found this to be true in a study comparing the output from electronic and face-to-face brainstorming teams.[128]

[128] Benbasat, I., & Lim, J. (2000). Information technology support for debiasing group judgments: An empirical evaluation. *Organizational Behavior and Human Decision Processes, 83*(1), 167–183.

Overall, the groups working with the software generated more ideas about the task compared to the groups working in a face-to-face setting.

Although this finding seems like good news for virtual teams and the electronic brainstorming software to support them, more recent research suggests that nominal groups do just as well, and perhaps even better, than groups using the software, at least in terms of the quality of ideas generated, if not the quantity. Henri Barki of Ecole des Hautes Etudes Commerciales in Montreal and Alain Pinsonneault of McGill University conducted a complex study of brainstorming in groups under several different conditions.[129] Some groups brainstormed verbally (face-to-face), while others were formed into nominal groups in which members never met or communicated with one another. Two sets of groups used electronic brainstorming software: one anonymously and one nonanonymously. Groups were asked to come up with as many original ideas as they could for a variety of topics that ranged in sensitivity, from "How can the spread of AIDS be reduced?" to "How can tourism be improved in Montreal?"

If the effectiveness of brainstorming sessions is measured in terms of idea quality rather than quantity, the nominal group did better than both electronic brainstorming groups, and also much better than the group who met face to face. Groups that used the electronic brainstorming software anonymously did somewhat better than the ones who participated nonanonymously. Though the researchers attempted to introduce variables that might improve the brainstorming sessions for the groups using the software, such as the sensitivity of the topic, none of them had any influence. Clearly, electronic brainstorming is superior to the face-to-face version, but it is not always superior to a nominal group in which independent minds focus on the same task without any interference, interruptions, or distractions from other people's chatter.

Why nominal groups might produce higher quality ideas than electronic group brainstormers is not clear. Perhaps nominal team members have more time to think and expand on their own notions, filling in details and weighing pros and cons. They don't have to look up at a collective screen to see what everyone else is contributing and try to alter their thinking to piggyback on someone else's creative idea. Also, people in nominal groups may be less likely to succumb to social loafing, because they have to turn in a product for which they are individually accountable.

---

[129] Barki, H., & Pinsonneault, A. (2001). Small group brainstorming and idea quality. *Small Group Research, 32*(2), 158–206.

Organizations continue to use group brainstorming – the face-to-face kind – long after the research demonstrated it was not as effective as nominal groups working on the same creative tasks. Adrian Furnham, of University College London, suggests a key reason may be that group brainstorming helps create buy-in and acceptance of the solutions to complex organizational problems.[130] Although the electronic brainstorming software certainly reduced some of the obstacles to success, the software itself may not be needed if the only goal is to create many high-quality ideas. Buy-in and acceptance are important components in group problem solving and decision making, so many organizations may continue to use group brainstorming for reasons other than a desire for innovative ideas. Buy-in and acceptance may be even more important for virtual teams, especially to encourage trust, so organizations may emphasize electronic group brainstorming for those teams in particular. In any case, it is clear that applying technological solutions to group work is a complicated affair, and we have much to learn about the intricacies of computer-supported cooperative work.

INEQUALITIES IN GROUP PARTICIPATION AND INFLUENCE

One of the more negative aspects that results from the social dynamics of groups involves inequalities of participation. When a team of people attempts to solve a problem and make a decision, certain people have more influence than others. In a face-to-face setting, their unequal influence might be due to physical appearance, gender, weight, ethnicity, age, or other characteristics that weigh heavily in the impression they make. From the standpoint of social cognition, people form impressions very rapidly when they first meet, usually relying on cues involving physical appearance. Tall, good-looking people are judged favorably even before they open their mouths to speak. The impressions then affect how people receive each individual's suggestions and how much influence each person has.

From the standpoint of trust, physical presence appears to be quite a plus, but it has mixed results with respect to other aspects of group work. Early research on computer-mediated communication, for example, demonstrated that groups who communicated only electronically were more likely to exhibit *status equalization*. People who were lower in status were more likely to speak up (electronically) and contribute more to the discussion than they were in face-to-face settings. Sara Kiesler and her colleagues performed some

---

[130] Furnham, A. (2000). The brainstorming myth [Electronic version]. *Business Strategy Review, 11*(4), 21–28.

of the first research on this topic.[131] They found that in three-person groups attempting to come to some decision, one person tended to dominate the discussion. However, when they communicated online, participation rates were more equal.

Virtual teams should benefit from this status equalization phenomenon, though they won't be completely immune. If they use the videoconferencing that helps build trust, for example, the effects of physical appearance on group dynamics will reenter the equation, although it will unfold rather differently. Picture the physical appearance that remote team members present on the TV screen in a small conference room. You can see your virtual teammates, but because there is just one camera, you see all of them at once, sitting around their own conference table. Each person – especially the ones farthest from the camera – appears quite tiny. You can't easily see who is talking because the images are so small, and the impression they make on you is quite different from what it would be if they were in the same room. The video contact may help improve the development of trust, but the impressions you form of those remote colleagues will not be the same.

Desktop videoconferencing, in which you can see a much larger headshot of your communication partners, also introduces some intriguing nuances for impression formation. The camera angle, for example, affects the impression people make and the biases that plague group discussions. Wei Huang, Judith S. Olson, and Gary M. Olson at the Collaboratory for Research on Electronic Work at University of Michigan experimented with camera angles that would make people on camera appear rather short or rather tall to the person on the receiving end of the transmission.[132] They randomly assigned one person in a pair to the "tall" camera angle, in which the camera was well below the person's eye level. The other person's camera made him appear "short" onscreen, because the camera was looking down from above. Before the videoconference began, each subject completed the Arctic Survival task, in which they ranked the importance of holding onto various items after they had crash-landed in an extremely cold and isolated landscape. Then each pair discussed the problem over the desktop videoconferencing link and arrived at a joint conclusion. The measure of

---

[131] Kiesler, S., Siegel, J., & McGuire, T. W. (1984). Social psychological aspects of computer-mediated communication. *American Psychologist, 39,* 1123–1134.

[132] Huang, W., Olson, J. S., & Olson, G. M. (2002). Camera angle affects dominated in video-mediated communication. In Proceedings of CHI 2002, Short Papers. New York: ACM Press. Retrieved February 1, 2003, from ACM Digital Library.

influence in this experiment was simply how close the joint conclusion was to each individual's initial ranking. Subjects were also asked whether they thought they were more or less influential on the task. Not only did the "tall" partners *think* they were more influential than their "short" partners, they *were*. The joint conclusions were closer to the "tall" person's original ranking than to the "short" person's. Apparently, the camera angle affected the behavior of both the "tall" and the "short" person. The "tall" person became more confident and influential, whereas the "short" one was more easily persuaded and perhaps intimidated. (Even in face-to-face groups, it might be wise for shorter people to choose chairs with a higher seat.)

BIASED DISCUSSIONS

Another common finding in group dynamics that impedes performance involves bias – the tendency for members to selectively choose which information they have that they will share with the group. Each person, of course, has tons of information that may be at least peripherally relevant to a problem-solving/decision-making event, so they must make many choices along the line. However, most groups try to seek consensus, so when the group starts leaning in a particular direction, individuals become less likely to bring up the "cons" of that direction – even when they would be especially relevant. Groupthink is an extreme example, but it happens in many group settings.

Ross Hightower and Lufus Sayeed found that biased discussions become even more biased when they are conducted online with groupware.[133] They formed three-person groups to review the qualifications of a set of candidates and collectively decide who was the best fit for the position. Each team member received a packet that had some information about each candidate drawn from the resumes, but the subsets they received were not the same. This meant that the team would need to share what they knew rather efficiently to come up with the best candidate. Some groups met face to face, whereas others communicated via online chat and also used the groupware's voting capabilities.

Regardless of how they were communicating, none of the groups were able to choose the best candidate because of bias effects. As the discussions proceeded, people were less likely to bring up negative information about the candidate who appeared to be "winning" in terms of the group

---

[133] Hightower, R., & Sayeed, L. (1995). The impact of computer-mediated communication systems on biased group discussion. *Computers in Human Behavior, 11,* 33–44.

discussion. They were also not likely to bring up positive information about the "losers," even though it would unbias the discussion and ensure the group had all the information they needed – both pro and con – about each candidate. As the group moved closer to consensus, each member made nonrandom choices about what piece of information to contribute, so the consensus was reached with very biased information in the end. For the online groups, however, the bias was especially strong, more than twice as large compared to that of the face-to-face groups. One reason for this may have been that the online groups had to do more work, in the form of typing, to make a contribution to the discussion, so they were even more selective about what they chose to share.

The Performance of Actual Virtual Teams

Virtual teams are on the rise, though based on research findings the difficulties of making them work well are not trivial. Nevertheless, people are adaptable and may be able to bypass the problems that arise when team members are not collocated and capitalize on the features that actually improve group dynamics and productivity for virtual teams compared to their face-to-face counterparts. The acid test for virtual teams is whether they are working in the workplace, not what happens in the laboratory. People have much higher motivation to do well in the workplace and they may find many ways to compensate for the lack of media richness and social presence. The findings from field studies of real, working virtual teams, however, confirm how the obstacles I've described can lead to performance problems. Results are mixed, but it is clear that virtual teams are more difficult to launch successfully than many expected.

VIRTUAL SOFTWARE DEVELOPMENT TEAMS

One collaborative research project that involved researchers at Bell Labs, Lucent Technologies, and the School of Information at University of Michigan, for example, investigated actual software development teams, working from four locations.[134] Geographically distributed software development has become more and more common in technology companies, and these workers were located at sites in the United Kingdom, Germany, and India. The researchers took advantage of a critical feature of software development

---

[134] Herbsleb, J. D., Mockus, A., Finholt, T. A., & Grinter, R. E. (2000). Distance, dependencies, and delay in global collaboration. In *Computer Supported Cooperative Work, 2000*. Philadelphia, PA: ACM Press. Retrieved February 3, 2003, from ACM Digital Library.

to help analyze the results of projects accomplished by team members who were all collocated and compare them to results achieved by teams with dispersed members. This was the "change management system," which is used to track the events that take place when modifications to complex software systems are requested. The change management system automatically tracks the initial request, along with all the logins of the people who submitted modified software code as the work progressed. From this system, it was possible to calculate the amount of time each modification request took, how complex the coding was, and how many people from each site were involved in each project.

The most striking finding was that projects requiring work from people who were not collocated took quite a bit longer than projects handled totally by people at the same site. The average modification request for single-site projects took about five days from the time the work started to the time it was completed. For projects involving people at more than one site, the work interval shot up to 12.7 days. The developers working with colleagues in another location reported various reasons for the delays. They had trouble finding the right person who could answer a question, they didn't receive answers quickly enough from people at distant sites, and of course, time zone differences made it more difficult to contact one another.

The software developers also ran into problems establishing trust across sites. For example, they were asked in a survey how much they agreed with these statements, both for their collocated team members and for those at the remote sites:

"I assist my coworkers with heavy workloads, beyond what I am required to do."
"My coworkers assist me with heavy workloads, beyond what they are required to do."

All workers generally agreed with the first statement, and they believed *they* assisted coworkers equally well regardless of where their coworkers were located. Everyone believed they helped out all their coworkers with heavy workloads, beyond what they were required to do. However, based on their responses to the second statement, the developers had differing opinions about the willingness of their coworkers to help them. They thought coworkers at remote sites were much *less* likely to assist *them*, compared to their collocated coworkers. Clearly, there is a disconnect in perceptions here, one that reflects the difficulty virtual teams have in developing trust.

THE FUNDAMENTAL ATTRIBUTION ERROR AND VIRTUAL TEAMWORK
Catherine Durnell Cramton, of the School of Management at George Mason University, finds that the *fundamental attribution error* is exacerbated for

virtual teammates, and this may explain why the developers thought they were being very helpful to their remote colleagues, but they didn't think their remote colleagues were being helpful to them.[135] Attribution involves the processes people use to infer what caused behavior, and whether they emphasize the person's basic nature and disposition or the specific context of the situation. Suppose, for example, you receive an email from the CEO saying the New Year's party was being canceled. What would you attribute that behavior to, and what factors would influence your choice? You could emphasize the CEO's disposition and conclude the CEO is a lousy leader who doesn't care at all about workplace morale, or you might attribute the CEO's behavior to a stingy nature. However, with more information about the context of the CEO's behavior, such as the knowledge that the CEO's spouse just passed away, you would be more likely to attribute the CEO's cancellation to situational factors rather than to dispositional ones.

One typical error people make in their attribution process is to overestimate dispositional factors when making attributions about other people's behavior and underestimate situational factors. A key reason for this is that they don't have broad-based information about the context of the other person's behavior, so they often don't know that an unusual situation might even exist. When Jack hangs up the phone on you, you assume Jack – whom you know little else about – is a jerk. That is his disposition. If you hang up the phone on someone else, you attribute your own behavior to the situation; the other party said something outrageous, and that caused you to behave rudely. You know much more about the context of your own behavior, of course, so it is far easier to see how the situation played a role.

Cramton and her colleagues found that people who work in distributed teams are more likely to attribute their remote colleagues' behavior to dispositional factors rather than to situational ones. After working together on a team whose members were either collocated or dispersed, each person was asked: "On this project, when team members did not meet my expectations, it could generally be attributed to 1) something within the team member, or 2) circumstances outside the member's control." The dispersed team members were more likely to choose number 1.

Remote colleagues are less likely to have knowledge of the context of their coworkers' behavior, so the fundamental attribution error is exacerbated. A team in India might be having a major monsoon that brings down the networks, but the team in the United Kingdom wouldn't know that.

[135] Cramton, C. D. (2002). Attribution in distributed work groups. In P. Hinds & S. Kiesler (Eds.), *Distributed work*. Cambridge, MA: MIT Press.

Instead, they would assume the India team was simply ignoring their email requests for information. Switching from asynchronous text-based communication to synchronous videoconferencing does not always alleviate the problem. One such conference involved a remote team in Oregon and a team at the corporate headquarters in California. The virtual meeting was to begin with the presentation of a videotape that was shown in California and transmitted over the videoconferencing link to Oregon. However, the transmission wasn't reaching the remote team in Oregon because of a technical glitch, so they saw only a blank screen. Unfortunately, the California team didn't know the Oregon team couldn't see the tape. The team members in Oregon didn't really want to interrupt to report the blank screen, especially because they suspected they were being intentionally excluded. The Oregon team thought they were not supposed to be invited, so they got up and left. When the videotape ended, the California team's monitor picked up the Oregon site again, but all they saw from California was the empty couch in Oregon, because everyone was gone. The empty couch remained on the California monitor throughout the meeting, reminding everyone in California how rude the Oregon teammates were.

Certainly many virtual teams work reasonably well, some exceptionally so. Also, many collocated teams fail miserably. The collocated team may not be an entirely fair comparison to judge the performance of virtual teams anyway, because the corporation may not be able to create the team at all if it must be created in the same geographical location. Virtual teaming allows corporations to bring together expertise in ways that were not possible in the past, so many teams can now benefit from expertise that is especially hard to find. Nevertheless, virtual teams face many challenges that can undermine their performance.

What Will Make Virtual Teams More Effective?

Based on what has been learned about the factors that derail virtual teams, we can propose some approaches that will help make their work smoother, both now and in the future. It is critically important to analyze these factors carefully, especially to guide technology innovations that will better support virtual teamwork and avoid foisting useless and expensive products on corporations. In fact, many of the factors have little to do with the capabilities of groupware or netcentric technologies. Instead, they have more to do with making wise decisions about the kind of work virtual teams should tackle and with providing effective leadership. Let's first look at the kind of work virtual teams can and can't do well.

COUPLED AND UNCOUPLED WORK

Gary M. Olson and Judith S. Olson use the concept of *coupling* to refer to how close the level of coordination must be among the workers on a team, and how frequently they need to communicate to achieve the right level of coordination.[136] Tightly coupled work requires team members to communicate often, to constantly be aware of one another's progress at a high level of detail, and to share information and work products quickly and nimbly. Highly complex tasks are tightly coupled when the problem is not well defined and alternative approaches and solutions must be evaluated collectively by people with different kinds of expertise. In software design and development work, for example, the team would include a range of people who understand functional requirements, people who have deep content knowledge in the subject, and techies who have specialized knowledge in areas such as database design, systems analysis, or application development.

People who are doing tightly coupled work benefit enormously from collocation as they continually communicate with one another using whiteboards, flip charts, and live prototypes displayed on a large computer screen. In the same room, they have a great deal of "real estate," in the form of walls, screens, and tables, to collectively analyze the artifacts of their work. They also have awareness of when other team members are available for the quick question or clarification, so even when they are not in the conference room they can quickly get the answers they need to continue with their part of the project. Some of the most successful projects involving tightly coupled work use the war room approach I described earlier.

Loosely coupled work has fewer immediate dependencies, and more structured and modular components to it. The successful work of one team member is not so heavily dependent on complex interactions with the rest of the team, and there are fewer ambiguities. Most projects have some portions that are tightly coupled and other parts that are loosely coupled, but they generally lean toward one or the other. Olson and Olson argue that virtual teams, at least with today's technology, are very ill-equipped to handle tightly coupled work. Assigning such projects to a distributed team could doom the team to failure because it would be almost impossible for the members to communicate as fluidly and spontaneously as they needed.

COMMON GROUND

Teams become more and more efficient as members learn more about one another and establish more *common ground*. This broad term covers cultural

---

[136] Oldson, G. M., & Olson, J. S. (2000). Distance matters. *Human-Computer Interaction, 15,* 130–178.

factors, local context, history of working together in the past, and many other features that help individuals communicate efficiently and smoothly. When a group of people are working together many communication efficiencies emerge when this common ground is in place. For example, one team member may say "deep-six that." With common ground established, the other team members know immediately what "that" is, and what "deep-six" means. Also, the speaker *knows* that they know it and also has some notion of whether he or she would offend someone on the team by making such an abrupt, colloquial dismissal of whatever "that" is (perhaps someone else's favorite suggestion). Common ground in the team saves much time and also helps reduce conflict due to misunderstandings and misperceptions.

Awareness of the state of one's coworkers is another component of common ground. Simply knowing they are around to ask questions and don't mind interruptions increases communication efficiency considerably. Being aware of their state of mind also helps. If you know your coworker's desk was just flooded by a pipe break in the ceiling, you will adjust your attributions about the cause of his or her behavior when the coworker seems a bit testy.

Olson and Olson also argue that virtual teams who have this common ground may work very well together despite the distances between them, because they have already established trust as well as communication efficiencies. However, the virtual team composed of people who have almost no common ground at all, because they come from different cultures, have never worked together in the past, and are geographically too distant to meet face to face will encounter very serious obstacles to success. Probably the fastest way to increase the common ground available to a team to maximize their effectiveness is to collocate them. For virtual teams, face-to-face meetings at the start of the project at least would certainly help.

EFFECTIVE LEADERSHIP FOR VIRTUAL TEAMS

What makes an effective leader for a virtual team? The leader must be aware of all the pitfalls of virtual teaming, from problems in trust development to communication ambiguities. The leader must do whatever possible to counteract them and help the team members become aware of them as well. Much of the research on virtual team leadership suggests that it requires a somewhat different approach compared to leadership in collocated teams. Generally, a structured and deliberate management style works better because the message will be clearer when transmitted over impoverished media. Virtual team members have trouble self-organizing, so clear instructions about the project goal, deadlines, and role assignments are usually needed. But the leader must also be deliberate about the "consideration" component that we discussed in an earlier chapter. Leaders must find ways to build those relational ties, trust, and common ground to make the group maximally effective.

Suzanne Weisband at the University of Arizona conducted a study of virtual team leadership in which business students at two geographically distant universities worked together on a four-week project to write a consensus policy document.[137] The teams consisted of two to four people, and each team included one or more members from both locations. Team members used a Web-based computer conferencing system and email to do their project, and the researchers assigned one of the students as the team leader. The team's performance was judged based on the quality of the paper, graded by several instructors who came to a consensus. The messages that were exchanged were also analyzed in depth based on their content, and messages from the leader were analyzed separately. Students also filled out a questionnaire after the project was completed and the paper turned in.

The results of this study demonstrate several aspects of successful leadership in the virtual team environment. First, the leaders of the high-performing teams were more likely to initiate task structure through their messages compared to leaders of low-performing teams, especially early in the project. They sent out messages that clarified the task objectives and set up deadlines and roles. Second, the more successful teams also had leaders who tried to increase group awareness and relational ties in various ways. Their messages included many statements that attempted to find out what the members of the team were doing, if they were having problems, or if they needed help. They also systematically tried to include everyone. One email in that vein read:

> "OK, I'll be looking for posts/principles from Rick and Matt on Saturday and from Josh on Sunday. If you are having any trouble at all or anticipate any future problems, let me know now rather than later. I can help in any way and take up any slack (if I know in advance). See ya!"

This is the same kind of tack that those who were able to develop "swift trust" used. The leaders showed consideration for the team members, their workloads, and also used a great deal of structure to reduce the ambiguities that plague virtual work teams. In a face-to-face setting, this might seem a

---

[137] Weisband, S. (2002). Maintaining awareness in distributed team collaboration: Implications for leadership and performance. In P. J. Hinds & S. Kiesler (Eds.), *Distributed work*. Cambridge, MA: MIT Press.

bit heavy-handed and overly authoritative. However, in virtual teams this seems to be the most promising approach to leadership.

A study by Timothy R. Kayworth of Baylor University and Dorothy E. Leidner of INSEAD in France on global virtual teams also pointed to the important role the leader plays in the team's performance.[138] They created virtual teams of five to seven students, each from locations in Europe, Mexico, and the United States. After the teams submitted their projects, all of the nonleaders completed surveys that assessed what they thought of the leader's effectiveness. The questions probed the participants' judgments of many aspects of the leader's behavior, including how clearly the leader communicated roles, how much influence the leader exerted on the team, how innovative the leader was, and how well the leader functioned as a mentor by showing empathy and concern for each team member. The measure of each team's success was the grade on the project.

The team members especially focused on the leader's mentoring capabilities and empathy when they were judging the leader's effectiveness. They also considered the leader's ability to clarify roles and communicate effectively as key ingredients of an effective leader. Leaders who scored low on these characteristics were judged less effective by their team, and teams whose members thought the leader was ineffective did not do well on the project.

Participants made telling comments about the leaders they judged to be particularly ineffective. Some of their comments show the importance of both consideration and structure in the virtual team environment:

> "[The leader] never wanted to know anything about us."
> "To him the topic was easy, but to us it was very complicated and difficult to understand."
> "I didn't feel like I was being pushed to do well. I must admit I didn't do my best because I didn't feel encouraged and pushed along."
> "Unfortunately, he did not follow up in a good, effective way in guiding the team . . . He should have given us more specific guidelines."

This research project also investigated the leader's perspective. Leaders found their virtual leadership role to be highly challenging, and their main problems focused on the motivation and behavior of the team members, the lack of control mechanisms, and technology hurdles. Leaders struggled with nonresponsiveness in some of the team members, and they were never

---

[138] Kayworth, T. R., & Leidner, D. E. (2002). Leadership effectiveness in global virtual teams. *Journal of Management Information Systems, 18*(3), 7–40.

sure if the problem was apathy, laziness, or technology. All but two were disappointed in the quality of their group's project, but as one might expect from attribution theory, they did not blame themselves. Instead, they blamed the situation. High on their list of factors that caused the less than sterling results from the leaders' perspective were the lack of motivation and responsiveness in the team members and the unpredictable technologies they were using. Hayworth and Leidner summarize the leaders' perspectives: "It is telling that the leaders saw themselves as helpless, powerless, and yet flawless."

Clearly, virtual teams will benefit from effective leadership tailored to their special needs. Leaders must recognize that consideration and structure are both still positive leadership behaviors, just as they contribute to effective leadership in face-to-face settings. However, they play out differently online and seem to require much more deliberate communications, focused attention, and clearer role assignments. Leaders underestimate the power of the nuances that can so easily be communicated with physical presence, and they are awkward at using the tools available in a virtual environment. It takes considerable skill with a keyboard to provide the kind of structured leadership and role clarity that virtual teams need without sounding too bossy and overbearing. It takes even more to convey a sense of empathy without sounding false or just goofy. Ending each message with a smiley face :), for example, will not carry the same message as ending a conversation with a smile.

TECHNOLOGY

The leaders did indeed have various problems with technology, and as we've seen throughout this chapter, many characteristics of the technology virtual teams are using introduce challenges for them. The Internet and all the netcentric innovations that have arisen along with it have a great deal of power to improve productivity, but the kinds of tools people use to participate in truly effective virtual teams are still rather limited. Mark S. Ackerman of the University of California at Irvine calls this the *social–technical gap*.[139] It divides what is needed to support virtual teams from what we can now support technically. The gap is due to limitations of the Internet and other components of the technological infrastructure and also to our limited knowledge of what is actually needed by the groups themselves. He writes,

[139] Ackerman, M. S. (2000). The intellectual challenge of CSCW: The gap between social requirements and technical feasibility. *Human-Computer Interaction, 15,* 179–203.

"Simply put, we do not know how to build systems that fully support the social world . . ." A face-to-face setting contains an almost infinite number of variables that can affect the productivity of a team. Identifying the critical ones that must be supported by technology so that virtual teams work well is a challenging process.

The technologies teams are now using, such as email, Web-based conferencing systems, interactive whiteboards, video- and audioconferencing, groupware, project Web sites, and instant messaging, can all make a contribution to the communication efficiencies of virtual teams; but they also introduce problems. Even videoconferencing, which is arguably the least impoverished in terms of media richness, has its share of problems and is unable to substitute fully for the physical presence of collocated teams. Some difficulties arise simply because the technologies themselves are not particularly robust and are sensitive to many configuration and transmission troubles that take time to solve. Setting up a desktop videoconferencing link, for example, is hardly as simple as popping your head into your coworker's cubicle to ask a question. The sensitivity and idiosyncracies of different workstations often mean that virtual team members spend a lot of time just debugging and tweaking their communication tools. They also must spend some time just to learn how to use them, even when they work perfectly.

No one is giving up, however. Much recent research is dedicated to aligning the innovations in technological tools to support group work with the social requirements, as these unfold and we learn more about what they actually are. For example, there has been much interest in developing technological means to support synchronous *awareness* of team members. In a collocated environment, knowledge of who's around at any moment in time appears to be one of those subtle characteristics of the communication environment that did not receive much attention, but that may be a significant feature that is missing in virtual teamwork. Knowing when your colleagues are within conversational range (even if the conversation is conducted by instant messages) is a security blanket and time saver. If you have a quick question you can just ask them, without having to arrange a formal meeting or send an email for which you might not receive a reply for days. Instant messenger software supports a low-bandwidth version of awareness, through its buddy lists. When a "buddy" signs on to the system, a sound file of a door opening plays and the buddy's name appears in the list of available buddies. When the buddy signs off, the door slamming sound file plays. Other strategies have also been used to support the awareness of presence. In game worlds, for example, players use avatars that they can move about on the screen. Other players in the same portion of the game can see and interact with the avatars that are "present."

One prototype to support the virtual workplace was developed by researchers from both the corporate and the academic communities.[140] The software, called "Rear View Mirror," supports instant messaging and synchronous group chats with a text-based interface, but it also supports "presence awareness" in a richer way compared to instant messaging. Team members have a "presence viewer" displayed on their computer screens that shows the photos of their team members. The border of the photo indicates the person's present state and anticipated availability. Green, for example, means the person is present, and yellow means temporarily unavailable. Red means the person is likely to be away for more than an hour or two. Rolling the mouse over a photo pops up a brief message that the team member can tailor, such as "I'll be away for about an hour." One lighthearted team member set his rollover to automatically change to "Missing, presumed working," when he was inactive for an hour.

Innovative technology to support virtual teams is not easy to introduce, and most people stopped using Rear View Mirror after a few months. Concerns about privacy were one reason some users were reluctant to adopt this software, even in trial mode. The presence viewer appeared to be a tool that could be easily used for worker surveillance, and German team members thought it might be illegal in their country. In any case, it had to be approved by a worker's council.

Another barrier to a successful adoption is one that haunts any technology that needs a critical mass to be useful at all. Groupware falls into this category; if all your group members are not using the new technology fully, then it becomes less useful for the whole team. New technologies, however, especially prototypes like this one for Rear View Mirror, are usually quite buggy so only the most tolerant and forgiving employees were willing to keep trying it in a workplace setting. They needed to get their work done after all. Yet to design effective technology for groups, the designers must have feedback from the users. This becomes a catch-22, because it is difficult to get the critical mass needed for virtual team members to learn whether the new tools will be valuable for them when they tackle group projects.

Software vendors hype and promote innovative technologies to support virtual teams, but not many relate the examples of failed attempts to

---

[140] Hersleb, J. D., Atkins, D. L., Boyer, D. G., Handel, M., & Finholt, T. (2002). Introducing instant messaging and chat in the workplace. In Proceedings of CHI 2002. New York: ACM Press. Retrieved January 15, 2003, from ACM Digital Library.

implement them. Managers who champion the projects within their own organizations naturally prefer to talk about successes rather than failures as well, so stories of the projects that collapse or fall by the wayside are not widely circulated. However, such technologies can be very difficult to launch and knowledge about the false starts is valuable.

Tomorrow's Virtual Teams

With today's Internet and technological infrastructure, virtual teamwork is a challenge, indeed. In their book *Virtual Teams*, Jessica Lipnack and Jeffrey Stamps point out that, "Virtual teams must be smarter than a conventional collocated team – just to survive."[141] The technologies available to support them are still in their infancy and are neither able to convey all the nuances of communication nor counteract the advantages of collocation. We cannot create life-size three-dimensional holograms of team members, for example, transmit the images over the Internet, and invite them all to interact within a virtual collaborative space. Also, we are still learning what aspects of the collocated team are most critical for the team's success and trying to embed at least those features into the technology.

The technologies will certainly improve, and what we are using today will seem very antiquated in the near future. However, some researchers believe that virtual teams will never be able to operate the same way that collocated teams do, regardless of how much futuristic technology we provide to support them. They will always be hindered by problems involving trust, the development of common ground, and the difficulties related to communications. Humans evolved and learned to work together in collocated spaces, and there may be just too many factors and interrelated characteristics of the face-to-face setting that simply can't be duplicated by people working with electronically mediated communication tools on different continents. Woody Allen may have been right when he quipped, 80 percent of success is just showing up.

Despite the obstacles, virtual teams are and will continue to be a significant trend in the workplace. In many circumstances, they add a critically valuable capability in the context of the work that people want to do. One of the finest and most productive implementations of virtual teamwork, for example, is the virtual collaboratory system used by space physicists. This community of scientists is located all over the world, and the measurements

---

[141] Lipnack, J., & Stamps, J. (1997). *Virtual teams: Reaching across space, time, and organizations with technology.* New York: John Wiley & Sons.

and images each one collects from the sensors and telescopes at their own sites are extremely interesting to their coworkers. Their collaboratory includes remote access to real-time data from the instruments, as well as maps, virtual "rooms" and "clubs" where the scientists can choose the displays they want to see and gather to jointly view and discuss the data.

The best approach is to continue to learn from the successes and failures of virtual teams, identify the problem areas, and explore what can be done to better support them. As the technologies improve, some obstacles will disappear – or at least shrink. Yet useful improvements can be made now by understanding the social and psychological issues that arise when teams are not collocated. Many of these issues can be addressed by changing what kinds of work virtual teams are assigned, how they are oriented, and how they are led.

8 E-Learning

With an Internet connection on the desktop at work and at home, you can join fellow students from around the world and take classes whenever you choose. The organization does not necessarily need to arrange classroom-based training for all its employees when new standards and procedures are required. When new people come on board, they do not have to wait until the next scheduled program they need to become effective in their new jobs. Just as the Internet offered opportunities to break through the boundaries of time and place for teamwork, it offers the same opportunities for classrooms.

Success for a knowledge-based workplace relies heavily on continual upgrading of skills, and organizations put considerable effort and funding into their training programs. Surprisingly, despite the promises and potential of Internet-based delivery of education and training, few organizations use it much for in-house corporate training. The instructor-led classroom-based program is still the norm in most places, though some analysts predict that the e-learning market is poised for explosive growth in the coming decade. Gartner Group, for example, predicts the market will grow to more than $33 billion by 2005. Others, however, think the reports of the death of distance in educational settings, as Mark Twain put it, are greatly exaggerated; bits and bytes can never replace live teachers.

Although employees might not yet have many opportunities to engage in e-learning for their in-house corporate training, they have an astounding number of alternatives for university-level distance programs which are growing rapidly. Many organizations provide tuition assistance for students who wish to pursue degrees, especially if they are job related. In the past, employees would need to enroll in a local college or university to attend class, usually at night, as a part-time student. After work, the employee grabbed a sandwich and drove to the college for the evening lecture, usually one or two nights a week. Gulping coffee to stay awake after a long day at work, the employee sat in the class listening to the professor, taking notes, and occasionally asking questions or engaging in discussion, until around 10 p.m. Classes might also be offered on weekends during the day, thus consuming the employee's Saturday free time. These so-called nontraditional part-time college students have little time to participate in aspects of college life beyond the classroom, such as student government, sports, fraternities, or clubs. Their numbers are quite large, however, much larger than most people suppose. A report from the U.S. Department of Education estimated that a whopping 73 percent of undergraduates could be classified as "nontraditional" based on their age, part-time status, whether they have dependents of their own, or other criteria that distinguish them from the full-time student who enrolled in college right after high school.[142,143]

It takes stamina and perseverance to succeed as a nontraditional part-time student. Attending classes two or three nights a week for several years to earn a degree, and studying in whatever free time is left after work and class, takes a singlemindedness of purpose that deserves credit. A single parent trying to complete a degree in this way struggles constantly with babysitter problems and exhaustion. A father misses his children's bedtime and the Saturday ball game, week after week, month after month. If the university is distant from the employee's home and place of work, just the additional time spent in the car is staggering. It is not at all surprising that when on-line degree programs emerged in the 1990s, the nontraditional students began flocking to them. The range of choices for university-based distance education is now extremely broad, and students can even complete all the coursework for an entire degree, such as a master's in business administration, without ever physically appearing at a campus.

E-Learning: A Virtual Tour

What is e-learning like? People who have not been involved in any distance education have a difficult time understanding what it might be like. Our approach to education has been solidly based on the live classroom experience

[142] Evelyn, J. (2002). Nontraditional students dominate undergraduate enrollments, study finds. *Chronicle of Higher Education*, June 14, 2002, A34. Retrieved April 4, 2003, from *Chronicle of Higher Education* Web site: http://chronicle.com

[143] Wirt, J., Choy, S., Gerald, D., Provasnik, S., Rooney, P., Watanabe, S., & Tobin, R. (2002). The Condition of Education, 2002. U.S. Department of Education Report, NCES 2002025. Retrieved April 4, 2003, from National Center for Education Statistics Web site: http://nces.ed.gov/pubsearch/pubsinfo.asp?pubid=2002025

and the collocation of students and faculty on a campus for so long that it is hard to imagine how education might work any other way. To better understand e-learning, let's take a virtual tour of an online graduate-level class, beginning with the experience from the student's perspective.

E-LEARNING FROM THE STUDENT'S PERSPECTIVE

Katie T., the single mother of a six-year-old boy, has been working in the human resources office of her organization for about a year. Her Atlanta company has a tuition reimbursement plan and she proposes to her supervisor that she begin a master's degree program in human resource management. Eager for career advancement, Katie also recognizes how much time this degree will take and how difficult it would be to attend classes at night and weekends because of her son. Like most people, she is skeptical of distance education and doesn't want to put in a lot of time to earn a "second-class" degree that won't be recognized or valued by employers. However, her situation is such that the convenience of online coursework is very attractive. In fact, she doesn't think a part-time program with a local university would even be possible, given her job and family responsibilities.

Katie decides to apply to a university in the Midwest, intending to enroll in their online master's degree program. They offer a variety of specialties, including human resource management, and the university is fully accredited so she feels more comfortable about the program. She fills out her application on the Web and also completes the forms for tuition reimbursement at work. Within a week she receives confirmation that she was admitted and the email and telephone number of her academic advisor. She calls, and talks at length with the woman about the human resources management track, which courses to take, and how the online program works. She gets back on the Web and enrolls in the first course, "Organizational Communications," entering her credit card number to pay the tuition. After downloading the syllabus, she clicks on the hyperlink to "buy textbooks now" and is taken to the university's online bookstore, where she chooses the books and enters her credit card number again to pay for them. Immediately she begins receiving automated emails confirming her registration and textbook purchases and assigning her a login name and password for her course.

The course, which runs for the fall semester (September to January), starts in two weeks. The syllabus shows the course requirements, readings, assignments, group project description, and term paper requirement. Katie, who has been out of college for six years, is nervous. How can she read all this, and how will she communicate with the teacher, the other students, and the members of whatever group she will belong to? From her desk at work, she logs in and works through the online tutorial to learn how to use the system to look at course materials, send assignments, participate in asynchronous discussion groups, chat in the chat room, and find online library materials. The system they are using tries to use many metaphors appropriate to a campus, so she sees terms like admissions office, reference desk, student café, faculty lounge, classroom, library, faculty office hours, and media room. She feels as though she entered a new universe, a digital counterpart to her old undergraduate college. During the tutorial, she practices with the text-based chat room and runs into another person who is also learning the system. Hiroshi K. is a Japanese American working at a consulting firm in Tokyo, and he is also a new student in the online program. They both have quite a shock when they realize they are in the same "class," even though they are on opposite sides of the planet.

She can't log into the Organizational Communications class just yet – it says "class begins on September 6" when they attempt to click on their class link. However, when the class opens, she heads straight for the link at the top, "Welcome to the Class, from Professor Jenkins." A warm letter typed in blue in a script-like font from the professor describes the topic of the class and also introduces the first assignment – "Introduce Yourself on the Discussion Board." Jenkins wants to be sure everyone can use the system and also wants to lay the groundwork for interactions by ensuring everyone reads and understands the class norms.

Katie is not sure what to write about herself, so waits until a few others post their intros. Most of them are nontraditional students like herself and write about their jobs, their families, and their interest in taking an online course. The discussion board fills up quickly and by the weekend, twenty-five students have posted their intros. Now that she knows more about her classmates, including how many there are, she gets more comfortable. It was disorienting at first not to be able to see them, but she reflected that their written intros were probably much more informative than their physical presence in a live classroom might have been. The professor comments occasionally in the intro discussion, always using her "signature" font so everyone will associate that font with her online persona.

The pace of the class gathers steam and it seems that assignments are due all the time. Katie goes through the material for each unit of the course as it progresses, which includes mini-lectures on the Web from Jenkins, audio files, or slide presentations, as well as tons of textbook reading. For her first assignment, she analyzes some business memos and uploads her analysis to the assignment drop box. Just reading everyone's postings in the discussion board takes a couple of hours a week, especially when the debate becomes heated. In October, the topic involved the ethics of email surveillance in the workplace and students became very agitated, describing some horror stories from their own companies. At one point, a student writes "Prof Jenkins, are you sure this class is secure? I wouldn't want my employer to read what I just posted."

Katie and Hiroshi are assigned to the same group, along with Larry, a forty-five-year-old ex-Marine in California. They want to meet online for a chat to get organized, but negotiating the time zones is a challenge. Finally they choose 10 a.m. east coast time, which is at least not in the middle of the night for anyone. Their project involves developing a proposal for a crisis management and communications plan, and they each volunteer for specific components. The class "resource room" includes some software that students can choose to download to support desktop videoconferencing for their group projects, and the trio uses this as well. They all share a laugh when they finally can see each other, because the impressions they had formed of one another based on their text-based interactions did not match up well with actual appearance.

The course has no final exam, but the twenty-page term paper requirement is quite extensive. Katie drops in to the chat room during one of Professor Jenkins's posted office hours to ask more questions about the paper. At work, Katie spends many hours searching through the online library for materials and finds good articles from journals such as *Harvard Business Review, Sloan Management, Journal of Human Resource Management,* and *Academy of Management Review.* Although she has permission to use a university library in Atlanta to check out books or find articles that are not accessible online, the drive is long, parking is impossible, and she'd prefer not to have to spend the time.

On the last day of class, Professor Jenkins extends her regular chat room office hours to congratulate the group for completing the course. She comments on all the group projects and makes jokes about some of the events that happened. At one point, a student asks what she looks like, and she encourages them to guess. Katie is already talking to the other students by email, discussing which professors are the best and which ones to avoid. Though none of the students have ever visited the campus or set foot in a class, they have taken the first step toward their master's degrees and are eager for the next.

Katie's experience with e-learning was positive and she had few problems, but online programs do not always run so smoothly. Sometimes the system goes down just before an assignment deadline, and students look frantically for fax machines to get their papers in on time. Sometimes the teacher does little to interact with the class except grade the assignments, so not much rapport develops. Flame wars occasionally break out in the discussion boards, leading to anger and resentment. Some students seem to just "disappear" and never contribute to the group project or the classroom, as you saw in the chapter on virtual teamwork. The classmates of the vanishing students have no idea whether the student is still in the class, and the professor might not know either. Potentially one of the most significant issues about distance courses is the sheer volume of reading matter in the textbooks, printed workbooks, online course material and mini-lectures, discussion forums, email, chat transcripts, and other sources. Many students feel overwhelmed by the information load, because they are comparing it to a face-to-face class in which the reading material is less extensive. Finally, the technology often causes headaches and frustration. Software designed to increase media richness that includes desktop videoconferencing, for example, can be agonizingly slow and difficult to configure properly.

E-LEARNING: THE TEACHER'S PERSPECTIVE

As the teacher, Professor Jenkins had a very different job compared to a teacher of a face-to-face class. For example, long before the class began, she had to create all her mini-lectures and slide presentations, format everything for the Web, and post them onto the server into the correct area. Her syllabus, class schedule, assignments, class policies, and class materials have to be ready to go on the day the class starts. Although she can add supplementary materials during the class, the copyright restrictions for posting current content online are cumbersome. A face-to-face teacher can make photocopies of an article that appeared in yesterday's newspaper, for example, and distribute them to his or her students during the class. The copyright laws that govern analogous distributions to students in online courses continue to undergo change and are quite confusing to teachers.[144] In any case all of this material must be created for online delivery, and posted to the online class, so the teacher must be reasonably fluent in Web development.

Once the class starts, the teacher must be the facilitator and moderator, finding ways to engage the students and keep them involved with the class and the material. She typically does not lecture, so her lively lecturing style is irrelevant. She cannot see the faces of her students so those nonverbal cues that tell her the students didn't follow the last point are invisible.

---

[144] Carenevale, D. (2003). Slow start for long-awaited easing of copyright restrictions. *Chronicle of Higher Education, 49*(29), A29.

For the face-to-face teacher, the core components of the course include classroom lectures, textbook and other reading material, library materials, some group work, videotapes, interactive discussions in class, tests, and term papers. These are the elements a classroom teacher blends together to create a dynamic learning experience. The lecture is the central component, and it has been for more than 700 years since it first started at the University of Paris. Although many alternative teaching and learning approaches have been proposed, the classroom lecture is overwhelmingly the dominant methodology for practically all educational settings.

Although some e-learning programs make use of "talking-head" videos of professors, or interactive videoconferences in which students can see a live professor on the screen, most do not. What happens to the teacher's role when there is no classroom lecture? The "sage on the stage becomes the guide on the side," and that guide has a different set of responsibilities. Instead of preparing the lecture, the teacher interacts constantly with students, individually, in study groups, or as a whole class. The teacher starts discussions, moderates them, answers email, joins chat groups, offers explanations, suggests additional resources, and generally spends many, many hours at the computer screen and keyboard, reading and typing.

When distance programs first began, many thought the teachers would get a break because they did not need to prepare lectures. As it turned out, however, the faculty workload for an online class is generally higher than it is for a traditional class, particularly the first time the teacher leads a particular course. There are two main reasons for this. First, the delivery method itself is time consuming. It is far easier to explain a concept to a group of students using speech and a blackboard than it is to develop a Web page to explain the same thing. In class, the faculty can draw diagrams, modify them in response to student questions, erase them, and interact with the students to check understanding.

The second reason for the higher workload is that the class itself is open twenty-four hours a day, seven days a week. In a face-to-face class, the professor might lecture for an hour and then leave five or ten minutes for questions before the class is over. Students in an online class can email the teacher anytime of day or night, and the questions can be as long as the student chooses to make them. Although the professor might hold synchronous office hours with a chat room or videoconferencing system, the email is always open. Some professors have given up in dismay when they see how much they must read and respond to in an online class. It seems that e-learning has unleashed a considerable amount of pent-up demand for interaction with the teacher. Shy students sitting in the back of the traditional classroom who might never have asked a question before feel much freer to ask them via email. Although this development is a positive one, the downside is the increased workload for the instructor.

Defining the Terms

Terms like e-learning, distance education, distance learning, telelearning, distributed learning, computer-based training have grown widely in use, though few people agree on their definitions. During the 1990s, for example, Bell Atlantic (now Verizon) installed a statewide "distance learning network" in Maryland, and its promoters and advocates equated this single approach with the totality of distance education. Actually, the "distance learning network" was only a collection of about fifty sites equipped with videoconferencing capabilities, including television monitors and cameras, each located in one room with about twenty seats. A small number of sites in the network could connect to one another at a time, and view the people in each small classroom at the other sites. The technology was not Internet based, and it was severely limited by regulatory and technical factors. For example, no sites in Virginia or Delaware could be included in the network, let alone India or Japan. Experiments like this one led many people to believe that "distance learning" was synonymous with synchronous videoconferencing, with a teacher at one site with some students, and additional groups of "remote" students gathered at a few other locations. This kind of confusion continued to arise because people mixed up the technologies used to implement a particular kind of distance education with the whole horizon of what might be possible.

The terms *distance education, distributed learning,* and *distance learning* all loosely refer to educational programs in which the teacher and student(s) are not in the same physical location. Such programs can be conducted in a great variety of ways and can involve many different technologies to mediate the educational experience. One variety might rely on a videoconferencing network, such as the one Bell Atlantic built, which would allow a trainer in a Baltimore bank headquarters to include employees in the Hagerstown branch in her training program. The remote students would be able to see and hear the video images of the teacher, and the teacher could see them. A very different kind of distance education might allow employees to log into a Web server anytime, work with some interactive multimedia instructional materials, and then take a quiz. The results would be recorded in the corporate database, and a trainer might review the results to guide the employee toward additional resources.

Yet another distance education experience might capitalize on some of the same technologies used by virtual teams to create an online "classroom." Students from around the world would log in to the "classroom" at the same time, and the instructor might appear as a talking head in the corner of the screen. The students would click on the "I have a question" button when they have a question, and the teacher's screen shows the icon of a raised hand next to that student's login name. At the next breaking point, the teacher allows the student to type the question into a chat window and all the others in the virtual classroom can see the student's question. After students log off, they might communicate using email or telephone to work on their group projects. Distance education programs cover an enormous range of educational experiences, from the snail-mail-mediated correspondence courses that began in the nineteenth century to the high-tech virtual classrooms of today. The key ingredient is that the teacher and student(s) are not physically collocated. (One of my colleagues considers his freshman economics class at a major university to be "distance education," because students in the back of a 500-seat auditorium can barely see him. It's difficult to call those back-row students "collocated.")

Figure 8.1 shows examples of technologies used to support different educational configurations in terms of place and time. Videoconferencing, for example, is a "same time, different place" technology, whereas email can

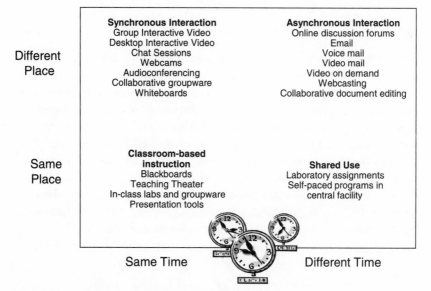

Figure 8.1. Matrix of e-learning technologies.

support "different time, different place." Some technologies, such as group-ware, can be effectively applied in most or all of the configurations. In a lab in which each person has a computer, a facilitator can use the group-ware for brainstorming or voting and follow it with live, in-person discussion. Geographically dispersed group members could use the same kind of collaborative software asynchronously from their desktops around the globe.

The figure shows technologies, not distance education programs, because the programs themselves often take advantage of more than one configuration. Students might begin their course with a face-to-face meeting in a classroom with the teacher but then move online to continue their interactions and coursework. Email is used heavily in most contexts, even when students see each other and their teacher frequently.

The term "e-learning" is becoming popular in the business world, and it usually refers to programs that contain content distributed in digital format over the Internet or other network. Interaction between instructor and student or among students is also mediated by the Internet, if it is part of the program. E-learning is thus the high-tech, net-enabled subset of the larger universe of distance education or distributed learning. Many organizations are adopting this term, partly to get away from the stereotypes and misconceptions surrounding the term "distance education."

Advantages of E-Learning Programs

The findings of a recent Gartner Dataquest end-user survey showed that e-learning approaches, with or without an instructor, were the least used of all training models, but most respondents also indicated that they plan to greatly increase their use of it.[145] The advantages of e-learning programs, compared to traditional face-to-face instructor-led classes, are many. Employees don't need to wait for the class to be scheduled, and they don't have to travel to a specific location. The pacing of the class and the speed with which material is presented can be individually tailored, and the fast learners do not have to wait while the rest of the group completes an in-class exercise. The material itself can also be individualized, so people having difficulty with a particular topic can receive additional training and practice on it, also without delaying other students. With an Internet connection at

[145] Igou, B. (2002). How enterprises select e-learning training providers. Gartner Dataquest Perspectives Note Number ITSV-WW-DP-0255.

the desktop, a worker can engage in training programs anytime during the day and review materials whenever they need to brush up on the topic. The instructor, if there is one, can be located anywhere and can communicate with currently enrolled students using a variety of technologies.

E-learning offers advantages for interactive communications and free-dom from the constraints of time and place. It also offers advantages over earlier computer-based training programs because of the way materials are developed, updated, and distributed. Earlier computer-based learning pro-grams were typically designed for the stand-alone computer and were dis-tributed on floppy disks and, later, on CD-ROMs. If the program collected data about student progress in the training program, it was stored on the lo-cal computer. As time went on, the advantages of converting the programs to networked-based software became more evident. The software could then be installed for the entire local or wide-area network, and employees could access it from the servers instead of installing it locally. The networkable software also permitted more useful course management systems to grow, so that the training managers and teachers could keep track of the progress of all employees in a single database.

When the Internet arrived and became widely accessible in the work-place and at home, the limitations of the existing crop of computer-based courseware became apparent. Courseware distributed on CD-ROMs could not easily be updated without distributing more disks, so the material could easily become out of date. It was expensive to create a new version because of the distribution costs. With Web-based learning materials, the information can be updated on the server and made immediately available to everyone throughout the organization, regardless of location.

With all these advantages, why has e-learning been slow to take off in the workplace? One of the most obvious reasons is the high cost of software that supports an e-learning environment, including progress tracking, content management systems, course management tools, and software to support interactivity. Another obstacle involves the cost and difficulty of converting stand-up training programs and courses into e-learning formats. Although it is not that difficult to put a workbook online and add a few quizzes for a sin-gle course, a typical corporate instructor-led training program is much richer and more complex than that. It might include print-based workbooks and textbooks, videotapes, classroom-based exercises, assessment instruments, guest speakers, group work, and an instructor to help the group navigate through the material and evaluate progress. The instructor can tailor the program to the group's needs, add up-to-date materials on the fly, bring in speakers to spark interest, and challenge individual students with direct questions. Making the leap from classroom-based to e-learning formats has been far more difficult than many people expected.

How Effective is E-Learning?

A major controversy for distance education programs involves their effectiveness, and the gold standard for effectiveness has generally been the face-to-face classroom-style experience. Literally hundreds of studies have been conducted that compare various types of distance experiences with in-class experiences, using a number of different dependent variables for the comparison. Thomas L. Russell of North Carolina State University has been compiling many of these studies and providing abstracts of them in his book, and also on a Web site called "The No Significant Difference Phenomenon." A companion Web site, called "The Significant Difference Phenomenon," lists studies that have found differences.[146] Although the majority of studies have not detected much difference between the distance learning formats and their in-class counterpart, many have found subtle differences. However, the studies vary so much in terms of the type of programs offered, the controls used in the study and the assessment instruments, that there is still plenty of room for debate.

Consider, for example, a study of two versions of a graduate class by Scott D. Johnson of the University of Illinois at Urbana-Champaign and his colleagues.[147] One course was taught via the traditional face-to-face lecture method, and the other was online. In terms of learning outcomes, there were no significant differences between the two groups, including the grades on the final projects, which were graded by judges who didn't know which class the student took. There was, however, a difference in the attitudes of the students. Those in the face-to-face class rated the quality of the course and their attitudes toward the instructor more positively compared to the students in the online course. This finding suggested that students in the online course performed as well as students in the classroom, but they didn't enjoy the experience as much.

Another study suggests that researchers will come to different conclusions based partly on whether the students are randomly assigned to the different formats or choose the format themselves. Stefanie B. Waschull at Athens Technical College studied students taking online or in-class versions

---

[146] Russell, T. L. (n.d.). The no significant difference phenomenon. Retrieved January 14, 2003, from http://teleeducation.nb.ca/nosignificantdifference/

[147] Johnson, S. D., Aragon, S. R., & Shaik, N. (2000). Comparative analysis of learner satisfaction and learning outcomes in online and face-to-face learning environments. *Journal of Interactive Learning Research, 11*(1), 29–49.

of a psychology class. In the first study, she allowed them to self-select the format.[148] She taught both formats herself and found that students in the online course were significantly more likely to fail the course. In the next study, however, she randomly assigned students to the formats and found no significant difference in performance measures.

In some settings, e-learning students do better than their in-class counterparts; in others their performance is poorer; and in many, there is not much difference. William S. Maki and Ruth H. Maki of Texas Tech University, however, have consistently found students in their Web-based classes to perform better on tests compared to those in the face-to-face class, though the online students like the class less, as other researchers have found. In a recent study, they identified one of the variables that may explain some of the contradictory findings about student performance. Because most of the material in an e-learning format is presented in text, graphics, and audio files, they hypothesized that students who were better able to comprehend these formats would benefit most from the Web-based courses.

In their study, students enrolled in introductory psychology courses that were offered either in class or on the Web.[149] Before the classes began, however, the students took tests to assess their multimedia comprehension skills. In addition to text comprehension questions, the battery included audio readings with questions about the content. The subjects' ability to comprehend graphics was assessed by showing them a series of slides that told a story with no words and asking them questions about the content.

Overall, the students in the Web-based class did somewhat better than the students in the face-to-face class, and as before, they liked it less. The performance advantage in the Web-based course, however, was mostly due to the very high performance of students who also had high scores on the multimedia comprehension battery. Those with low scores showed no performance advantage at all.

BEYOND APPLES (LIVE CLASSROOM) AND ORANGES (E-LEARNING)

The study by William Maki and Ruth Maki points to the importance of looking more closely at the details of e-learning programs, including the abilities and learning styles of those who choose to participate in them as well as the way the material is presented. Debating whether distance

---

[148] Waschull, S. B. (2001). The online delivery of psychology courses: Attrition, performance, and evaluation. *Computers in Teaching, 28*(2), 143–147.

[149] Maki, W. S., & Maki, R. H. (2002). Multimedia comprehension skill predicts differential outcomes of web-based and lecture courses. *Journal of Experimental Psychology: Applied, 8*(2), 85–98.

education is as effective as in-class instruction and the lecture method has not been terribly productive, especially because most of the research has not been designed in a way that would allow researchers to compare apples to apples and draw conclusions about why students were performing differently, even if they were. For example, the online courses may have different assignments, different due dates, and different teachers, and students are not generally randomly assigned. However, much of the research helps elucidate the characteristics of distance programs that are especially well received and create an effective learning environment.

The debate has also been somewhat politically charged, which makes it even more difficult to objectively assess the effectiveness of e-learning approaches. For example, the American Federation of Teachers ran advertisements in the *Chronicle of Higher Education* and other newspapers that spoofed distance education and questioned its validity. The ads featured Father Guido Sarducci of *Saturday Night Live* fame joking about the "5-minute university" and suggesting it was about to become a reality through questionable online degree programs. The ads read, "Just because it is technologically feasible to deliver a college program through distance learning doesn't make it educationally sound." At the request of the American Federation of Teachers and the National Education Association, the Institute for Higher Education Policy undertook a review of the research on distance programs.[150] Their report found that much of the research that reported "no significant difference" was deeply flawed because it lacked control groups and other typical experimental conventions. The A.F.T. promoted the report, but advocates of distance programs pointed to the potential for bias because of the political motivations of the sponsors. Also, advocates point out that in-class instruction certainly has many flaws and varies considerably in quality. Not all students do well in that setting, either.

As we discussed in earlier chapters, the Internet's role in disintermediation has been a crucial one, and education is one of the most contentious arenas in which the process is unfolding. Consumers who want to purchase wine via the Internet don't have much sympathy for the wine distributors who want to block the practice to protect their business model. However, disintermediating live classroom teachers along with all the other potential benefits that may come from physical presence on a college campus is another matter. Learning is a "deliverable good" that is far more

---

[150] Phipps, R., & Merisotis, J. (1999). What's the difference? A review of contemporary research on the effectiveness of distance learning in higher education. Institute for Higher Education Policy. Retrieved February 12, 2003, from http://www.ihep.org/Pubs/PDF/Difference.pdf

difficult to quantify and assess compared to cases of wine, and changing the distribution channels by reducing or eliminating the role of live teachers and the physical campus may have significant effects on the quality of the whole product. Much of the controversy surrounding distance education and the studies that compare it to traditional approaches involves concerns about the elusive definition of educational quality and also reflection on what it means to teach and to learn in the Internet age.

The logical next step for e-learning programs is to move beyond the debate that pits in-class formats against e-learning formats and ascertain what it is about distance programs that works well, for whom it works, and why. What characteristics of the face-to-face setting should we be trying to replicate as closely as possible, because the technology is capable of doing it and the capabilities are important for e-learning success? Which ones simply can't be replicated in any meaningful way? What kind of subject matter is most appropriate for e-learning? Finally, what can we do with Internet-based e-learning that we can't do with an in-class format, and how can we leverage the new capabilities for education? In one sense, this is like asking what would best go into an "amazon.edu," one that does not replicate the classroom (or bookstore) environment except in certain particulars but that capitalizes on other features of the Internet to bring fresh capabilities to the educational table. The most obvious one, and the one that continues to attract so many part-time students with full-time jobs and family responsibilities, is the elimination of the nightly commute to class and the babysitter bills. The convenience of anytime-anywhere coursework is a critical feature, not just for these nontraditional students but also for the employees who need just-in-time learning at their desks and have little time to attend more formal corporate training programs.

Another potential advantage of e-learning over traditional classes led by live instructors involves mass customization. We saw in previous chapters that many e-commerce vendors are using the approach to tailor products and services to each individual based on the information the customer provides, or on information that is collected from the customer's Web browsing habits. Carol A. Twigg, Executive Director of the Center for Academic Transformation, makes this point forcefully: " . . . as long as we continue to replicate traditional approaches online – and continue to treat all students as if they were the same – we will once again find the "no significant difference" phenomenon vis-à-vis quality."[151]

---

[151] Twigg, C. A. (2001). Innovations in online learning: Moving beyond significant difference. The Pew Learning and Technology Program. Retrieved May 6, 2003, from: http:/www.center.rpi.edu/PewSym/Mono4.html

Individualized instruction tailored to the needs of each student has certainly been tried before, and it is no surprise that people vary in the way they learn; in their preferences for different kinds of media and learning environments; and in their need for interaction, hand-holding, or feedback. It is a fundamental principle in education, but unfortunately, it has not been used routinely or very effectively because of the cost. A teacher – student ratio of 1 to 40 does not support a great deal of individual assessment, materials tailoring, or one-on-one mentoring. Our lack of knowledge about how learning styles interact with course materials and formats has also inhibited individualization of instruction. However, mass customization should become more cost effective and easier to do, just as it has in the world of e-commerce. As we learn more about how to optimally match the learning environment with the student, we can better design course materials, taking full advantage of all the capabilities the Internet offers, from individual assessment and detailed records of student activity to multimedia and interactive courseware and high-bandwidth communications.

The Challenges of E-Learning

E-learning in all its varieties will play a very significant role in the workplace. Many more organizations will develop e-learning approaches for corporate training, much as the U.S. Army has already done for more than 400 courses – from basic skills to management training. Also, many more employees will enroll in distance programs offered by institutions of higher education, taking advantage of tuition reimbursement programs and the fast connections on their workplace desks. The advantages are much too powerful to ignore, ranging from increased convenience and accessibility to reusability of learning modules to savings on travel budgets. The challenges, however, are not trivial.

CONTENT IS KING

The quality of the digital content distributed over the Internet is a critical ingredient for e-learning initiatives, but the amount of high-quality material available online is small. At the moment, much of the content from commercial and academic sources is still dominated by paper and books. The online content providers are fragmented and struggling with diverse approaches and business models, and most of the material being generated by these providers is not cataloged in any formal way, as it would be if it had received an ISBN number and were cataloged in a library. There are also few mature review processes in place for digital content, so that training managers, teachers, or students can learn what reputable reviewers have to say about the quality of an online course. A corporate training manager who identifies a need for some employees in all the branch offices to learn more about accounting, for example, has a difficult time identifying all the potential options, let alone evaluating them.

Who is developing digital content for e-learning? In higher education, most faculty began doing this themselves when they wanted to venture into distance learning. They built Web sites to contain their syllabi and mini-lectures, slide shows, graphical images, audio files, and even little videos. In more extensive programs, the faculty may work with instructional designers and software developers to bring an online course to life with improved usability and a more professional look, using the course management system provided by the university. By the late 1990s, a number of commercial outfits entered the fray, developing and selling "off-the-shelf" generic courses that could be delivered over the Web in areas such as information technology and financial services. In some cases, the companies adapted computer-based courseware to the online environment, and in others, they built new courses. Many courses are self-paced, whereas others involve a group that moves through the syllabus on a schedule, guided by an instructor. Custom course development is also growing in popularity as large companies seek to offer e-learning that is tightly coupled with their organization's policies, procedures, and mission.

A major category of digital content that has been growing – albeit slowly – is the digital library. Although the quality of a course in many subjects, such as basic HTML skills, might not require access to a comprehensive library, e-learning programs for more advanced material – especially in academia – must have library support. How does the student in the rural bank branch office, who enrolls in a tax accounting class with tuition benefits from the bank, write a term paper or research the case studies that are assigned? If she has access to a university's library, she can go there, but online access to these materials would be far preferable to her. Increasingly, journal articles from sources such as *Accountancy* or *ABA Banking Journal* are being moved online, so students can conduct searches and view the online versions of articles they need. Books, however, are more difficult to access, although increasingly, publishers are finding ways to publish e-books, especially the more recent titles for which they have electronic versions already. Netlibrary.com, for example, offers full-text access to books from a large number of publishers, including Cambridge University Press – the publisher of this book.

How do people gain access to this digital content? The obvious answer is by using their Internet browser from the desktop. But this question leads to many of the issues we discussed in previous chapters, especially about changing business models swirling around digitally distributed information products. The marketplace for digital content is still very much in flux, and many access strategies and business models are present in the mix.

One model, for example, is individual enrollment in a course, which would provide access to the course content for a period of time. Anyone can log into DigitalThink.com, for example, and pay $99 to take an online course in the legal aspects of human resources management. Another model is an individual subscription to a publisher's collection of materials. The person might pay a monthly fee on their credit card to maintain a login and password to that publisher's site to gain access to all the materials available. Recognizing that many people are not just interested in the works published by a single company, aggregators have also emerged. They develop license arrangements with a number of publishers and then sell subscriptions to the whole collection.

Another approach is the organizational gateway, which is used by many universities. The organization becomes its own "aggregator" and pays the subscriptions for many collections of digital content appropriate for its student body. Students receive logins and passwords that identify them as members of the university community. They can then access an enormous range of materials. From my desk at Johns Hopkins University, for example, I can access a staggering variety of digital content that is not available on the open Internet to most Internet users, including papers in academic journals, proceedings of conferences, articles in newspapers and general interest magazines, e-books, statistical files, and business intelligence. You will see in the references that many of the sources for this book were electronically retrieved.

The methodologies by which content owners protect their content and content consumers pay for it are fragmented, confusing, and changing all the time. Digital rights management, called DRM, is a dynamic area for vendors and publishers who want to find ways to protect their copyrights, and numerous experiments are underway to track usage of information products such as software, music, and also educational materials. In education, for example, Netlibrary uses a digital rights management approach that relies on the metaphor of a physical book. Organizations buy a certain number of "copies" and the software prohibits people within the organization from "checking out" more than the number of copies on hand. Digital versions could, of course, be accessed simultaneously by as many people who want to view them, but the book metaphor creates a context for managing digital rights that people are familiar with.

Some approaches to DRM, however, have caused howls of protest, such as the cumbersome activation scheme that software giant Intuit introduced to protect its tax preparation software. Buyers had to activate the software after installation by connecting to Intuit's Web site or entering all the codes into the telephone keypad, and it could only be activated once. Consumers whose hard drive crashed or who upgraded to a new computer could not reload and reactivate without jumping through many hoops, questioned by sometimes hostile and suspicious customer service reps at the company. The software Intuit used to create this rights control mechanism also came under fire as users experienced system crashes and then could not uninstall it.[152] Consumers, students, and educational organizations do not want unwieldy schemes like this one that will frustrate them, limit their access and reduce the usefulness of the product, or invade their privacy. Sorting out all of the rights issues and bringing some sanity and equitability to the digital content arena are critical challenges ahead for e-learning initiatives.

COPYRIGHT, OWNERSHIP, AND THE "CUT AND PASTE" PHENOMENON

Copyright issues rear again as a challenge for e-learning from the standpoint of ownership. Consider a courseware module intended to teach students how to compute mean, mode, and median. The business statistics instructor at a local community college has been covering this topic as part of his in-class course and now wants to include it on the Web site he will make for his new distance class. He creates a Web page, then gets some assistance from one of his students to write a little interactive applet he envisioned. The applet shows students a group of employees along with their annual salaries and allows students to change the salary of the CEO. The mean, mode, and median salary are automatically computed, so the student can quickly see how easy it would be to give different impressions of the "average" salary in the organization, by choosing one or the other measure of central tendency. His colleague looks at the Web site and sends him an email with a little anecdote she wrote about "lying with statistics." He cuts and pastes it out of the email and adds it directly to the Web site. The faculty who worked on this, as well as the student programmer, used both their home computers and their computers at the university to build the site.

Who owns this digital content?

---

[152] Machrone, B. (2003). Turbotax and DRM: Why it matters. *PCMagazine, 22*(6), 55.

The issue might never become important if no one wants to buy or use the site (which is true of much of the content on the Web). But suppose a publisher approaches the instructor to buy the content for an off-the-shelf course they are building for corporations? The difficulty of untangling ownership issues in the digital, "cut and paste" world of content, has caused headaches and led to many lawsuits. The copyright and ownership issues have, for the most part, long been settled for live, instructor-led courses, but those models run into problems when we try to apply them to the digital setting. An instructor, for example, can be videotaped and his presentation archived on the Web for a future distance class, taught by someone else. Is that instructor entitled to royalties? Suppose a new instructor wants to update the statistics Web site to teach another section of the class. Should that instructor have the right to modify the original digital content? The logical approach to these issues is to decide in advance, through contracts or agreements, who owns what and who would be entitled to compensation for the use of the works. Universities, for example, having been burned by legal battles over such ownership issues, now attempt to negotiate ownership details in advance and put the agreements in writing.

Another troubling copyright issue for e-learning involves an educator's use of materials for the class. If the business statistics instructor has a video-clip of a highly paid CEO that he borrowed from the library, can he digitize it and add it to the site? He would be able to show the clip in his live classroom, thanks to the Copyright Act of 1976 and its so-called "classroom exemption" clause. That exemption, however, stipulates that the use of the copyrighted material in an educational setting has to occur in a non-profit institution, and only in a face-to-face classroom with students and teacher physically present. But can he make the clip accessible to his e-learning students who are enrolled? Copyright laws as they are interpreted for educational settings have not been able to keep up with the e-learning environment, although new laws are emerging that attempt to make materials more accessible while still protecting intellectual property rights. The Technology, Education, and Copyright Harmonization Act (TEACH Act) attempts to expand and clarify how educators can use copyrighted material in e-learning formats. For example, it removes the requirement that the classroom be a physical location.[153]

---

[153] Gasaway, L. N. (2001). Balancing copyright concerns: The TEACH Act of 2001. *Educause* Review, November/December, 82–83. Retrieved online August 15, 2002, from http://www.educause.edu/ir/library/pdf/erm01610.pdf

Finally, the easy accessibility of digital content, and the ease with which anyone can cut and paste portions of it into new products, creates a related challenge for educational settings: plagiarism. This has always been a problem and did not begin with e-learning, but the Internet has certainly made it far easier to do. Anyone can copy paragraphs out of a digital work they find on the Web and paste them into a term paper. Also, numerous Web sites offer to sell whole term papers for a fee, though they typically use a less incendiary name for their service, such as "research assistance." The Internet, however, offers a countermeasure for plagiarism. For a small fee, instructors can submit a paper to an online service that will compare the text to millions of online resources from which it could have been plagiarized, including the term paper mills. The report that comes back color codes the paragraphs that match existing work beyond reasonable credibility, and includes the URL address that may have been the source.

TECHNOLOGICAL CHALLENGES

E-learning has gone through many growing pains, technologically speaking. Arguably, the earliest incarnation of e-learning was a computer-aided multiuser instructional system called PLATO, dating back to the 1960s. This novel software platform was developed at the University of Illinois at Urbana-Champaign by the Computer-based Education Research Laboratory (CERL). The system evolved quickly, with its own authoring language, its own dedicated terminals with specialized keys for students, and a growing library of courseware modules and digital content. Much of the latter was developed by faculty and students who wrote modules that dealt with topics in mathematics, philosophy, foreign languages, and many other subjects. PLATO included early forms of groupware for collaborative work and discussions, and an online community of devoted adherents grew up around the project. Control Data Corporation, now defunct, took over the PLATO project and it re-emerged as CYBIS in the 1980s, with a more modern look and feel. By then the system had thousands of courseware modules, though many of them were already outdated.

PLATO and its various descendents died out, along with most of the aging courseware, proprietary terminals, and tangled royalty and payment schemes. The technological infrastructure for PLATO was part of the problem – it required an expensive mainframe and dedicated terminals. The authoring tools and user interfaces were proprietary and arcane. It took a considerable amount of intellectual energy, commitment, and capital to build a course, install the equipment, debug the network connections, set up the classroom administrative options, and train people to use the system. Courseware was often buggy, and connections would drop, frustrating students who were far more interested in learning the content than in beta-testing a new delivery format. When PLATO became commercialized under Control Data Corporation, lengthy negotiations and bitter legal disputes over licensing and access rights further disenchanted prospective users.

Despite the troubles PLATO encountered, interest in network and computer-based distributed learning certainly did not fade away, though its resurgence had to wait for widespread Internet access, better authoring tools, and the user-friendly Web. Now, the e-learning technology landscape includes a wealth of options, perhaps even too many. Initially, content developers learned to enjoy very capable authoring tools that would help them format pages for the Web, organize their materials, and insert multimedia elements. Courseware management systems entered the picture, which offered far more capability for the instructor and student to manage and navigate the online course. In addition to the authoring tools, these systems added progress tracking, test delivery, online discussion boards, assignment drop boxes, chat rooms, calendaring systems, virtual classrooms, and other features that made it easier to create the class, interact with students, manage class progress, and assess student learning.

The next generation of e-learning suites includes software products that allow instructors to manage the learning environment even more successfully, particularly for larger organizations that have or intend to have a broad portfolio of e-learning opportunities for their employees. For example, some of them offer content management capabilities so authors can easily deal with many versions of the same course module and collaborate on the creation of course materials.

An important technological challenge for e-learning will be to develop strategies and standards for courseware and online course management systems, especially to make it easier to catalog, share, and reuse valuable content. More standardization will also help ensure survivability despite changes in or even the demise of a particular platform. When courseware is developed in a proprietary format, as it was for PLATO, it relies completely on the continued existence of that infrastructure for its own life. Some Web-based course modules have also fallen into that trap, so modules built for one course management system have not been easily ported to another. We saw much courseware retired because it didn't survive the transition from Windows 98 to Windows 2000. Browsers also evolve and change, and courseware written and tested for one version may no longer work on the next, or on a competing browser product. The course management systems themselves are proprietary, so user profiles, usages statistics, and other kinds of tracking technologies are incompatible from system to system.

Efforts are underway to develop standards for development to reduce this confusion, so the courseware and systems developed are not so rigidly tied to particular platforms and can be reused in flexible ways. These efforts will improve accessibility, so that instructors hunting for modules on specific topics can locate the options and find what they are looking for with much less effort. Survivability and portability should improve, so that modules developed within one learning management system can be moved to another. For example, the Advanced Distributed Learning Initiative launched by the Department of Defense has been working out a set of standards called SCORM (Sharable Content Object Reference Model) to improve interoperability of course content modules. SCORM is built partly upon work by the Instructional Management System (IMS) project, which began in 1997 as an initiative of Educause, the nonprofit organization that promotes intelligent use of technology in higher education. XML (extensible markup language) plays a key role in these standards and will facilitate interoperability and interaction with other kinds of systems that are developed for Internet delivery. As IT professionals humorously point out, the great thing about standards is that there are so many from which to choose. Like most of the standards intended to ensure interoperability on the Internet, e-learning standards are still evolving and in flux. However, demand from savvy customers who want to purchase e-learning suites and digital content should nudge vendors toward the goal of interoperability.

Is Less More?

Students in e-learning programs have much to say about what works and what doesn't. In a chat session during online office hours, a student said, "This whole thing will work much better when we can all use videoconferencing and see each other." Another quickly responded, adding the comment to the scrolling chat screen, "You must be kidding – I'm in my pajamas and I want to stay that way!"

As learning management systems and e-learning suites become more feature-laden, there is a tendency to add many kinds of technology capabilities for students and to make more and more materials available. They can check the various discussion boards, join a group chat, watch some video clips in the multimedia room, enter a collaborative document editing area to work on their group project, respond to a class survey, vote on an issue, and check out the endless list of links in "additional resources," each of which takes them to another Web site filled with its own content. Noriko Hara and Rob Kling of Indiana University conducted an ethnographic study of students in a Web-based distance course and found an alarming number of students who were frustrated and in distress, especially because of communication problems, technical problems, and general overload.[154] Some were confused by the interfaces, the learning curves, and the vast array of options available to them. Many were overwhelmed by the sheer volume of messages and material they were expected to read.

These remarks and findings point to the need for caution. E-learning works better when simplicity is the guideline, so instructor and students can focus on the content rather than on the interfaces or gee-whiz technical capabilities, and so they can avoid drowning in too much irrelevant material and distractions. As the software, the standards, and the Internet itself mature, the capabilities may become more seamless so that students don't have to struggle for an hour figuring out how to download a plug-in that is needed to view one of the instructor's videos, or tinker with browser configurations. E-learning programs will be most valuable to the workplace and its employees if they stay focused on their main goal: learning.

---

[154] Hara, N., & Kling, R. (2000). Students' distress with a web-based distance education course: An ethnographic study of participants' experiences. CSI Working Papers, Center for Social Informatics, Indiana University. Retrieved July 10, 2002, from Indiana University Web site: http://www.slis.indiana.edu/CSI/Wp/wp00-01B.html

9 Workplace Surveillance and Privacy

"You have no privacy. Get over it."

– Scott McNealy, CEO of Sun Microsystems

The Internet and netcentric technologies open a window for the employee from the workplace to the rest of the world, but the window is not one way. Just as the employee can reach out electronically to anyone else on the globe with access to the network or to any Internet-connected source of information, the employer – and anyone else with the right tools – can use the same window to look in to observe and record the employee's activities. We are only just beginning to appreciate the implications of this feature of netcentricity, and what it may mean for privacy, productivity and performance, security, organizational relationships, management, stress levels, workplace violence, and job satisfaction. With the growing sophistication of the electronic devices that can be linked to the network – with or without a wire – surveillance programs in the workplace have multiplied and become much more powerful and pervasive. McNealy's alarming message is a chilling reminder of that immense power.

The American Management Association (AMA) surveys companies annually about their workplace monitoring and surveillance practices, and the number of companies that report active monitoring has been rising steadily. In 1997, about 35 percent of the companies were actively engaged in some type of surveillance of employees, which might include recording telephone conversations, storing and reviewing voice mail messages, examining computer files and email messages, and making video recordings. By 2000, this figure more than doubled, and almost three quarters of U.S. firms actively monitor their employees with electronic surveillance tools of one kind or another. Over half also monitor employees' use of the Internet, by logging Web sites visited or other types of tracking.[155]

How Are Employees Being Monitored?

According to the AMA surveys, Internet connection monitoring is the most commonly used form of surveillance, and more than half of the companies surveyed reported they monitored what sites people visited and how long they stayed. In 2000, the second most common form of surveillance involved the telephone. Forty-four percent reported that they logged time spent and number of calls made, but much fewer actually recorded the telephone conversations themselves (11.5 percent). In the follow-up conducted in 2001, however, monitoring of email messages overtook telephone monitoring. Almost half of the companies in 2001 reported they stored and reviewed email messages.

Other relatively common practices include storage and review of computer files and video surveillance for security purposes. Such cameras might be placed in hallways or over doorways to catch thieves walking out with equipment. Video was also used by some companies in the context of evaluating job performance rather than security, but by far fewer firms (11.7 percent). One of the least used surveillance techniques involved the storage and review of voice mail messages, though that also has been growing.

MONITORING THROUGH AUTHENTICATION

Employees are monitored through routine authentication processes when they attempt to gain access to resources, such as a building or a computer system, though the terms "monitor" and "surveillance" are not generally used in this context. To be sure employees are who they say they are, an employer can use one or more authentication strategies to authenticate them. These rely on three types of tests that assess what the person *knows*, what he *has*, or what he *is*.

Many authentication strategies use the first test, by asking the employee to type in a username, password, and PIN. If no one else knows those pieces of information, the employer can both authenticate the employee

---

[155] 2000 AMA Survey: Workplace Monitoring and Surveillance, and 2001 AMA Survey: Workplace Monitoring and Surveillance Policy and Practices. Retrieved February 15, 2003, from American Management Association Web site, AMA Research: http://www.amanet.org//research

and monitor the employee's activities whenever the password is used. Employers can also authenticate by relying on what an employee *has*, such as a driver's license, a passport, a social security card, or an identification card with a signature, magnetic stripe, photograph, microchip, or radio tag. Finally, employers can use what the person *is*, by confirming some characteristic of the employee that can be recorded and is individually unique for that person. A fingerprint, retinal scan, handprint, a face scan, or DNA would all qualify, as would a nod from someone who knows you personally and who is already trusted by the company to identify others.

The authentication strategies that verify you by what you know, what you have, or what you are vary with respect to security. Passwords are notoriously insecure because they can so easily be obtained or guessed. An astonishing number of people use their own name or the name of their spouse, child, or pet as their password. Technically inclined people add to that list references from favorite sci-fi books and movies, such as the call letters for the Star Trek Enterprise (NC1701). Also, because everyone has to come up with so many passwords, they often use the same one repeatedly for all the computer systems they want to access, or they recycle passwords from a small pool of favorites. Bruce Schneier, author of the classic *Applied Cryptography*, suggested that a very easy way to break into thousands of corporate networks would be to launch a free pornography Web site that only required visitors to create a username and password to access. Chances are, the visitors who registered would enter the same password they use for their corporate network, and they might also log in from work where the downloads take less time. Voila! The Web master of the porn site now has valid usernames along with their passwords and corporate network addresses.[156]

Authentication is critical for security and for keeping track of who does what in a corporate database. When an accounting clerk working in the financial system adds a charge to a customer account, the system will automatically stamp the database record with the clerk's username and the time of day so proper audit trails are created. The username is taken from the login name, so the clerk doesn't have to enter his initials on each record. In the past, the clerk would only log in to the system when he was going to enter transactions and would log out when he was done. The login name would only be used to record what the clerk did within the financial

---

[156] Mann, C. C. (2002). Homeland insecurity. *Atlantic Monthly, 290*(2), September, 81–102.

system. Now, however, because the network and the netcentric services support practically everything we do at work, the clerk logs in to the whole network as soon as he arrives and doesn't log out until he leaves work. The login name is not just available for stamping the financial transaction record, it is available to the system all day long. It can be used to track and "stamp" anything the person does on the computer, whether work related or not, and whether or not a stamp is required by the financial auditors. If you use the Internet to check on the weekend weather, the system has information about your whereabouts and what you are doing. If you use it to search for medical information about AIDS, the system can track that as well. Before the net, if we wanted to hear the weather report when we were at work we would have turned on the radio or picked up a newspaper. If we needed information about AIDS, we would head for the library or a doctor. Now we log in, authenticate, and leave tracks.

COMPUTER-BASED DESKTOP MONITORING

The growing sophistication of netcentric technologies makes the monitoring process easier to do, less costly for employers, more comprehensive, and also more timely. This is especially true for people who use a computer connected to a network most of the day. *Desktop Surveillance*, for example, is an inexpensive software product sold to companies that supports a host of surveillance options that can be configured by management based on the corporation's policies. It can monitor each employee's Internet use, block different kinds of sites, record time logged in and out, and alert administrators when an email goes out with any key words identified by management as triggers. The software can also be configured to take "snapshots" of what is on each computer screen at different times during the day, which would make it possible to view online chat sessions that aren't logged. Although the data collected would be immense, managers can also program the software to record every single keystroke each employee presses.

Another product, called *Surveillance Anywhere* from Omniquad, promises to track computer activity on any tagged computer, wherever the employee uses it. When the employee connects to the Internet, the log files and screen shots are transmitted to the employer's secure server and managers can check on them at any time. This means that an employee who uses a laptop provided by the company at home or on the road can also be under surveillance, even if they are not using the corporate network. Computer-based surveillance and Internet connection monitoring are becoming so prevalent that a new software industry, called *employee Internet management* or EIM, has grown up to respond to the demand. The market is expected to grow to a $562 million business by 2004 according to analysts at International Data Corporation's Internet Security Division.[157]

The technologies allow employers to examine just about anything an employee does with the computer, both by reviewing log files of activity and by monitoring keystrokes or screen shots in real time. The software or hardware in some cases can be installed directly on the employee's computer, or it can be installed remotely. For example, some monitoring software is installed using the "Trojan horse" approach. A user who wants to install a piece of software that is not related to monitoring may download it from the server, or open it from an email attachment. When the nonmonitoring software is installed, the monitoring software can be installed along with it, with or without the user's knowledge. Once in place, the monitoring software can record events, take snapshots, and transmit the information to the server – typically the system administrator – whenever the user is connected to the network. Clearly, technology is widely available to surreptitiously install monitoring software throughout an organization. Management has choices and decisions to make about informing the employees.

EMERGING VIDEO TECHNOLOGIES

Newer video-based techniques have become more cost effective, and they add significant capabilities to workplace surveillance possibilities. Video cameras, for example, have been used for some time, but the widespread availability and low cost of the button-sized Web cams have changed the dynamics of video-based workplace surveillance. The larger cameras installed mostly for security purposes are relatively easy to spot, but the tiny Web cams can easily be placed in inconspicuous locations. The images from such cameras can be transmitted through wires or wirelessly to central servers, viewed in real time, or stored for later review.

Increasing capabilities in facial recognition software have made video surveillance even more effective, especially as a means to identify and authenticate individuals through facial scans. The use of face recognition software by officials during the 2001 Super Bowl in Tampa, Florida, attracted considerable attention to this increasingly sophisticated video monitoring

---

[157] Katchaliya, R. (2001). Workplace surveillance: A $562 million dollar market by 2004. Retrieved April 12, 2003, from Privacy Foundation Web site: http://www. privacyfoundation.org/workplace/business

strategy, and the event triggered heated debate.[158] Law enforcement officials were able to store face scans of known terrorists, runaways, and sexual predators in a database and compare scans of people in the crowd to their files in real time. The scans operate somewhat like fingerprints, and geometrically identified points on the face are coded and stored for comparison purposes, much like the mathematically coded swirls, points, and bifurcations on a thumbprint. Viisage's "FaceFinder" product was also used in Florida's Ybor City as a means to identify possible criminals. Newer products in this technology line will permit storage of millions of facial scans for retrieval and comparison to live images.

Facial recognition technology represents a significant change in authentication capabilities, primarily because it is nonintrusive. Unlike fingerprints, it can be used to create a database record and then identify individuals in real time with or without their knowledge. It can also be used remotely, as in distance education programs, to authenticate the individual who is sitting at a computer terminal and taking a test. In the workplace, this kind of technology can be used for authenticating individuals as they enter buildings or access resources, or as a screening device before hiring.

LOCATION-AWARE TECHNOLOGIES

Technologies that can track and transmit an individual's location are also emerging. For example, cell phones are *location-aware* in the sense that there are means to identify the location of the cell phone. (A restaurant that has your cell phone number could call you when you are driving by around dinner time to tell you about tonight's specials.) Global positioning system technology (GPS), which triangulates signals from satellites to pinpoint an object's location anywhere on the planet, is becoming more cost-effective and is being built into many different devices. Automobile navigation systems make excellent use of GPS technology and can be used to navigate from one point to another. The driver enters the destination address, and the system computes the route, the driving distance, and the approximate time of arrival. The map appears on the small screen, showing the starting location. Once on the move, the navigation system issues friendly voice commands at just the right moment to remind the driver when to turn right or left, based on knowledge of the car's current location. GPS capability is also being added to personal digital assistants, so route mapping and driving directions can be linked to actual appointments entered into the date book.

---

[158] Keller, B. (2001). Face recognition software: Anti-terrorism tool and more. Gartner Research Services, Note Number COM-14-1814. Retrieved April 10, 2003, from Gartner Research Services.

SMART OBJECTS AND AUTO-IDENTIFICATION TECHNOLOGIES

The supranet that I discussed in earlier chapters expands the definition of the network well beyond the devices that are now linked to the Internet and other networks via wired or wireless connections. As technologies emerge that reduce the size and cost of computer-based intelligence, chips can be installed that will create many new categories of edge devices that go well beyond computers, cell phones, PDAs, Web cams, or beepers. These will make objects (including human beings) smarter, in the sense that the objects are capable of interacting with the network and other edge devices. These smart objects will play their own roles in the network, including as surveillance tools.[159]

Radio-frequency identification (RFID) is one of the technologies that makes objects smart so they can communicate with networks on their own. The e-tags used to allow cars to go through highway toll booths without stopping to hand over cash are one example of RFID. Another nonmilitary application of RFID is in livestock tagging, and many more are under development.

An e-tag is somewhat similar to a barcode, in the sense that both can be read electronically and both can be used to identify a particular item. However, the e-tag has an onboard silicon chip, which means that data can be written to the chip after installation. Also, e-tags do not need a line of sight to be read, as traditional barcodes do. Depending on the size of the e-tag and whether it has its own battery power, the tag can be read from much greater distances – hundreds of feet in some cases. Although passive tags can only be read, the active tags have both read and write capability so new information can be added as the object ages. Companies are racing to develop RFID technologies and e-tags that can be used in many new applications such as smart cards for security control, management of fleets, airline ticketing and baggage identification, package delivery, and hazardous waste tracking. For highly mobile work environments such as trucking or shipping, e-tags are enormously useful. When a physical object can – by itself – report its location, its identity, its movement history, its owner, and other characteristics, innovative applications are inevitable.

In the workplace, e-tagging will be used for tracking and identifying nonhuman physical objects and also for humans. They may be used to

---

[159] Magrassi, P., & Berg, T. (2002). A world of smart objects: The role of auto-identification technologies. Gartner Strategic Analysis Report, Note Number R-17-2243. Retrieved April 10, 2003, from Gartner Research Services.

add security controls in the workplace and to track patients in hospitals or institutions. Teachers may want to use them for field trips in which a few guides are responsible for keeping tabs on dozens of youngsters. The chips might also be placed in the kids' luggage or sports equipment bags to maintain surveillance on them as well.

Why Monitor the Workplace?

Corporate management has always monitored employees in one way or another, just to provide supervision if nothing else. The new tools, however, give management vastly more power and scope for surveillance, and one reason corporations are using them is simply that they are available and easy to implement. Yet surveillance is a complicated matter in the workplace, with both positive and negative consequences and important ethical implications. A comprehensive surveillance program may identify those "cyberslackers" who waste company time and bandwidth with their Internet shopping and portfolio management, but such a program may have hidden costs that are more difficult to capture, including reductions in workplace morale and productivity, higher turnover, and increased vulnerability to invasion of privacy lawsuits. How are employers evaluating the pros and cons, and why are the pros outweighing the cons in so many companies now?

Employers reported five major reasons for implementing surveillance programs in the American Management Association's survey. Ordered in terms of the companies' views of their importance, these were legal liability, security concerns, legal compliance, productivity measurement, and performance review. The fact that legal liability was listed as the most important reason and productivity and performance were at the bottom of the list may surprise many people. Monitoring has typically been used as a supervision strategy, and as a means for management to evaluate the performance of workers, ensure high levels of productivity, and provide feedback. However, the picture changed in the 1990s, particularly because of the important roles that email and the Internet began to play in the workplace.

LEGAL LIABILITY

A key motivation to launch electronic workplace surveillance programs involves legal concerns. The concerns are not about lawsuits by employees who might claim invasion of their privacy, but about litigations because of what their employees are doing that the employer does not know about, but should. Attorney Robert Mignin and his colleagues, writing for the *Employee Relations Law Journal*, describes the employer's obligation frankly: "Not only do private employers have a broad right to monitor the so-called work-related 'private affairs' of their employees, but the law, in many instances, virtually requires them to do so."[160] The laws they refer to relate especially to an employer's responsibility to prevent unlawful conduct by their employees, including engaging in harassment or negligently hiring people who do harm to others.

The legal history of an employer's liability in harassment cases is quite tangled, but the cases have generally affirmed that employers can certainly be held liable for the harassing behavior of their employees. When an employer learns of a situation that involves workplace harassment, it is the employer's responsibility to take corrective action to remedy the situation or face legal liability. However, the circumstances under which these principles apply are still rather murky. It is not entirely clear whether an employer knows, or should have known, about a harassment situation. One such case, *Ellerth vs. Burlington Industries*, involved a woman who was harassed by her supervisor with numerous sexually offensive comments and who eventually resigned because she found the situation unbearable. Even though the supervisor's threats to cause her problems if she didn't comply with his requests were never carried out and she never complained to anyone while she worked there, she sued Burlington for the harassment after she resigned. The District Court found in favor of the company. She appealed, and the Court of Appeals reversed the decision. The Supreme Court then affirmed the Court of Appeals decision, finding that the company could be held legally liable for harassment, even when she didn't report it.

Another key case in 1998 that followed a similarly tortuous path of court reversals involved a woman who worked as a lifeguard for the city of Boca Raton, Florida, and who was sexually harassed by two of her supervisors. In this case, the District Court ruled in her favor, but the Court of Appeals reversed their decision. The Supreme Court reversed the Court of Appeals, ruling that the city was indeed liable for the harassment of its employees.

One issue important in both cases involved the difference between "quid pro quo" harassment versus the more general "hostile work environment." Typically, courts had held employers liable for the former, but the latter was

---

[160] Mignin, R. J., Lazar, B. A., & Friedman, J. M. (2002). Privacy issues in the workplace: A post-September 11 perspective [Electronic version]. *Employee Relations Law Journal, 28*(1), 7–23.

more difficult to prove, because the employee had not suffered any loss of job or reduced compensation because of the harassment. Neither woman was a victim of quid pro quo harassment, because there was no evidence of any job discrimination or demotion. Another issue that made these two cases unusual was that neither woman had complained to the company or city during the time the harassment was going on, so the employer apparently did not know about it. The Supreme Court thus concluded that a worker could hold a company liable even though the worker does not complain, and even though no negative consequences result. Both of these ingredients became a warning to employers that they needed not only to have harassment policies clearly in place; they must also be sure they were being enforced. Many companies interpreted this to mean that they had a much larger and broader responsibility for monitoring the workplace for signs of harassment, even when no one complained. Ellen Bravo of the National Association of Working Women pointed out that companies had been taking a "hear-no-evil, see-no-evil" attitude that's been a big problem in the workplace. The Supreme Court has taken away the incentive for employers "to bury their heads in the sand."[161]

A third case shows how the courts are looking at activities that occur outside the workplace, in cyberspace. The first female captain of Continental's A300 aircraft filed a hostile work environment complaint against the company because of harassing and insulting gender-based comments that were posted by other Continental employees on an electronic bulletin board, called "Crew Members Forum." The board was hosted by CompuServ, not Continental, and pilots had to pay privately to subscribe to it. Nevertheless, Continental had selected that provider to host other services for the pilots, so it was convenient for pilots to also use CompuServ for other things. The New Jersey court granted Continental's motion to dismiss, and the appeals court agreed, stating that Continental could not be held vicariously liable for the pilots' defamatory comments on the bulletin board because the company did not require its employees to access it. However, the New Jersey Supreme Court disagreed and reversed the decision. Their conclusion was that:

> "Although employers do not have a duty to monitor private communications of their employees, employers do have a duty to take effective measures to stop co-employee harassment when the employer knows or has reason to

[161] Grimsley, K. D. (1998). For employers, a blunt warning. *The Washington Post*, June 27, 1998, A10. Retrieved April 10, 2003, from http://www.washingtonpost.com

know that such harassment is part of a pattern of harassment that is taking place in the workplace and in settings that are related to the workplace."[162]

The implication is that an electronic bulletin board, even though hosted outside the workplace in cyberspace, can still be a setting "related to the workplace."[163] Also, finding out about co-employee harassment is not very easy without actually monitoring employees' communications.

Though these legal decisions may have been positive in some respects, they ushered in a rapidly growing trend toward workplace surveillance that few predicted at the time. Employers, fearing lawsuits, stepped up their surveillance programs dramatically, and as easy methods to implement electronic surveillance became available, they adopted them. Jeffrey Rosen of George Washington University Law School argues that the emphasis on the employer's role in preventing a "hostile environment" in the workplace has backfired. He writes, " . . . its inadvertent side effects now threaten the boundaries between the public and private spheres. It is wrong, in a liberal society, that sexual expression without tangible employment consequences – overheard jokes, private e-mail, and consensual affairs between colleagues – should be monitored by employers and punished by the state."[164]

SECURITY CONCERNS AND COMPANY LEAKS

Employers cite security concerns as the second most important reason for monitoring the workplace. This covers a broad range of issues that overlap somewhat with the legal concerns, but some of them are focused on protecting the company's secrets, especially from internal leaks. For example, the Denver Broncos implemented *eSniff*, a widely used software surveillance product. The monitoring was designed to make sure playbook secrets were not passed around via email or leaked outside the team. The administrators entered the words "first 15" into the database of phrases they wanted the system to track, to be sure any use of that phrase would trigger alarms. "First 15" is shorthand for the first fifteen plays planned for the next game.

---

[162] Tammy S. Blakey vs. Continental Airlines, Inc. (June 1, 2000). Supreme Court of New Jersey, 164 N.J. 38; 751 A.2d 538; 2000 N.J. LEXIS 650. Retrieved April 10, 2003, from LexisNexis Academic Database.

[163] Feldman, C. (2000). Minimizing employer liability for employee Internet use. *Los Angeles Business Journal*, July 31. Retrieved April 10, 2003, from FindArticles. Com database.

[164] Rosen, J. (2000). Fall of private man. *New Republic*, June 12, 22–29.

Leaks of company secrets have been a problem in the television industry as well, in which employees who have access to scripts have shared them with fans before they played on the air. For instance, *X-Files* scripts were auctioned on e-Bay before they aired on television, at least before the studio began monitoring email traffic.

Since 9/11, security has received much greater attention in the workplace and more aggressive monitoring is the consequence. Concern about the potentially illegal activities of employees, for which employers could be held responsible, has become especially heightened in the wake of terrorist acts of 2001. The Patriot Act, subsequently passed in the United States, gives law enforcement agencies far greater power to begin electronic surveillance of an office or workplace without a court order and without warning even the employer in advance. Law enforcement officials searching for evidence of terrorist activity by monitoring the computer systems of a workplace may also find evidence of other illegal activities, such as downloads of copyrighted music or child pornography. Employers are thus even more motivated to make sure their systems are squeaky clean and contain no compromising information.

Concerns about Productivity

Although legal liability and security are the primary reasons employers are moving toward electronic monitoring, concerns about productivity are also very compelling. The Internet has an endless variety of amusements and attractions that can easily divert employees from productive work. Many employers consider "cyberslacking," in the form of off-task Internet surfing, to be a major problem in the workplace. Employees can hunt for their next job online, communicate with family and friends, check their portfolios, bid on auctions, gamble, engage in day-trading, shop, or just surf. Some have started sideline businesses on E-bay and spend considerable time posting their inventory for auction and tracking the bids. On the darker end of the spectrum, employees also spend time downloading pornography or viewing XXX-rated Web sites, or exchanging copyrighted music or software illegally. When Xerox learned of abuses in their workforce, they found some employees who spent eight hours a day cyberslacking, getting literally nothing done on the job.

CYBERSLACKING: HOW MUCH IS GOING ON?
The extent of cyberslacking in the workplace is very difficult to estimate. Vendors of surveillance software estimate on the very high side, naturally.

One company labeled cyberslacking an insidious, profit-eating virus, costing corporate America more than $1 billion a year in wasted computer resources, and that figure doesn't even include the billions wasted due to lowered productivity. Software maker Websense estimated $63 billion in lost productivity, but such numbers have to be taken with a grain of salt, given their source.

Anonymous surveys of employees suggest that most admit to at least some personal Internet surfing during work time. Vault.com's informal survey suggested that 90 percent of the respondents did some recreational surfing during office hours, and most workers also use their company email for the occasional personal email.

Much of what we know about the extent and cost of cyberslacking comes from relatively unreliable surveys, and also from anecdotes. One manager in an Arizona factory, for example, was convinced one of his employees was using her computer for too many personal projects, even though the company had a policy stating that the Internet was for business use only.[165] The employee vigorously denied the charges, but when the manager began monitoring Internet usage, the statistics painted a very different picture. The manager could provide exact dates, Web sites, and the amount of time the employee was spending at inappropriate sites.

Glen Eastman, employed by Compaq for nineteen years, was fired for a different kind of Internet abuse. His managers found emails in his account indicating he was starting an airplane-repair business on the side. Cyberslacking in the form of job hunting is particularly troubling to employers. One employee of a Hollywood movie studio, who for obvious reasons preferred to remain anonymous, told a reporter, "The bulk of my time online is spent looking for work elsewhere." [166]

A DILEMMA FOR EMPLOYERS

Should employers establish policies that prohibit all cyberslacking to stop what they think could be a productivity hemorrhage? Personal Internet surfing on the job might detract from productivity, but it can also improve workplace morale and save employees time. In some cases, it *increases* productivity because workers can accomplish personal errands online without taking long lunch breaks, leaving early, or logging "sick days." Employers

---

[165] Vanscoy, K. (2001). What your workers are really up to [Electronic version]. *Smartbusinessmag.com, 14*(9), 50–54.

[166] Naughton, K., Raymond, J., Shulman, K., & Struzzi, D. (1999). Cyberslacking. *Newsweek, 134*(22), 62–66. Retrieved February 15, 2003, from Academic Search Elite Database.

that restrict all personal use and implement comprehensive monitoring programs are sending a message to the workforce, intended or not, that the corporation does not trust its employees.

Walter Block of the Department of Economics and Finance at the University of Central Arkansas believes there is little new about cyberslacking. Employees could play poker or solitaire with physical cards long before they could play games on the net, and they could use a typewriter to write personal letters during work time. He states, "Yes, in the days of yore one could not shop while still at the desk or workbench. But an employee could peruse advertisements in the aforementioned newspapers and magazines, clip them out, and plan on a shopping spree."[167]

Block's points are valid, but the context of slacking off is dramatically altered because of netcentric technologies. When slacking is monitored by a supervisor, the employee knows when the supervisor is around, looking over his shoulder. When the network is doing the monitoring, it is far more pervasive. Another difference in context involves what it means to "look busy" in the age of desktop computers. The visual cues that managers can use to observe and evaluate whether employees are on task are quite different for cyberslacking compared to more traditional versions of goofing off at work. Two employees who set up a chess game or deal a hand of poker at work would be far more visible compared to one who was playing against a computer in a small, easily minimized window on the computer screen. In fact, while at work, an employee who is enthusiastically viewing the computer screen and typing rapidly on the keyboard appears to be working very hard to a manager who passes by. If the manager starts to glance at the screen, the window with the gambling casino on it can be quickly minimized with a keystroke. The same manager who passed the next employee who was reading a book at his desk might assume he was the slacker, not the Internet surfer. A security guard once popped into my office when I was reading a book and remarked, "I see you're not busy now so I'd like to ask you about the locks outside." When I am working at the computer, colleagues are much more likely to approach with, "Sorry to interrupt you but . . ."

Block suggests that employers should use a profit-maximizing strategy to make decisions about how much cyberslacking should be tolerated and proposes that managers use a trial and error approach. If productivity declines with a very restrictive policy, employers should loosen up. However, organizations create considerable confusion in their workforces when they

---

[167] Block, W. (2001). Cyberslacking, business ethics and managerial economics [Electronic version]. *Journal of Business Ethics, 33*(3), 225–232.

are vague or inconsistent about such policies, and also much dissatisfaction when they are slippery about what kinds of monitoring is underway and how the information is used.

Many organizations state in their policies that "some" or "limited" personal Internet use is permitted but leave it to the supervisors to determine who is exceeding this rather vague guideline. This approach, however, is gaining popularity because it is flexible. It leaves judgments about an employee's productivity in the hands of the managers who should have a broader understanding of the individual's overall contribution, accomplishments, and time demands. An employee who puts in many hours of work on the weekend, for example, would not deserve a reprimand for finishing up the holiday shopping online during work hours. Nevertheless, the policy would cover egregiously inappropriate use.

Electronic Performance Monitoring

Concerns about performance fell low on the list of important drivers for surveillance programs, according to the AMA survey. Yet historically, the main reasons for monitoring employees revolved around management's interest in improving and evaluating performance. Clerical workers and others who perform relatively simple, repetitive tasks, have been the most likely to be monitored electronically, along with people who communicate with customers on the phone who may have conversations taped for later review.

Electronic monitoring gets mixed reviews with respect to its effectiveness as a means to improve performance. It has been linked to increased levels of performance but also to higher stress levels in some studies. Monitored workers often report that the experience is highly stressful for them, especially if they think their performance is being individually assessed and graded in some way. Also, some research suggests that workers who are monitored for performance are less satisfied with both the job and the supervisor.[168]

MONITORING, SOCIAL CONTEXT, AND STRESS

The results from research on performance monitoring are complex, partly because monitoring occurs in the workplace, which is a social context with many variables that can interact with the surveillance experience. The

[168] Aiello, J. R., & Shao, Y. (1993). Electronic performance monitoring and stress: The role of feedback and goal setting. In M. J. Smith & G. Salvendy (Eds.), *Human-computer interaction: Applications and case studies*. Amsterdam: Elsevier Science.

monitoring may occur while individuals are working together in groups, or it may affect individuals working alone. Managers can choose to aggregate the monitoring results for large groups of employees as a means to assess group performance and target overall process improvements, or they might use the results to evaluate individuals.

In one laboratory study, for example, John R. Aiello and Kathryn J. Kolb of Rutgers University attempted to tease out some of the social variables that interact with monitoring on employee behavior and attitudes. They assigned participants to one of nine different groups to work on a data entry task and assessed their typing skills before the experiment began. Then they manipulated the social context of the task and the nature of the monitoring. Individuals were assigned to one of three different social contexts. In the most "social" context, the researchers put the subjects together into teams and gave them activities to perform that would lead to group cohesion and a sense of group identity. For example, the teams worked together on a brainstorming project to come up with new ideas for using the student identification card. Then the team members were asked to respond to a "pseudo-projective" test individually, which involved answering questions about the meaning of an inkblot. After a period of time, the researchers gave each group bogus positive feedback about their performance, telling each group that their performance was "among the best of the groups who had participated to date." They also received bogus feedback about the inkblot results: Each team was told that they had received unusually similar scores on that assessment, and their "inner traits" must be quite compatible. The goal of these deceptions was to encourage group identity and cohesion.

The second social context involved a nominal group or aggregation, in which the team members performed similar tasks in the presence of their group members but did not interact, and did not receive the bogus feedback. The control social context was not social at all – individuals worked alone, with no one else present.

The researchers also manipulated the type of monitoring the participants were led to believe would occur. Some were told the supervisor would be electronically monitoring the performance of their individual work, while others were told that only group performance scores would be evaluated. The control groups were not told anything about monitoring at all.

In terms of performance, the monitoring had complex effects depending on how skillful the subject was at the data entry task to begin with. Those who were highly skillful did more work under individual monitoring and far less when they were not being monitored at all. Those who were least skilled to begin with did better when they were not monitored. Stress levels were highest for those who were individually monitored and lowest for those who were not monitored at all. Subjects, who were monitored as groups, fell in the middle in terms of stress. People who worked in the cohesive groups also reported lower stress levels.

This study suggests that people who are doing tasks they find relatively easy show better performance if they are monitored, but their performance will suffer if the tasks are more complex. Monitoring, especially individual monitoring with no social group present to provide some measure of support, appears to add a stressor. The effects of this stressor depend partly on the complexity of the task. When the task is easy, the stressor increases the level of arousal so performance increases. For a complex task, however, the optimal level of arousal is lower, so the added stress makes performance decline.

FOCUSING ATTENTION ON QUALITY OR QUANTITY

In industrial settings, a key reason for comprehensive workplace monitoring programs is to improve productivity in assembly lines. These programs watch for slowdowns or bottlenecks and make changes to eliminate the problem area. Then, of course, the bottleneck moves somewhere else, and the process starts over. This approach has dramatically improved the speed of the process, but it also introduces considerable stress for the workers whose work is constantly expected to get faster and faster. It also creates an intense focus on whatever aspect of performance the monitoring program is evaluating. When an electronic monitoring program assesses just a few of the components that go into an employee's performance, it is reasonable to assume the employee will shift focus to the monitored assessments and ignore or downplay the others. For example, the assembly line worker would ignore quality if the monitoring program measures only the *number* of widgets installed per unit time.

Jeffrey M. Stanton and Amanda L. Julian investigated how workers reacted to electronic monitoring programs that emphasized either quality or quantity in a laboratory study involving a data correction task.[169] The subjects attempted to make corrections in a database containing mailing addresses by comparing each record to paper forms. All of them were told that both accuracy and speed were important for the task, but subjects received different instructions about what the electronic system would be monitoring during the task. Different groups were told that the system would record

---

[169] Stanton, J. M., & Julian, A. L. (2002). The impact of electronic monitoring on quality and quantity of performance. *Computers in Human Behavior, 18,* 85–101.

quantity, quality, both, or neither. The measurement of quantity involved a tally of the number of addresses they attempted to correct, whereas the measure of quality assessed how accurately they corrected each of the records they attempted.

For the most part, the students allocated their efforts based on their perceptions of what the monitoring system was monitoring, not based on the initial instructions from the "supervisor" about both quantity and quality being important. Subjects who thought quantity alone was being monitored tackled the largest number of records, but their quality score was among the lowest. They also emphasized quantity somewhat more when they thought the monitoring system was watching both quantity and quality. When the subjects were asked about their satisfaction with the task, the ones who thought quality was what the system was monitoring reported the most satisfaction. Those who thought the system was just measuring quantity were the least satisfied with the task. However, they did report the highest motivation to perform and complete it.

WHY USE ELECTRONIC PERFORMANCE MONITORING?

In the workplace, findings like the ones I have been describing present a difficult dilemma for employers, because electronic performance monitoring systems have both negative and positive impacts on workers. They can get employees to move faster on the simpler tasks, and they can promote and document positive behavior. A video camera on a bank teller and customer, for example, helps ensure a high level of customer service in addition to protecting the bank from robbers. However, such systems tend to reduce job satisfaction, and they may also discourage employees from focusing on important components of performance that are not measured by the electronic monitor. Unlike a live supervisor, who can assess many aspects of an employee's performance, the electronic performance monitor would only be able to assess certain aspects – especially those that are easiest to measure quantitatively.

Some employees – perhaps burned by biased performance evaluations in the past – say they are in favor of electronic performance monitoring because they believe it will be a fairer and less subjective measure of their performance compared to the supervisor's opinion. Some also use it to monitor their own output and adjust their work patterns based on the feedback. They see it as little different from other quantitative measures of performance, such as total sales volume or number of returning customers. Nevertheless, many employees find electronic performance monitoring to be offensive and intrusive, and they resist its implementation in the workplace.

The Internet and Disinhibition

The Internet and netcentric technologies have enabled a dazzling array of capabilities for workplace surveillance. Ironically, the same technologies have drawn out behaviors in employees that make employers extremely concerned about what their workforce is doing. As I discussed in much greater depth in *The Psychology of the Internet*,[170] the Internet is a social environment in which people are acting and interacting in sometimes startling ways. An environment and its characteristics can strongly influence how a person chooses to behave. We have generally underestimated how the characteristics of the Internet itself affect our behavior, the way we interact with one another online, and how we form impressions of other people.

Early research on computer-mediated communication demonstrated that when people are interacting over an electronic medium – whether it is a chat session or email – they can become disinhibited. They may type remarks that they would not have uttered in a face-to-face setting because the social cues that create constraints or encourage civility are lacking. Sitting at a computer terminal, people's sense of self-awareness is lower, and the feedback they receive from coworkers is neither immediate nor high in media richness. For example, if I send a joke by email, I can't see your arched brow if you interpret the joke as offensive, so I can't immediately retract it or apologize. The Internet environment does not support the nuanced feedback that we constantly use to gauge the impression we are making, or the effects of our actions on others. If you don't reply to my emailed joke, I might assume that you found it amusing or passed it along, when in fact, you were deeply offended.

In some cases, the disinhibiting influence can lead to very troubling behavior in the workplace. For example, a worker at Dow Chemical complained about seeing an offensive email on a coworker's screen, and the company responded by looking into the email of more than 7,000 employees. The enormous collection of violent pornography they found astounded management and union officials. More than fifty employees were fired, and hundreds were suspended for their inappropriate behavior. The employees were passing images around via the net, and they believed their email was private. Corporate email is not private, but a more fundamental question is whether the same workers would have used postal mail – which is

[170] Wallace, P. (1999). *The psychology of the Internet.* New York: Cambridge University Press.

private – to pass around 8×10 pornographic glossies. Or would they have just handed a stack of photographs to a coworker in the company rest room? I doubt it. The characteristics of the email environment, with its physical distance, misleading perceptions of privacy, and lowered self-awareness, are such that individuals may sometimes engage in behavior that would be highly uncharacteristic in a face-to-face setting. The environment itself causes disinhibition.

The American Management Association's workplace surveillance surveys have found that a surprisingly high number of firms have taken disciplinary actions against employees for unacceptable use of email or the Internet. More than 46 percent, for example, have disciplined an employee for sending sexually suggestive or explicit material via office email, and more than a third report action against employees for downloading or viewing pornography. Were all these people hiding porno magazines in their office desks before the Internet came along, and management just didn't stumble upon it? Or did the disinhibiting effects of the Internet environment combine with the easy availability of sexually explicit material online to promote this kind of inappropriate workplace behavior?

The disinhibiting influence of computer-mediated communications also makes email, in particular, a prime target for investigators who are searching for evidence in criminal or civil suits. Despite endless warnings about the lack of privacy in corporate email, and numerous high-profile cases in which email became critical evidence in lawsuits, employees continue to send incriminating, or at least injudicious, email. Archived emails provided crucial evidence against Microsoft in the government's antitrust suit, for example. Employees frequently discussed extremely aggressive tactics in their emails that were later resurrected by prosecutors to demonstrate antitrust activity. The main thrust of that prosecution involved Microsoft's attempt to integrate Internet Explorer browser into the operating system as an attack on Netscape's browsing software. Ironically, despite that bitter experience from the release of internal emails, more incriminating emails from Microsoft continue to emerge years later and are leaked to the press. One released in May 2002 suggests that tactics similar to the ones used by Microsoft against Netscape would be used against the streaming media industry, which allows users to view video footage or play music online.[171]

Email communication plays a major role in government investigations, such as those involving Enron, WorldCom, and Arthur Andersen. On

[171] Wilson, D. (2002). More embarrassing Microsoft email. May 3, 2002. Retrieved February 10, 2003, from CNN Web site: http://www.cnn.com

August 29, 2002, *The Washington Post* featured snippets from three emails exchanged by WorldCom execs that pointed to attempts to cover up accounting frauds. The first is a simple and routine email from a staffer who emails a copy of a report on capital expenditures to the finance managers of the company, not realizing that it contained incriminating information. The second is from Buford Yates, WorldCom CPA, who was director of general accounting, and who has since been indicted for conspiracy to hide operating expenses in the capital budget to make the company look far more profitable than it was. His email, in reply to the forwarded report but directed only to David Myers, WorldCom controller, reads, "Where do I sign my confession?" Myers follows up abruptly, to two other finance managers: "Why did you distribute this report? I thought we were never again distributing this ... do not distribute again."[172]

The Internet's power to promote disinhibition is apparently quite strong. It can blind people to a normal concern for prudence and confidentiality, even when they know their messages will be archived. They might even be published in the newspaper or required by subpoena. Events like these make the case for workplace surveillance even more compelling.

Developing and Implementing Monitoring Programs

In response to the many drivers I've been discussing, the widespread adoption of workplace surveillance programs occurred very quickly and continues to expand. Many corporations are making serious blunders as they rush to incorporate the latest surveillance technologies, alienating employees, drawing fire from privacy advocates, and facing litigation for invasion of privacy.

CLARIFYING THE POLICIES

One troublesome blunder is failure to clarify the policies the corporation maintains with regard to computer use, Internet access, and monitoring procedures. Although most corporations have acceptable use policies for information technology in place, many of them are buried in employee handbooks and not widely circulated. Some read like legal documents, so even if employees are confronted with them as soon as they log in, they will click the "I AGREE" button without ever reading them – much like they do when they install new software and a window appears that displays

---

[172] Krim, J. (2002). Fast and loose at WorldCom. *The Washington Post*, August 29, 2002, A1, A12–A13.

ten pages of fine print to state the license agreement. This exchange on a Vault.com discussion forum about Internet surfing shows how vague employees often are about their corporation's appropriate use and surveillance policies:

Surfing while Working
Author: Anonymous
Date: Sep 19, 2000 9:13 PM EST
Has anyone gotten in trouble for surfing at work? I surf and so far it has been cool. Anyone else have different experience?

yeah
Author: Anonymous
Date: Sep 20, 2000 12:09 PM EST
I had a UM from another team tell my PM and UM that I was surfing. Watch your back.

Use Common Sense
Author: Anonymous
Date: Sep 24, 2000 9:52 AM EST
I've heard that IS runs jobs at the end of the month to look at Internet usage. Associates have been fired for going to inappropriate (i.e. porn) sites while on the job.

However, if you are on the Internet checking out your stocks or getting some other type of information you should be okay. Just try to keep your usage down and close out the Internet window when you're not using it. High usage will raise a red flag. It would probably be a good idea not to go job hunting through the Internet from work.

FYI: I've been in TBA for 5 years and I justify my Internet surfing as "If [company name] expects me to work these long hours, they need to expect me to take care of some of my personal things while I'm at work."

Another message, from a different thread, showed that the corporation was monitoring their employees' use of the Internet even when it didn't appear to involve use of corporate resources at all. In this case, the employer was monitoring external job posting sites:

Big Brother
Author: Anonymous
Date: Sep 27, 2000 6:55 PM EST
Not that big brother, the other one.
I heard a very disturbing trend at [company name]: policing the world outside of [company name]. A friend of mine was pulled into a jointwork room to "discuss" why her resume was on the internet. She had told her manager that she wasn't happy or challanged with her role, and thought this to be the right thing to do. Not only did the manager get mad, because it made her look bad, but HR wanted

to know when it was posted, what she was looking for, and her timeframe. They stated that they needed to do future planning and wanted to know when her last day would be. Needless to say, she left that week. Have you ever worked with a recruiter that won't talk to you because you work for [company name]? There is a new trend that [company name] is not only paying firms to not work with you, but that they also expect those firms to then tell [company name] who you are.

BE CAREFUL – We're not in Kansas anymore, Toto.

Many employees are not certain what is allowed and what is not, what kinds of monitoring are in place, and what might be done with the information. Corporations should be very upfront about their policies and communicate them in clear language. They should also ensure employees know that policies will be enforced and disciplinary action taken if warranted. Telling employees that all nonbusiness use of computer and network resources is prohibited, but then never enforcing that policy is an approach that can create confusion and paranoia in an organization. The man who was fired from Compaq after nineteen years for the three emails involving his personal business was especially bitter because others in the office were also using corporate resources for private entrepreneurial activities – selling Amway products. Though the "everyone else is doing it" defense does not hold up in court, the inconsistency can create difficult problems for workplace morale.

DESIGNING THE POLICIES

Deciding what policies to establish and how to monitor behavior depend partly on the nature of the organization. There is no "one size fits all." Some corporations may need extremely tight restrictions for security or liability reasons, and they may also have compelling reasons to implement very comprehensive surveillance programs. Others may prefer to use Internet access and personal use as perks to encourage employee commitment and retention. These same organizations may choose not to monitor at all and rely instead on traditional supervision and supportive human resource departments to make sure that employees who do have complaints about a hostile work environment will air them.

Research in organizational behavior and psychology has clearly demonstrated that employee participation is a key ingredient in obtaining buy-in and acceptance, especially for controversial and sensitive practices such as workplace monitoring. When employees have a voice in the design of policies, they are more likely to consider them fair and accept them. Elizabeth A. Douthitt and John R. Aiello of Rutgers University found this to be the case in a laboratory study.[173] Students were assigned to either the high-voice or low-voice condition, in which they had varying levels of input about how their work on an experimental computer analysis task would be designed, evaluated, and monitored. The "high-voice" group was able to communicate their opinions to the supervisor and make various choices about how the work should be done, but the "low-voice" group had no such opportunity. The subjects who were invited to participate in the planning viewed the evaluation process as fairer, compared to those who had no options. Both groups found the task reasonably satisfying when they were not monitored, but only the high-voice subjects thought so when the monitoring was going on. In fact, their satisfaction with the task was even higher under the monitoring condition than it was when they weren't monitored.

PROVIDING RATIONALE AND WARNING

Corporations can also make missteps when they fail to explain *why* they are implementing a surveillance program, or start it up without telling the employees about it. Some corporate managers may think they shouldn't warn employees because they want to catch a suspect in the act, and the warning would cause the employee to clean things up before the monitoring begins. However, the loss of trust among all employees will likely outweigh the benefits of trapping a single offender.

Audra D. Hovorka-Mead and her colleagues in the Department of Management at University of Wisconsin at La Crosse found that advance notification and clear rationale were critical ingredients in the reactions of employees to a monitoring program in a field study at an amusement park.[174] The lifeguards were told in advance that they would be monitored by nonemployee private detectives using video cameras. The lifeguards all knew when the detectives were on the premises making tapes by using their walkie-talkies to give their coworkers the heads up. In contrast, the ticket agents, food service personnel, and gift shop employees were not told about the monitoring in advance. Many of them only found out about it when management began using the tapes for disciplinary action later in the summer for misdeeds recorded on tape, such as letting someone into the park

---

[173] Douthitt, E. A., & Aiello, J. R. (2001). The role of participation and control in the effects of computer monitoring on fairness perceptions, task satisfaction, and performance. *Journal of Applied Psychology, 86*(5), 867–874.

[174] Hovorka-Mead, A. D., Ross, W. H., Jr., Whipple, T., & Renchin, M. B. (2002). Watching the detectives: Seasonal student employee reactions to electronic monitoring with and without advance notification. *Personnel Psychology, 55*, 329–362.

without a ticket. All the seasonal employees filled out questionnaires to assess their opinions of the monitoring and also to find out whether they intended to return to work for the park the next year.

The surveys showed that those who had advance notification of the monitoring thought the process was fairer and that the consequences were more just in terms of the performance evaluations and reprimands. The employees who were told in advance also felt that they were more valued by the organization. Their beliefs about the fairness of the monitoring procedure were critical to whether they said they intended to return. The researchers followed up the next year and found that the employees' predictions about not returning were not just bluffs, at least not for most of them. More than half of the workers who said they would return actually did, but less than a fourth of the ones who said it was unlikely they would return because of the monitoring came back the next year.

Employees also react to monitoring more favorably if the employer provides a good rationale for implementing it. In a follow-up study, Hovorka-Mead and her colleagues conducted a lab study that assessed how seasonal workers perceived hypothetical scenarios in which the quality of the justification for monitoring varied. A high-quality justification, for example, read:

> "The supervisor explains that this type of monitoring is necessary to insure the safety of those entering the park – that lives might be at stake and hidden monitoring was important to see if employees (either ticket agents or lifeguards) were actually performing their duties properly; thus the monitoring could save the organization several thousand dollars in liability insurance."

This rationale was convincing. It led the subjects to conclude that the monitoring was fair and necessary, both in terms of how it was being implemented and how it would be used to evaluate performance. Even a weaker justification in which the supervisor explains that "management just wants to make sure employees are following the rules" was far better than no justification.

The conclusion from this and other research studies is that employers will have more success if they allow employees to offer input on a surveillance system, provide them with advance notice, and ensure they explain the reasoning behind the program. Many managers have assumed that most employees would object to monitoring no matter how they implemented it, so they did not give sufficient attention to factors that would increase employee acceptance.

EMPLOYEE REACTIONS TO MONITORING

As the research shows, employee reactions to surveillance vary considerably, and some of the variance depends on how the program is introduced, how the information is used, and whether a compelling rationale is offered. When a corporation introduces it with care, many employees think it is appropriate and necessary. Jeffrey M. Stanton and E. M. Weiss conducted an exploratory study of employee comments, made anonymously in response to a question they posed on the Web:

> "Next, please discuss any technology your company uses to track your work performance. Some companies use computer monitoring, email monitoring, phone monitoring, security cameras, and/or geographic tracking (for example, of company trucks used by employees). Your company may use technology to track your work in other ways as well. How are these technologies useful or helpful to you? How are they annoying, undignified, or disturbing? Or perhaps you don't even notice these techniques in use?"[175]

Note that the question prompted respondents to think of both positive and negative aspects of their company's monitoring program. The researchers used content analysis to code the open-ended comments and developed a coding scheme to categorize the different reactions. About half of the respondents said they were not monitored at all, and of those that were, most of the comments indicated that the employee was not bothered by the monitoring. Most thought it was appropriate and justified. Some, however, were far more concerned, especially when the rationale and policies were vague. One employee commented,

> "I know that email sent via the company server is not confidential and could potentially be monitored. I also know that the Web sites you visit and how much time you spend at them are known to the MIS people. However, I don't know if they are being monitored with the intention of tracking your work habits or for other reasons. It's a little disconcerting that your private emails or your Web research that you do off hours could be tracked if someone really wants to."

Anthony M. Townsend and James T. Bennett point out that employees strongly object to the highly pervasive monitoring that seems to be driven by the company's profit motive. The monitoring becomes a "paranoia-inducing organizational omniscience of every aspect of an employee's

---

[175] Stanton, J. M., & Weiss, E. M. (2000). Electronic monitoring in their own words: An exploratory study of employees' experiences with new types of surveillance. *Computers in Human Behavior, 16,* 423–440.

life . . . [Employees] begin to see themselves as the inmates of a technological panoptikon."[176] Clearly, corporations that implement programs without thinking through the ethical implications, rationale, and consequences
with respect to employee reactions, are going to have problems.

The Honorable Edith H. Jones of the United States Court of Appeals wrote
an especially scathing letter to the chairman of the Committee on Automation and Technology because of the way that committee had implemented
a monitoring program for the judiciary. She endorses the need for certain
kinds of monitoring, but objects strenuously to many of the features of the
program – especially the way it was introduced. Here are key excerpts from
that letter, dated August 18, 2001:

> We objected to the following features of the program . . . .
> (5) The program was ordered and directed from Washington without prior
> knowledge of or notice to or consultation with any but a very few judges.
> (6) Finally, the Internet monitoring was neither revealed to all the judges
> at the time it was undertaken, nor was its operation satisfactorily and fully
> explained after the fact. . . .
>   I suggest that the Committee step back from these recommendations, take
> a deep breath, and recall that one of the first principles of leadership is to fos-
> ter trust and mutual respect among one's team members. In an organization
> like the federal judiciary, with our highly trained, well-educated employees,
> surely we can expect more of ourselves and our team members than these
> benighted privacy-invading recommendations imply.
> Very truly yours,
> Edith H. Jones

Judge Jones's comments reflect the views of many knowledge workers.
Employers will do better to confront the dilemmas of workplace surveillance
by involving the workers in the design and implementation of the program
and carefully considering the rationale for it.

Workplace Privacy: An Oxymoron?

What expectations should employees have about privacy in the workplace?
Historically, the notion of a right to privacy in the workplace for employees
is a relatively recent idea, and in many countries, employers and employees
are just not quite sure what it means. In Canada, for example, it is not clear

---

[176] Townsend, A. M., & Bennett, J. T. (2003). Privacy, technology, and conflict: Emerging issues and action in workplace privacy [Electronic version]. *Journal of Labor
Research, 24*(2), 195–205.

who actually owns email sent or received by an employee via the employer's computer system. Also, the laws surrounding an employer's rights to monitor the workplace are not at all settled. Legislation in Canada is likely to tightly guard the context of surveillance to protect employees, including requiring employers to obtain employee consent before implementing any program.[177]

In the United States, notions of privacy derive from the Fourth Amendment of the Constitution, which protects "the right of the people to be secure in their persons, houses, papers, and effects, against unreasonable searches and seizures," but this principle has not been extended to private sector employees – only to public employees. The reasoning behind the special protection for public employees is that their employer is the government, and the Fourth Amendment protects against unreasonable government intrusion.

For private-sector employees, state laws and case laws have been the major guiding factors in the United States, and these have increasingly diminished the zones of privacy that a worker can expect in the workplace. The courts have generally ruled that the workplace is not the employee's "castle" in which privacy should be protected – it is the employer's castle. The rulings have usually been decided based on whether the employee had a reasonable expectation of privacy and whether the employer's intrusion would be considered excessive and unreasonable. However, employers have been given considerable leeway by the courts with respect to what constitutes an expectation of privacy and what is reasonable. For example, Pillsbury management informed its employees that email would not be monitored. One would suppose that the corporate policy would be interpreted as leading to "an expectation of privacy" by the courts. Yet in the ground-breaking case of *Smyth vs. Pillsbury Company*, the court ruled that it was perfectly within reason for Pillsbury to fire Smyth based on what his managers found when they peeked into his email account, despite the policy. According to the ruling, a reasonable person would not consider the company's interception of the messages to be a substantial and highly offensive invasion of privacy, even though the company said it would not intercept them. The court added that the company has an interest in "preventing inappropriate and unprofessional comments or even illegal activity over its email system which outweighs any privacy interest the employee

---

[177] Corry, D. J., & Nutz, K. E. (2003). Employee email and Internet use: Canadian legal issues. *Journal of Labor Research, 24*(3), 233–256.

may have in those comments."[178] And, as you saw earlier, the courts have determined that in some cases it should be more than just an "interest." It is the company's legal responsibility to prevent many kinds of unprofessional conduct.

DATA IN TRANSIT, DATA AT REST

Conceptually, there is some difference between monitoring information in transit and reviewing it once it is digitally stored. For example, laws prohibit people from recording ongoing telephone conversations without permission, which employees grant when the employer states that phone monitoring is part of the company policy. These same laws have been used to argue that email should not be monitored without consent – at least while it is in transit. The caveat, of course, is that email is stored on the server for a period of time, and it could be stored other places as well, such as on the recipient's local computer. Decisions in some court cases have revolved around this difference and decided against employers who were intercepting data in transit but in favor of them when they looked at the same data when it was at rest.

The distinction between data in transit and data at rest emerged from Title III of the Omnibus Crime Control and Safe Street Act of 1968, which was later amended with the Electronic Communications Privacy Act. The goal of those acts was to protect the content of communications in transit from being disclosed or intercepted, to prohibit "wire tapping." Technology continues to advance, however, and legal language that is too specific and too tied to current technology is bound to get into trouble within a short time. For example, what about wireless devices? Does "content" include the URLs logged by surveillance systems when employees visit Web sites? Are voice mails in transit or at rest? What about screen shots of instant message conversations or status reports from global satellite positioning systems?

The trend toward diminished employee rights to privacy in the workplace has not been 100 percent, however, and some states have passed their own laws to counter the trend toward lack of workplace privacy. These are intended to provide employees with some protection, though they do tend to create a patchwork quilt of rules and regulations. California, for example, adds restrictions to federal law about what employers can legally do in the workplace. That state's privacy laws prohibit recording of communications

[178] McEvoy, S. A. (2002). Email and Internet monitoring and the workplace: Do employees have a right to privacy? *Communications and the Law,* June, 2002, 69–80.

unless "all parties" consent, rather than just one, as required by Title III. Also, California prohibits recording of communications without reference to an employer's ordinary course of business. That is, employers must have a business rationale for workplace surveillance.[179]

Despite the trend toward favoring the rights of employers, there have been some cases in which employees have successfully argued that employer intrusion into their private affairs was excessive. This especially occurs when the employer scrutinizes personal communications for their content, not just for the extent of personal use of corporate resources. Also, employers and employees sometimes settle complaints without taking the issue into court, either through labor review boards or through human resources departments.

EVOLVING PERSPECTIVES ON THE ETHICS OF SURVEILLANCE

Workplace electronic surveillance raises numerous ethical concerns, especially about unbridled incursions on individual privacy. The technology enables employers to watch over and record much of an employee's life, whether or not it has some relationship to the person's working life. The fuzzy line between work and nonwork that I discussed in an earlier chapter adds to the difficulty of determining where a person's work life starts and private life begins. A corporation executive attempting to make an ethical decision regarding workplace surveillance has many pros and cons to weigh and many unknowns about potential harm and benefit to employees, customers, and stockholders. The factors that go into that decision are also evolving and changing.

The legal climate has certainly laid more responsibility on the employer, to know what the employees are doing – even in settings only loosely linked to work – and protect people from hostile working environments. The events of late 2001 and 2002 in the United States have had even more significant effects on people's thinking about workplace surveillance and privacy in general. The terrorist attacks led to an easy passage for the Patriot Act in the United States, which gave law enforcement officials much broader authority to monitor communications and conduct surveillance, both inside the workplace and out. The introduction of anthrax spores into the mail system in late 2001 launched another set of concerns, this time about the safety and security of employees who open the mail. Then, the

---

[179] Caragozian, J. S., & Warner, D. E. (2001). Privacy rights of employees using workplace computers in California. Retrieved August 15, 2002 from Privacy Rights Clearinghouse Web site: http://www.privacyrights.org/ar/employees-rights.htm

accounting scandals at Enron and other companies, and the widespread use and destruction of email that could document criminal activity, added new elements to the debate about surveillance.

In different ways, each of these forces contributed to a change in the way people balance the need for security and protection and the desire for privacy. For example, the notion that it is better to let ten guilty people go free than to convict one innocent person has given way to a heightened desire for security and for greater protection against the horrible acts that any one of those ten people might do – even if they have done nothing illegal yet. This shift has certainly changed how private citizens react to potential invasions of privacy by law enforcement. Now, most people would welcome a highly sophisticated video surveillance system that could spot terrorists in an airport or at the Super Bowl. In the past, many would have objected to this technology. In the workplace, the balance has also shifted. A corporation whose surveillance system identified someone who was buying bomb-making equipment, communicating with known terrorists, or inflating profits on annual reports would be considered a hero. When surveillance contributes to security, and when it is used to catch greedy executives and ensure accountability, employees welcome it.

The difficult task ahead is to stay in control of that balance, even as it shifts, based on our interest in increased security, protection, and accountability. Is it better to let just five guilty people go free rather than to convict one innocent person? Can we find better ways to protect that innocent employee from unfair treatment in the workplace? It will not be long before surveillance of some kind is used in just about every workplace, and possibly every public place as well. As Richard Hunter of Gartner Group said about the use of technology for surveillance in *World Without Secrets*, "Once you start, you tend to keep going."[180]

---

[180] Hunter, R. (2002). *World without secrets: Business, crime, and privacy in the age of ubiquitous computing.* New York: John Wiley & Sons, p. 262.

10 The Changing Context of Employment

Edward L. and several of his friends sensed that the company where they worked would be downsizing quickly, maybe even filing for bankruptcy. The company was an application service provider, or ASP, that hosted software applications for many clients. In 1999, this industry was one of the Internet era's rising stars, and clients were eager to let them handle the technological infrastructure for their businesses. Thanks to the Internet and netcentric technologies, companies did not need to maintain all their IT equipment and personnel on their own premises any longer, and many chose to outsource this headache-inducing function to an ASP. The user, after all, doesn't care whether the customer database is located on a server in the basement of the building, tended by the company's own employees. Their main concerns are about reliability, responsiveness, and anywhere-anytime access.

By 2002, however, many ASPs went bankrupt and others were merged or downsized. Edward managed the help desk where he and his team solved technical problems clients experienced when they ran their applications. His clients contacted the desk by phone, email, instant message, or pager, and he frequently solved their problems by remotely viewing their screens. From the diminishing call volume, he guessed he would soon be out of a job. He turned to the Internet for his job search, and seeing few openings that matched his skills posted by companies, he submitted his resume to the Web site of a large staffing agency with offices in a nearby city. His resume was reviewed, polished, and added to their database, and within a couple of weeks the agency sent him out on two interviews. Within a month, he signed a contract with the staffing agency and began work at a financial services company where he works in a call center that troubleshoots customer problems with a new online banking application. The company's offices were too far for a daily commute, so he stayed at a motel during the orientation period. After that, he began to work from his home office most of the time, traveling to the company site just once a week.

The Internet's impact on Edward's working life and career prospects shows up in several places. The ASPs would never have emerged at all without netcentric capabilities. His role in the ASP and his position would not have existed. He would not have had the help desk tools, such as remote access to a desktop computer, to do his work without the Internet. When the downturn came, he used the net to find new options, many of which were themselves created by the Internet's e-commerce capabilities. Finally, the net expanded his working options by making telecommuting feasible for a person with his skills.

The net also may have had more subtle influences on Edward's life. He was attracted to technology and eventually e-commerce because the pay was higher and job opportunities were greater. He began taking courses in these subjects at a local community college, even though he already had a bachelor's degree in history. When he accepted the position at the ASP, the recruiter promised many perks, including stock options and access to the company swimming pool and exercise room. Like most of his coworkers, Edward was extremely committed to the company and felt like a valued member of a dynamic, high-performance team. Now, he is "working" for one company, but actually employed by another. The ambiguity is troubling, especially because his wife is expecting their second child, but Edward remains optimistic about the future.

Employment Trends and Technology

Few subjects have been so hotly debated as the relationship between technological innovation and employment trends. Technological unemployment and displacement have been going on since the beginning of recorded history, when wheeled carts replaced human backs. Now, innovations in information technology and telecommunications are generating waves of creative destruction that have put many people out of work and moved others into new occupations.

THE FASTEST GROWING OCCUPATIONS
The fact that most of the fastest growing job categories directly involve computers testifies to the importance of technology in this latest wave of

creative destruction. According to recent projections from the U.S. Bureau of Labor Statistics, the ten "hottest" jobs, which means those with the highest projected growth rates, are those listed in Table 10.1.[181]

This list tells a compelling story about the forces affecting employment opportunities. Technology dominates the picture, and we especially need more people to support the infrastructure, develop the applications, and keep users happy and productive by providing responsive help desk support. The earnings ranks for the technology-related occupations are high or very high, and most require substantial education – usually a bachelor's degree. The only fast-growing occupations in this list that are *not* technology related are caregivers and medical assistants, and they are at or near the bottom of the earnings ranks. The population is getting older and sicker, and we will need many more lower paid workers to provide care. These positions require far less education and also will not pay particularly well.

It is instructive to look more closely at exactly what people in those fast-growth technology-related occupations will be doing. They will not be building or repairing PCs for the most part. Instead, they will be developing, supporting, and helping people use netcentric technologies and their applications. Those systems administrators will be launching new servers, installing updates for Web server software to patch security holes, and adding functionality. The network administrators will be diagnosing bandwidth bottlenecks and constantly fine-tuning configurations to improve throughput and performance. The systems analysts will be working directly with business users to translate their models into workable e-commerce sites with highly convenient, personalized, and secure functionality. And most of the "desktop publishers" will be designing Web sites, not magazine layouts. The overpowering influence of the Internet shows up clearly in this list of fast-growing occupations.

Though most of the fastest growing occupations require significant levels of education, people with less education will still be able to find work. In fact, the majority of new job openings will be for people who don't need much more than on-the-job training, simply because these occupations are already quite large. Even with slower growth rates, these occupations will see many new position openings. Nevertheless, the projections show that the workforce of the future needs more education. In 2000, for

---

[181] Hecker, D. E. (2001). Occupational employment projections to 2010. *Monthly Labor Review,* November, 57–84. Retrieved April 12, 2003, from Bureau of Labor Statistics Web site: http://www.bls.gov/opub/mlr/2001/11/art4full.pdf

Table 10.1. *The Fastest Growing Jobs*

Rank	Occupation	Growth Rate 2000–2010	Education and Training Requirement	Earnings Rank*
1	Computer software engineers, applications	100%	Bachelor's degree	1
2	Computer support specialists	97%	Associate's degree	2
3	Computer software engineers, systems software	90%	Bachelor's degree	1
4	Network and computer systems administrators	82%	Bachelor's degree	1
5	Network systems and data communications analysts	77%	Bachelor's degree	1
6	Desktop publishers	67%	Postsecondary vocational award	2
7	Database administrators	66%	Bachelor's degree	1
8	Personal and home care aides	62%	Short-term on-the-job training	4
9	Computer systems analysts	60%	Bachelor's degree	1
10	Medical assistants	57%	Moderate-term on-the-job training	3

* From U.S. Bureau of Labor Statistics. Earnings ranks refer to 1 = very high ($39,700 and over), 2 = high ($25,760 to $39,660), 3 = low ($18,500 to $25,760), and 4 = very low (up to $18,490). The rankings are based on quartiles using one fourth of total employment to define each quartile. Earnings are for wage and salary workers.

example, 29 percent of all jobs required a postsecondary vocational award or an academic degree. However, in the next ten years jobs that require at least the vocational award or academic degree will account for 42 percent of all job growth.

UPS AND DOWNS IN TECHNOLOGY EMPLOYMENT

Though the long-term outlook for technology-related occupations is rosy, the ups and downs in the e-business world have created a very volatile employment picture. Edward, for example, was about to be one of the hundreds of thousands of tech workers caught up in creative destruction and laid off in 2001, even though his skills were in great demand the year before. In one short year, the number of technology jobs shrank by 5 percent, and the majority of those who lost their jobs were in technical support. The demand for IT workers fell especially quickly in the California heart of the dot.com boom – down 71 percent. In 2002, however, industry executives are projecting another upturn, and company executives anticipate once again having trouble filling their job openings.[182]

Despite the volatility, the generally accepted wisdom in the United States and most other developed countries is that IT workers are in short supply. We are not providing sufficient education in math and science in the early grades, and too few people are going into these fields. In 1998, the outcry about the IT worker shortage reached very high levels. High-tech industries lobbied Congress to remove immigration constraints on IT workers, so more people from India, Philippines, Korea, and other countries could obtain H-1B visas to work in the United States. In 1998, the U.S. Congress raised the annual limit for these visas from 65,000 to 115,000 for high-tech workers, though several groups argued vigorously against the change. The Federation for American Immigration Reform, for example, protested that the statistics that the industry associations were using to document a worker shortage were flawed, and the real motivation was to bring in workers who would work for less. Opponents of the immigration measures also argued that the U.S. industries should do more about their human resource policies for IT workers who were U.S. citizens rather than import new people from abroad.

Is there really an IT worker shortage? During the late 1990s, industry execs complained of ferocious bidding wars to recruit IT talent, so they certainly thought so. Labor economists have attempted to tackle this question in many different ways. One approach is to look at trends in the *share* of employment that people with technology skills hold, especially new college grads. Since 1989, the relative share of employment by math/computer science college graduates rose gradually until 1995, and then it rose more

---

[182] Kary, T. (2002). Study sees IT worker shortage in 2002. c|net news.com, May 6, 2002. Retrieved April 3, 2003, from c|net Web site: http://news.com/2100-1017-899730.html

quickly. Engineers, however, saw their share of employment slip over the same period. This means that the college grads with math or computer science backgrounds saw rising demand for their skills, especially after 1995, but those with a different kind of technological background – engineering – experienced less demand. However, Lawrence Mishel, Jared Bernstein, and John Schmitt, authors of *The State of Working America 2000/2001*, point out that the rising demand was hardly confined to math and computer science grads. Most professionals and white-collar workers also saw greater demand for their labor in the late 1990s.

Another statistic that might point to whether IT workers are in shorter supply now is the extent of their wage premium. In 1984, men in IT occupations earned about 16.6 percent more than their counterparts with similar levels of education and experience, working in similar industries. This wage premium has not changed much through the 1990s, so economists do not see a strong case for a fast-growing IT worker shortage. If IT workers have become so hard to find and so much in demand, their wages would have shown a larger premium in recent years. Mishel and his colleagues summarize what they believe the economic statistics show about the IT worker shortage: "All in all ... nothing spectacular seems to be taking place, although the last few years may anticipate large changes ahead."[183]

SOME I.T. IS BETTER THAN OTHER I.T.

Economic analyses use a very broad brush, and they aggregate large numbers based on groups that can be quite heterogeneous. IT workers are not just "computer gurus" who know the magic required to make networked computers and all their applications run properly. They have widely different skills.

For example, those "IT workers" include COBOL programmers who were desperately needed to fix aging legacy systems before the Y2K cutover. COBOL, which stands for "COmmon Business Oriented Language," is a programming language developed in 1960 under the auspices of the Department of Defense. It has been widely used to build applications for mainframes to support payroll, personnel, accounting, transactions, and other business functions. Because of disk space limitations, those applications developed in the 1960s and 1970s used two digits for year rather than four, so a year such as 1979 was stored as 79. This was fine as long as the applications could safely assume that "19" preceded the two-digit year. Few predicted

---

[183] Mishel, L., Bernstein, J., & Schmitt, J. (2001). *The state of working America 2000/2001*. Economic Policy Institute. Ithaca: Cornell University Press.

that those applications would survive so long, so at the time it seemed like a reasonable way to conserve disk space. But the applications kept going and going, decade after decade. Instead of replacing those systems, most companies patched, expanded, and improved their COBOL-based applications. As 2000 approached, some companies raced to retire the old systems, whereas others chose to fix up their old systems by adding staff who knew COBOL and could delve into the millions of lines of code.

After that last spike, the demand for COBOL programmers dropped. They are not likely to have much wage premium, assuming they have a job at all. In contrast, people with "hot" skills in technologies needed for e-commerce will continue to be in great demand. The statistics showed that demand for engineers fell compared to math/computer science grads, but they can't easily break down the demand for different types of IT skills.

The type of skills and the kinds of technologies with which the applicant has experience have become key sorting factors for IT recruiters. When a company wants to hire a new IT worker through a staffing agency, the company identifies the actual technologies the person will need to know. The agency does a key word search through its files of digitized resumes to tag candidates who mention that particular technology on their application. The technologies and the key word searches are astonishingly specific, usually including the brand names of the actual products. If the company needs a database administrator and they use Oracle's database, the search will look for "Oracle" as the key word, not "database," and certainly not just "computer." Someone who knows a competing database environment – SQL Server, for example – will not be in the finalist list. Job applicants learn quickly to include a very long list of technologies in their applications, even if they only have a passing acquaintance with each of them.

Changing Employee – Employer Relationships

Another significant employment trend involves the changing relationship between the employee and the employer. When I worked in Japan in the 1980s, when lifelong employment with a single company was still very common for college-educated men, a Sony engineer introduced himself to me by saying, "How do you do, I am Matsumoto, I belong to Sony." Matsumoto-san clearly believed he was in a tightly bound relationship with his employer, and he had good reasons for thinking so. He didn't identify himself by his profession or specialty, but as Sony's man named Matsumoto. Matsumoto worked very hard, staying at the office past 9 p.m. on many evenings. He socialized mainly with other Sony employees, and his family outings were often sponsored by the company. "Belonging to Sony" was not just a current job description, it was an honor and it gave him bragging rights. Sony, after all, is a major international company that has its pick of the new college grads. He fully expected to stay with Sony his entire working life and retire with a decent pension. Perhaps "belong to Sony" is a bit strong, but that is how the Japanese words can be translated to English (Watashi wa Sony no Matsumoto desu).

That kind of employee–employer relationship represents a strong bond – one that incurs obligations and responsibilities on both sides. In the United States, this bond between employer and employee was never quite so strong, and in both countries, our impressions of how widespread such a bond was are exaggerated. Japan's women, for example, never had relationships like that with their employers, nor did the many people who worked in small businesses, often as subcontractors to the giant corporations. In any case, the bonds have grown much weaker over the past three decades, and the trend is not likely to abate.

JOB STABILITY AND SECURITY

Patterns of job stability in the United States show up in the analyses of long-term employment. Since the 1960s, the median number of years men stay with a single employer has been dropping steadily. Men between the ages of forty-five and fifty-four averaged about twelve years with the same employer in 1963. By the mid-1990s, that figure dropped to about nine years. For women, the picture is different, partly because their job opportunities have changed dramatically in the postwar period. Women have always had a lower median job tenure compared to men, and since the 1960s the median job tenure for them has been increasing in the United States. Nevertheless, younger women show a decline in the median years with the same employer since the 1980s. Like men, they too are changing jobs more often. The share of people in the labor force who have worked for the same employer for a very long time has also dropped. In 1979, almost half of all men had been in their current job more than ten years. By the mid-1990s, this figure dropped to 40 percent.

Workers switch jobs for a variety of reasons, many voluntary. They may see better prospects with another firm and want to increase their salary or expand their portfolio of skills. People who lose their jobs through layoffs or other reasons, however, often pay a high cost. When they find a new job, it may pay less than the old one or offer fewer benefits. People expect many involuntary job losses in periods of high unemployment and recession, such as the early 1990s. However, the rate of involuntary job loss did not subside when that recession ended. Even when unemployment figures dropped, the rate of involuntary job loss continued to increase.

THE CONTINGENT WORKFORCE

When long-term employment opportunities decline, people are more willing to accept nonstandard employment. This could involve contract work, part-time work, temporary and contingent work, or on-call work. Businesses use different strategies to hire people in these nonstandard categories, including the staffing agency arrangement that Edward entered. They might hire people as "temp casuals" for a season, or have them sign an independent contractor agreement with a specific scope of work, time period, and payment. They also might offer many part-time or on-call arrangements. Benefits are often not part of the agreement. In 1999, about 25 percent of the workforce was considered "nonstandard," and their wages were generally lower than counterparts doing similar jobs, but with full-time regular employment.

Do people in nonstandard employment settings want to switch to regular full-time jobs? Many do, but certainly not all. Their work arrangements and personal interests are widely varied, and some choose nonstandard employment for flexibility or other reasons. For example, 57 percent of those who work for temporary help agencies said they were not satisfied with their current work arrangement and would prefer standard work. However, other categories of contingent workers, especially those whose pay is actually higher than their counterparts with full-time regular jobs, are pleased with their work arrangements. Among independent contractors, for example, only 8.5 percent said they would prefer standard work. More than 90 percent are satisfied.

RISE OF THE "DEPLOYEE"

Those independent contractors represent an intriguing group of highly educated talent that bears closer analysis. Many of these people appear to prefer their working arrangements to a more traditional employer – employee model, despite the uncertainties. They can move fluidly from project to project, working for themselves, as part of a staffing agency, or perhaps as shorter term employees of the company. Regina Casonato and Diane Morello of Gartner Group call these people *deployees* to distinguish them from employees.[184]

Deployees operate in the context of a more worker-centric environment, one in which they have considerable freedom to choose their own projects,

[184] Casonato, R., & Morello, D. (2002). Management alert: A certain employee type, "deployee," is changing the IT workforce. *InSide Gartner*, Note Number IGG-07242002-03. Retrieved February 14, 2003, from Gartner Intraweb Database.

working environments, and colleagues. The employer cannot simply assign them a task, as they might for a more traditional employee, and expect the deployee to perform it. Instead, the worker has greater freedom to pick and choose projects for personal reasons, including a preference for acquiring certain kinds of new skills or collegial contacts that might add value to the individual's own intellectual and social capital.

From the business perspective, the availability of highly talented deployees who can land running on complex projects can be enormously beneficial. They may pay them very well, but they don't have to commit to an employment relationship that reduces flexibility or adds legal burdens. The word "deploy" conjures up the strategic movement of military troops to hot spots on the globe. The troops must be ready for action on a moment's notice and can be moved to wherever they might be required. Deployees share some of those characteristics, though employers can't order them to perform.

Job stability and security have both decreased along with the waves of creative destruction that accompanied the Internet. That bond with the employer – however exaggerated – has declined considerably. People cannot expect to work for the same employer for an entire career, if they ever could. They can expect more volatility and job changes. Those waves of destruction have also affected the way employers and employees relate to one another, and the employee has not always been the loser. Although many people have become contingent workers involuntarily, others are choosing the deployee path. For them the waves have opened up novel and attractive ways of working and learning and, of course, new challenges for their managers.

Challenges in Managing New Employment Relationships

Linda, Edward's manager in his current position with the financial services company, has more than her share of personnel headaches. She is responsible for fourteen people, all of whom report directly to her. At least that is what the organizational chart shows. However, Edward and two others were placed there by staffing agencies for a six-month period, with options to renew. Four others landed in her shop when her company bought out a smaller bank last year, and the acquisition included strong legal language to protect the rights of the bank's employees. Two more are part-timers and one is actually an employee of an insurance company that partners with her corporation in some area, including online services. The rest are full-time regular employees who have been with the company from one to six years.

All but the most recent hire joined the company before she did, two years ago.

MANAGING THE MOTLEY

A heterogeneous crew like this is not unique in organizations, yet it is almost completely ignored by theories and principles of human resources management. The team has a bewildering mix of "employees" who have different agreements, contractual obligations, and emotional ties to the company where they are physically working. These people are not just diverse in terms of cultural or ethnic background. They are working within quite varied employer–employee contexts that are nearly impossible to manage with a single strategy.

Researchers studying human resource management strategies generally use either "soft" or "hard" approaches to the field. The soft approach examines HR policies and their consequences to determine which constitute overall best practices across many companies. The emphasis has been on developing commitment in employees, building teamwork, encouraging participation, treating people fairly and equitably, and nurturing talent with investment in training and education. The underlying theme is that employees should be considered an asset, like capital or factories, and the company should take good care of them and invest in their growth and development. Many surveys have been conducted to identify HR practices that correlate with various measures of success, but typically, each company gets to respond only once. Usually, the survey is sent to the HR manager, who responds for the entire company. There is little opportunity for the company to explain that some workers are treated one way, others another way, and still others a third way.

Another approach to studying human resources management is to examine how companies use different strategies depending on their industry, the level of competition, or other aspects of the context in which they conduct business. This is the "hard" or contingent approach, and it assumes that a best practice can only be best within a certain set of circumstances. In one context, for example, a somewhat ruthless set of HR policies may lead the company to become a success, especially in a frenzied competition in which new services must be launched on Internet time just to keep up. A colleague who was chief information officer at a telecommunications firm told me his HR strategy for the IT staff was to hire them young, pay them well, give them a few days of training, and then burn them out within eighteen months. The norm was at least twelve hours of work a day, and on-call almost every weekend. In another industry with different characteristics, a more successful HR strategy would be to emphasize training, employee commitment, and retention.

Neither of these approaches has much bearing on the motley crew Linda was leading. Jill Rubery and her colleagues at the Manchester School of Management in the United Kingdom point out all the HR issues that are not adequately addressed by current HR approaches in settings with such heterogeneous employment relationships *within* a company, and frequently in a single department.[185] Discipline, for example, may vary depending on the type of employee and the kind of relationship. A contract worker might be terminated for the same offense that would lead to a letter of reprimand for another worker whose terms of employment were different. Compensation will also be different. Some workers may receive benefits in the form of company-sponsored health plans and retirement pensions, and other workers will not. The putative manager, Linda in this case, is not really the supervisor for some of the workers. Edward, for example, works for the staffing agency, and Linda's company is their client. Legal responsibilities for the health and safety of the people on Linda's team are equally murky. Most of these laws have been developed within the context of a traditional employer – employee relationship and do not easily clarify who would be responsible or liable if workplace injuries occur.

OUTSOURCING THE PEOPLE

The staffing agency for which Edward works is an example of a burgeoning business called the professional employee organization, or PEO. Prominent among such companies is Adecco, a Swiss human resources solutions company that places millions of technical, professional, clerical, and industrial workers in companies throughout the world. The people are called "associates" and Adecco envisions them as information age entrepreneurs. The company Web site describes the traditional model of employer – employee relationship as obsolete and sees the growing need for more business flexibility in human resources than what that model could provide. Adecco also seeks to deregulate the workplace, lobbying for change in many outmoded laws that limit flexibility in employment relationships.

Essentially, client companies that work with staffing agencies are not just outsourcing human resource functions, such as payroll or benefits processing. They are outsourcing the people themselves. Peter F. Drucker is alarmed

---

[185] Rubery, J., Earnshaw, J., Marchington, M., Cooke, F. L., & Vincent, S. (2002). Changing organizational forms and the employment relationship. *Journal of Management Studies, 39*(5), 645–672.

by this growing trend, especially by the rapid expansion of the services PEOs offer.[186] He suggests that many companies are certainly choosing PEOs because they add flexibility to their workforce deployments, but they have another reason that has nothing to do with their own business models or need for flexible hiring. Governments have added so much regulation to the traditional employer – employee relationship and so much reporting to ensure compliance, that companies switch to PEOs to get out from under a crushing paperwork and data-gathering burden. He cites U.S. Small Business Administration figures showing that the cost of government regulations, required paperwork, and tax compliance for smaller businesses was around $5,000 per employee in 1995, and that doesn't include the employee's wages or benefits.

In that context, people categorized as employees whose role is regulated by so many government agencies, become less of an asset and more of a liability. By outsourcing the relationship itself, PEOs allow managers to attend to the business and let someone else worry about the paperwork and all the other regulatory responsibilities of an employer.

Though PEOs are providing an important service, Drucker worries that knowledge-intensive companies may lose the commitment and advantages of the most important asset they have, their intellectual capital. To what mission is the deployee committed? Not the staffing agency's, certainly. The agency acts like an agent for these people, and agents can be replaced quickly. Nor would a deployee be committed to a particular company, expecting to be there only for a year or two and then possibly move on to new work somewhere else. Drucker warns, "If, by off-loading employee relations, organizations also lose their capacity to develop people, they will have made a devil's bargain indeed."

Changing Organizational Forms

What is the best way to design an organization and structure the relationships among the people who work there? The conventional bureaucracy and the relationships it defines have been sorely challenged by the changes wrought by technological advances and the Internet. In the context of the new employer – employee relationships, the bureaucratic organization creaks badly. Communication patterns that formerly followed the hierarchical chain of command now can easily bypass those lines on the organizational chart and generally do.

---

[186] Drucker, P. F. (2002). They're not employees, they're people [Electronic version]. *Harvard Business Review, 80*(2), 70–77.

John Child of the University of Birmingham and Rita Gunther McGrath at Columbia University attempted to capture several of the key features that differentiate conventional and emerging organizational forms.[187] For example, the conventional organization would rely on hierarchy, concentrated power, and top-down goal setting, but the emerging forms stress teamwork, distributed power, and decentralized goal setting. Many organizations that adopt components of the new forms are experimenting with ways to deal with uncertainty and change in employer – employee relationships as well as with all the other aspects of the business climate. They are finding ways to deal with ambiguity, paradox, and contradictions. While bureaucracies attempt to *buffer* the organization against uncertainty by building strong foundations, clear chains of command, and orderly relationships, the newly emerging forms are attempts to *embrace* uncertainty to achieve faster response and more flexibility. In a conventional bureaucratic organization, for example, the employee handbook would lay out the terms and conditions of employment clearly, and its precise wording would be used to settle legal disputes. In some of the new experimental forms, there may be a handbook, but it would probably be gathering dust and rarely updated. It also wouldn't apply to many people working in the organization. If anyone were responsible for maintaining it, that person would not be aware of all the fluctuating employer – employee relationships in different groups.

Other aspects of the emerging forms take into account the expectations of knowledge workers, whatever their employment relationship. They expect high levels of participation in decision making, empowered teams, horizontal working relationships, and some ability to set their own goals. A university's decentralized organization typifies some of these contradictions and paradoxes. The president's office may control very little of the actual university budget, much of which is controlled by faculty, who win large grants from agencies like the National Science Foundation to conduct research, employ staff, and train students. The chair of the department has little control over the tenured faculty, who can usually pick and choose the projects they work on and the courses they teach. The adjunct faculty, however, are in a very different employer – employee relationship with the university. They may teach several courses each semester on a contract basis, but the university can't count on them. Collegial and collaborative projects emerge frequently, but not usually because of any central, top-down

[187] Child, J., & McGrath, R. G. (2001). Organizations unfettered: Organizational form in an information-intensive economy. *Academy of Management Journal, 44*(6), 1135–1149.

directive. Howard Frank, Dean of the Robert H. Smith School of Business at University of Maryland, College Park, emphasizes the importance of tolerating – even encouraging – contradictions, paradoxes, and "messiness" in this kind of environment. He encourages activity he calls "stuff," in the form of new research projects, collaborations, partnerships, technology initiatives, lecture series, labs, grant proposals, or courses. Coordination might be weak, and the left hand might not know what the right is doing all the time. Nevertheless, the environment may support innovation and enthusiasm among knowledge workers in ways a more bureaucratic design can not.

ENTERPRISES WITHOUT BOUNDARIES

The newly emerging forms present challenges to the very definition of the term "organization." As companies enter partnerships and alliances, as they outsource many of the functions that were formerly performed by employees, and as they work with PEOs to staff their own base of knowledge workers, the boundaries of the organization become more and more permeable and fuzzy. The growing sophistication of networks to support virtual teamwork and business-to-business interaction are enablers of this greater permeability. The new forms, sometimes called *virtual enterprises*, can be hard to pin down and even harder to define.

One characteristic of the virtual enterprise is its emphasis on flexibility and fleet-footed response to change. Through outsourcing and other partnership arrangements, the virtual enterprise can off-load many functions, downsize to its core capabilities, and focus on innovation. The large, traditional bureaucracy is the lumbering dinosaur, bent for extinction and unable to adapt to climatic changes. The small virtual enterprise is the proto-mammal, scampering around the dinosaur's feet and readily adapting to environmental change.

Outsourcing is one way in which the virtual enterprise trims down. Functions needed by the business but peripheral to its central mission are candidates for outsourcing. These may include janitorial services, the cafeteria, payroll and benefits processing, and security. Functions closer to the core are also being outsourced, including information technology, help desks, and Web site administration. And as I described earlier, the PEOs offer companies the chance to outsource any of their categories of employees, from clerical staff to the CEO.

Partnerships and alliances are other ways that convert boundaries around an organization into a permeable membrane. Two companies might make an agreement to jointly develop an innovative technology because each has capabilities needed for the project. Collaborative teams are set up, often as virtual teams, consisting of people from each firm. When the technology is developed, more agreements are needed to commercialize it, market it, license it, and share the profits.

STRENGTHS AND WEAKNESS OF VIRTUAL ENTERPRISING

Henry W. Chesbrough of Harvard Business School and David J. Treece of the Haas School of Business at the University of California, Berkeley, argue that the virtual enterprise has significant strengths in some areas but is very vulnerable in others.[188] Its strengths lie in incentives and responsiveness. A virtual enterprise can quickly tap into the marketplace for talent and resources it needs to respond to a new opportunity. Then it can offer incentives to those people or companies, incentives that could easily outpace anything a larger bureaucracy would offer one of its own employees. In contrast, the large bureaucracy attempting to build the in-house capability might not be agile enough to compete on Internet time.

A downside of the virtual enterprise is that coordinating all the partnerships and alliances becomes extraordinarily difficult, precisely because of those incentives that drew them together in the first place. Each player operates on the basis of self-interest. They are not in the game to help the large organization succeed because there is no large organization. It is just a virtual enterprise. The social dilemmas I discussed in earlier chapters apply here, though on a larger scale. When the self-interest of group members is at odds with the group's collective interest, obtaining their cooperation to advance the group goal can be enormously difficult. It requires considerable trust, and that is not easy to build in virtual teams. It is also not easy to build in virtual enterprises.

Virtual enterprises are very agile at introducing and embracing certain kinds of innovations, but they can be very ineffective for other kinds. When an innovation is relatively autonomous, meaning it affects only a small component of an entire process and its introduction won't create ripples or breakdowns everywhere else, the virtual enterprise handles it well. An innovation in computer monitors, such as the flat panel display, can easily be incorporated into Dell's marketing as long as it doesn't require any changes to the ports on the back of the CPU. Dell can quickly add or replace agreements with suppliers and offer its customers the new technology under the Dell brand. In contrast, the larger bureaucracy may have difficulty with such

---

[188] Chesbrough, H. W., & Teece, D. J. (2002). Organizing for innovation: When is virtual virtuous? [Electronic version]. *Harvard Business Review, 80*(8), 127–135.

autonomous innovations because it can't react as quickly. GM, for example, took a long time to adopt disc brakes compared to more decentralized automakers because it had strong vertical relationships with suppliers who were steeped in the older technology.

However, virtual enterprises cannot easily launch innovations that are systemic, ones that require change in most or all of the parts. Because the collection of self-interested players is difficult to coordinate and no one is in charge at the top to settle conflicts, systemic innovations can flounder. Chesbrough and Teece suggest that the most successful virtual enterprises have not generally been a loose consortium of players with relatively equal power. Instead, some powerful company "sits at the center of networks that are far from egalitarian." They do not outsource everything, especially not capacities that contribute to their most important competitive advantage. In other words, someone is calling the shots and can insist that partners cooperate, even if their cooperation requires behavior that is not in their self-interest. They may not "own" their partners, but they do have considerable influence over how their partners behave.

Another vulnerability for virtual enterprises, or any enterprise that adopts decentralization and distribution of power, involves accountability. In the wake of the accounting scandals of Enron, WorldCom, and other big businesses, corporate stakeholders are extremely concerned that someone is in charge who can oversee the integrity of the organization and can be held accountable if problems arise. The control structures of the large bureaucracies, whatever their weaknesses, can do a better job at this than the loosely coordinated enterprises composed of many units with their own agendas. The board of directors holds the CEO responsible, who in turn holds VPs responsible for their units. When there is no clear hierarchy in terms of authority, there are also fewer lines of accountability.

The Volunteer Organization

The emerging organizational forms take account of the changing employer – employee relationship. Employees – especially those with the most valued knowledge and skills – are not necessarily motivated by higher pay, promotions, benefit packages, or promises of lifelong job security. Peter Drucker suggested that organizations are beginning to resemble symphony orchestras more than anything else. The conductor may not even be able to play the violin at all and must rely on that person's expertise – and the talent and perseverance of everyone else in the orchestra – to be successful. The violinist can sabotage the performance if the conductor is annoying or autocratic, and today's knowledge worker can do the same thing to an autocratic manager.[189]

Drucker proposed that new organizational forms resemble collections of volunteers committed to a cause more than a pool of people attached to a company and working for a paycheck. In that sense, a corporation can learn a great deal from the way the Salvation Army or Catholic Church operates. We can also gain insights from another highly successful volunteer organization of knowledge workers: the open source movement.

THE OPEN SOURCE ORGANIZATION OF VOLUNTEERS

Open source is a broad term that generally refers to software that is licensed and distributed as a public good. The Open Source Initiative, a nonprofit corporation dedicated to managing and promoting the open source approach, lists several criteria about distribution that must be met for the software to be considered open source. For example, the license must not restrict free redistribution of the software, and the program has to include its source code so others can review it and improve upon it. The software must not be a "black box," whose inner workings are known and understood only by company employees who sign nondisclosure agreements. The guidelines also require the software to be licensed without discrimination to any people or groups, or to specific industries. An open source developer could not, for instance, prohibit certain businesses, or any business for that matter, from using the product.[190]

Several well-known software products are open source, including the Apache Web server software and the operating system Linux, named for its originator Linus Torvalds. These products were not developed in the secure labs of Microsoft or behind closed doors at IBM. They evolve, and continue to improve, through the labor of thousands of volunteer developers who contribute their time and expertise to create good, reliable software. The underlying principle is that the best software will emerge from an environment in which thousands of programmers can review the code, redistribute it, find its bugs, modify it, and improve it. The more people who work on software code, the better it will be. This contrasts sharply with, for example, the closed model used by Microsoft. The code for the Windows operating system is closely guarded and never distributed.

---

[189] Drucker, P. F. (1998). Management's new paradigms. *Forbes, 162*(7), 152–170.
[190] The Open Source Definition, Version 1.9. (2002). Retrieved March 15, 2003, from The Open Source Initiative Web site: http://www.opensource.org

Why do people become volunteers in the open source movement? Although some are paid employees of companies who work on open source projects, most are not. They hold other jobs to earn a living and work on open source software as volunteers. A large part of their motivation is the satisfaction of contributing to a worthy cause in a way that many believe is both more productive and more effective compared to the closed development model. Much commercial off-the-shelf (COTS) software is very buggy because it is developed in isolation and not enough people have a chance to fully test it before it is released. Once thousands of people begin using it, the bugs become apparent.

Another strong motivation is the desire to establish and maintain a good reputation among highly talented peers. Much open source development work and discussion takes place on the Internet, through newsgroups and mailing lists especially, and a capable programmer whose work is praised by peers receives valuable psychic income. The history file on open source projects includes the names of people who make significant contributions, and being listed on several projects is an important accomplishment.

Involvement in open source projects becomes a passion for participants, and most feel strongly that the initiative is not just an alternative approach to software development. It is a mission, one that has considerable grass roots momentum to counter the greedy excesses of corporate giants. The Open Source Initiative Web site features one of the most dramatic conflicts between the open source movement and more conventional and competitive business tactics, outlined in the "Halloween" documents. In 1998, some Microsoft internal documents discussing open source software were leaked to Eric Raymond, one of the leaders of the open source movement and author of *The Cathedral and the Bazaar*, a book that contrasts the two different software development strategies.[191] Raymond gave the documents to the press and, of course, distributed it widely via the Internet. The memos confirm that Microsoft execs believe open source to be a viable way to create software, and they also think it can be a serious threat to their business model. One memorable line reads, "OSS [open source software] is long-term credible . . . FUD tactics cannot be used to combat it." (FUD refers to fear, uncertainty, and doubt, a technique used to raise concerns about software reliability.)

Despite the voluntary nature of most contributions, open source projects are not chaotic free-for-alls. Many do have open membership, and anyone

---

[191] Raymond, E. S. (2001). *The cathedral and the bazaar: Musings on Linux and open source by an accidental revolutionary.* Cambridge, MA: O'Reilly.

can get involved just by participating and contributing something. They are not egalitarian or democratic, however. Most are organized with governance structures that are quite different from traditional corporations, but which can be remarkably effective in maintaining order, establishing goals, and settling disputes. Projects have leaders, or more usually leadership teams, who have earned their reputations and are often elected by the community of developers themselves. The leaders can exert considerable authority over the path the project takes.

In a more conventional employer – employee relationship, an uncooperative, untalented, or troublesome worker might be reassigned or terminated by the project leader or manager. On an open source project, however, leaders handle such unsuitable volunteers somewhat differently. The leadership teams can use their social influence and standing in the community to promote compliance with norms. In severe cases, they can shun, expel, or humiliate volunteers who won't conform. This can be worse than being fired.

Consensus is another important ingredient for open source projects, and it is not always easy to achieve. Voting is commonly used, after a period of online discussion in which the volunteers defend their viewpoints. Peter Wayner studied the open source movement and found that disputes and their resolution can be time-consuming, contentious events. He writes, "The group is filled with many strong-minded, independent individuals who aren't afraid to express their opinions. Flame wars spring up again and again as people try to decide technical questions like whether it makes more sense to use long integers or floating point numbers to hold a person's wealth in dollars."[192]

LESSONS LEARNED FROM VOLUNTEER ORGANIZATIONS

M. Lynne Markus and her colleagues point out that open source projects would appear to be operating under conditions that would favor low-quality contributions, freeloading, and unstable membership.[193] Nevertheless, they are often quite successful, thanks to the many procedures, community norms, institutions, and processes the groups have learned to use over time. They exhibit certain characteristics that resemble the newly emerging organizational forms, so their practices are well worth examining. For example, they rely heavily on the intrinsic motivation of knowledge workers who

[192] Wayner, P. (2000). *Free for all*. New York: HarperBusiness, p. 161.
[193] Markus, M. L., Manville, B., & Agres, C. E. (2000). What makes a virtual organization work? [Electronic version]. *Sloan Management Review, 42*(1), 13–26.

want to work on something for their own reasons, especially to build a reputation with people they admire, rather than on extrinsic motivators in the form of pay, benefits, or formal promotions. Also, they emphasize open and fluid membership on projects, so they can attract specialized and outstanding talent for specific jobs. Nevertheless, they maintain a stable core of participants.

Another important best practice for the volunteer organization, at least if one judges from the open source movement, is that the leadership's decision-making processes are transparent and visible to the whole group. They are not democratic organizations, but the rules are relatively simple. The primary means of ensuring conformity and maintaining order are social control and group pressure.

The lessons learned from the open source movement can only take us so far in envisioning new organizational forms. There are ways to make a profit within the context of open source, but as one proponent pointed out, making money with open source software is "nonintuitive." Nevertheless, companies like Red Hat have succeeded, in their case by offering training, support services, and custom programming to companies using Linux. The most important lesson from open source, however, is not how to make money, but how to deal with human motivation and governance in an organization of volunteer knowledge workers.

Another quote from Microsoft's internal memo published as part of the Halloween documents points out the power of the open source model to organize knowledge workers in the age of the Internet and win their passion, commitment, and energy:

> "The ability of the OSS process to collect and harness the collective IQ of thousands of individuals across the Internet is simply amazing. More importantly, OSS evangelization scales with the size of the Internet much faster than our own evangelization efforts appear to scale."

People still need a paycheck, but the vitality of volunteer organizations and their power to evangelize a mission and recruit new members demonstrate that the paycheck is not the only reason for working hard. The emerging organizational forms recognize this important lesson.

11 The Netcentric Workplace: Future Trends

The years surrounding the turn of the millennium have been turbulent, to understate the case. Trying to keep up with the events has led to CNN-itis and news addiction, and the cable programs are capturing even more viewers than they did during the O. J. Simpson trial. Against this backdrop, the Internet has been penetrating many aspects of our workplaces and working lives, sometimes quietly, sometimes stormily, but relentlessly nonetheless. I once asked my audience during a speech whether they, or anyone they knew, had ever chosen to cancel their organization's Internet access, once they had been connected. One remarked, "Are you kidding? That would be like disconnecting the electricity." Although individually, people choose to take a hiatus from email, the Internet, and all the netcentric technologies that keep us connected to work, almost everyone comes back. For organizations, disconnecting is all but impossible, and a key reason often given is that the Internet makes us all more productive. Or does it?

The Internet and Productivity

Economists' definition of productivity is "output per man-hour of labor," or the value of goods and services produced in a period of time divided by the hours of labor used to produce them. Considerable effort has been devoted to studying how to measure productivity, how to analyze their patterns, and what factors influence the patterns over the years. Productivity is important because it is closely related to improvements in standard of living: When we produce more per hour of labor, our standard of living collectively increases. The growth in productivity is especially important. Each year, we expect to become more efficient thanks to technological improvements, better training, or just learning from previous mistakes. Growth is accompanied by rising standards of living.

The trends in productivity growth have shown some intriguing changes since World War II. From 1948 to 1973, average productivity growth was very good, almost 3 percent per year. After the war, many technological advances were ready to be exploited by returning soldiers who quickly went back to school for further education. In 1973, however, productivity growth slowed and remained slow for almost twenty years. The reasons for the slowdown are not clear. One factor may have been the entrance of a large number of inexperienced baby boomers into the labor force. In any case, slower productivity growth meant that people had to lower their expectations about standard of living. This was the period in which people no longer expected to enjoy a higher standard of living compared to their parents. Although people came to view this slower growth as normal, they were surprised again in 1996, when productivity growth accelerated.

Robert E. Litan and Alice M. Rivlin, economists at the Brookings Institution, have been studying productivity issues extensively, and they point out that this sudden acceleration is somewhat mystifying.[194] Information technology clearly plays a role, but businesses had been investing in computers and telecommunications for many years before 1996. Robert Solow, the MIT economist, quipped in 1987, "We see computers everywhere except in the productivity statistics." It was difficult to imagine why such enormously useful technologies did not have more impact on the output per man-hour of labor earlier, but their effects began to show by the mid-1990s. At this time, information technology investments were accompanied by several other significant economic conditions: low inflation, low unemployment, and tight labor markets. The tight labor contributed to a climate in which businesses were under great pressure to improve productivity because they couldn't just hire more workers. Low inflation made greater investment in riskier technology implementations more likely by reducing interest rates, thus lowering the risk of investment. As Litan and Rivlin put it, "The economic stars were realigned."

The stars became misaligned again in the middle of 2000, when the economy sputtered and productivity growth dropped. This time, the causes appeared to be related to the delayed effects of a restrictive monetary policy established by the Federal Reserve Board that began the year before, higher energy prices, and the precipitous nose dive in the stock market, led by the dot.coms. The terrorist attacks of 2001 along with the accounting scandals

[194] Litan, R. E., & Rivlin, A. M. (2001). *Beyond the dot.coms: The economic promise of the Internet*. Washington, DC: Brookings Institution Press.

of 2002 pushed the economy, and productivity growth along with it, even further into the doldrums.

THE INTERNET'S ROLE

As one of the century's most disruptive technologies, what role did the Internet play in the sudden acceleration of productivity in 1996? Probably not much, at least not in the beginning, because technologies take a long time to have an impact on productivity in an economy as large as that in the United States. Although the timing looks suspiciously like the Internet played a key role, most businesses did not even have Internet access until the mid-1990s. Its effects on productivity in the workplace were most likely minor in 1996, but it may have made larger contributions toward the end of the 1990s when computers were increasingly interconnected via the net. And the potential for future contributions to productivity are very promising, despite the slump.

Transforming the Economy, Old and New

The Brookings Task Force on the Internet, led by Litan and Rivlin, attempted to predict the role the Internet would play in the economy and how its effects would unfold in the future. The group included scholars knowledgeable about each of the eight sectors of the U.S. economy, which collectively account for more than 70 percent of the gross domestic product. Many of them were reluctant to offer even remotely precise predictions, given the youthful age of the net and the many variables that could derail diffusion of the Internet's capabilities. Although precise figures were difficult to predict, their insights about how the net would eventually affect all of these "old economy" sectors are very valuable. The new economy dot.coms came, and most of them subsequently went. Some of the companies that were pure Internet plays survive, but if the net is going to truly affect the economy and workplace productivity in signficant ways, it has to reach into its heart. Let's take a look at a few examples and explore how these fundamental economic sectors may be affected by the Internet in the years to come.

MANUFACTURING

Some industries may not appear to be likely candidates for leveraging the power of the Internet, but these may turn out to be the ones that are transformed the most. Manufacturing is a key example. Cisco, the manufacturer of networking equipment whose logo reads "Empowering the Internet Generation," pioneered many Internet-enabled improvements in manufacturing. It made complete sense for them to capture and apply Internet capabilities, given the importance of their products to the infrastructure, and they claimed significant cost savings as a result. Cisco used the net to provide customer support, to improve internal business processes, and especially to streamline the management of their supply chain.

Brookings Task Force member Andrew McAfee of the Harvard Business School points out that Cisco looks like a world-class manufacturer to most of the world, but most products that Cisco distributes are never seen or touched by Cisco employees.[195] What Cisco employees do, however, is manage the integration of their suppliers by disseminating and analyzing information about forecasts, production schedules, shipments, quality control reports, and manufacturing activity. Cisco does not own most of the physical assets used in the production of those routers. Instead, the company manages the processes by which all the players cooperate to design, manufacture, market, deliver, and support their products. The term "e-supply chain" doesn't even fairly describe the kind of transformation that is occurring in manufacturing. For Cisco, and for firms that will follow this model, the chain is not a linear sequence in which information and products flow from one partner to the next in line, like an assembly line in warp drive. Instead, all the partners in the network have instant access to all the information they need. All the players know immediately when orders are placed or problems arise at any node in the network.

Dell's methods for building computers to order takes advantage of this kind of networked supply chain. Unlike most other PC manufacturers, Dell does not carry large inventories of stock. Instead, customers go online or call by phone to let Dell know exactly what kind of computer they want. Each buyer selects their preferred customizations from a list of choices. The Web site has dozens of options, and customers simply click a radio box to choose a rewritable CD drive for their new computer, or a DVD player. Dell begins assembling the needed parts almost immediately and ships the computer to the customer within days. Dell has very little investment in inventories of these component parts, which is especially important in the computer industry in which aged equipment is very difficult to unload. For example,

---

[195] McAfee, A. (2001). Manufacturing: Lowering boundaries, improving productivity. In R. E. Litan & A. M. Rivlin, (Eds.), *The economic payoff from the Internet revolution.* Washington, DC: Internet Policy Institute, Brookings Institution Press.

once a faster modem is available, few people will choose the slower one at *any* price. Those boxes of computers with 28K modems, made by other manufacturers and stacked in warehouses for distribution to retailers, were very difficult to sell after the 56K modem was released. Getting caught with a warehouse full of obsolete computer inventory is a costly affair, one that Dell generally can avoid thanks to the way they implemented their Internet-enabled sales and supply chains. Dell can also get excellent prices on the parts it purchases from suppliers through competition in e-markets, thus keeping the cost of the parts down as well.

Can the automotive industry benefit from the same kinds of Internet-related efficiencies? Compared to the computer buyer, the car-buying public is used to far more variety in designs, features, and capabilities. In many ways, the computer is less complex than a car. The computer is also more modular, and most of the modules are relatively standard. This means that a person can piece together components purchased from any number of suppliers and make a computer that functions. Cars, however, are not as modular and their parts are not generally standard or interchangeable. The savings and productivity improvements that were generated by the "build-to-order" computer approach made possible by the Internet are likely to be much more difficult to generate in the automobile industry. Nevertheless, the Internet will certainly offer opportunities for savings. Charles H. Fine of MIT and Daniel M. G. Raff of University of Pennsylvania predict considerable savings from better efficiencies in almost every component of the industry: procurement and supply, product design, manufacturing, and retail distribution. The number of car dealerships will certainly decline, as will sales commissions. Taken together, the price of a car could fall by as much as 13 percent thanks to the gradual impact of the Internet on this industry.

TRUCKING

Transportation is another old economy industry, and trucking makes up a majority of this sector – contributing more than 3 percent of the gross domestic product. Trucking firms are already using the Internet in many different ways, and 1999 was proclaimed the "Year of the Internet" by *Transport Topics*, an industry magazine. The Internet's support for gathering, analyzing, and disseminating information have helped trucking companies improve productivity by reducing waiting times at docks and warehouses and avoiding empty miles in which trucks carry small or no loads. This is especially important in an industry as fragmented and geographically dispersed as trucking, and where information transparency and integration could offer huge gains.

How do these gains actually emerge? Transplace.com is a logistics management alliance created initially by several large trucking companies who decided to explore how the Internet could maximize their productivity and efficiency. By aggregating their buying power, and also their information about logistics and the requirements of their customers, they are able to create *dense network efficiency*.[196] The efficiency comes about because of three factors. First, they need a critical mass of virtually unlimited shipper freight and carrier capacity, and the Transplace.com e-market place creates that. Second, they need the Internet to reach out to and connect the people who want to ship something with those who have trucks. Third, they use optimization technology to make sure the network of trucks is used in the most productive ways, by reducing waiting times, matching loads to available excess cargo space, and reducing those deadhead runs with empty trailers.

Anuradha Nagarajan and colleagues at the University of Michigan foresee some future gains from the Internet for the trucking industry, but these are likely to be modest because most of the gains have already occurred.[197] What may be far more significant, however, is the contribution a more efficient trucking industry can make to productivity and growth in other sectors of the economy – e-commerce in particular. The level of trust in e-commerce increases considerably when customers receive real time shipping status information about their purchases. A substantial portion of these indirect gains still lie in the future.

HEALTH CARE

If your workplace is within the health care industry, you know how heterogeneous, inefficient, and fragmented the flow of information can be. It is often a frustrating mix of multiple manual forms, carbon copies, handwritten prescriptions, computerized billing, and manual appointment systems, along with Internet-enabled communication networks. The Internet has contributed a great deal in some areas, but almost nothing in others, at least not yet.

---

[196] Transplace, The Market for Transportation Services. (n.d.). Retrieved April 16, 2003, from Transplace Web site: http://www.transplace.com/aboutUs.jsp

[197] Nagarajan, A., Canessa, E., Mitchell, W., & White, C. C. III. (2001). Trucking industry: Challenges to keep pace. In R. E. Litan & A. M. Rivlin, (Eds.), *The economic payoff from the Internet revolution*. Washington, DC: Internet Policy Institute, Brookings Institution Press.

For patients, an enormous amount of medical information is now available on the Web. The National Institutes of Health maintain very rich information resources about disorders, treatments, medications, and many other health-related topics for patients and providers, as do several commercial sites. As in other industries, e-markets are springing up that promise to drive down the price of supplies for buyers and make price comparisons easier.

Other areas of the health care industry, however, are mired in time-consuming and error-prone paper transactions and record keeping, mixed with incompatible computerized systems that have few standard formats. As such, they are very promising targets for improved productivity through greater standardization and interaction via networks. Standardizing insurance claim forms, for example, would make it far easier to develop Web-based systems to replace the current manual forms so providers could instantly see what treatments were covered under the patient's policies. Better information flow and more integration could also bring improved patient care and save lives. If physicians entered their prescriptions into a database, or even on a handheld PDA, fewer errors would be made. Also, if the emergency room had immediate access to an accident victim's medical history, better treatment would be possible.

Obstacles loom very large for any rapid Internet-related improvements in this industry, however. Privacy of medical records is a key issue, and privacy is easier to protect in a fragmented information environment in which disparate pieces of information collected at different times cannot be integrated into a whole picture. In a netcentric world, the safeguards that protect medical records from misuse, but make them available when they are needed for patient care, will take time to implement. Lack of standardization in medical forms and records is another hurdle. The coding schemes that identify treatments, disorders, drugs, allergies, and other ingredients of health care are not well standardized, so handoffs of information between health organizations is anything but seamless.

The traditional working style of physicians is a potential obstacle, especially because much of the current health care infrastructure is tied to that working style. For example, a typical model involving the dispensing of prescription drugs begins with the patient scheduling a visit with a physician for an in-person evaluation. The physician would review the patient's history, conduct an examination, do some tests, and then write a prescription for medication on a piece of paper, which the patient hand carries to the pharmacy to be filled. The policies covering insurance reimbursement for this standard model are well documented by the insurance companies, and the rules are set out in computer programs. However, what happens when the patient goes online for a consultation? The online physician could obtain the patient's history and symptoms with a Web-based form and then write an e-prescription for regulated substances, to be filled by an Internet pharmacy and delivered by mail. The insurers have little experience with new models of health care and might not recognize it as a qualifying medical visit. Although telemedicine promises to be a valuable addition to health care, there are many issues to work out and safeguards to develop.

Some of the old economy industries are in a position to make large changes in the way they do business so they can exploit the power of netcentric technologies to improve productivity. Others, however, will be delayed, or will experience little impact from the Internet. In most, however, the impact will be mixed. The Internet will bring efficiencies to the procurement process in any kind of business that buys supplies, because of e-markets. It will also offer opportunities for much greater potential access to customers on a global basis for businesses that are seeking them.

The processes that go on in the workplace and in different industries will change at varying paces, and these are critical to any improvements in productivity. The physical characteristics of the workplace also affect productivity, and changes here are likely to be varied and uneven as well.

Offices of the Future

Most of this book has been about how emerging netcentric technologies affect and reshape how we work, how we communicate, what tools we use, where we work, and the many challenges that these changes are creating. But what will all these changes mean for the physical characteristics of the workplace? Will the workplace of the future look like Captain Picard's ready room on the starship Enterprise, with a tiny voice-activated computer display, spotless and uncluttered surfaces, a shelf full of archaic and rare books (kept only for their sentimental value), and an all-purpose communication device worn on the shirt? Now, many workplaces are a cluttered affair, even for knowledge workers keen on organization and orderliness. Desks and offices are filled with an odd combination of nineteenth-, twentieth-, and twenty-first-century paraphernalia. Bulky computer screens, tangled cables, keyboards, Web cams, PDA cradles, and mice sit side by side with telephones, pencils, ink blotters, paper clips, manila folders, in- and out-boxes, and overflowing filing cabinets.

Figure 11.1. Private office at Leland & Faulconer Manufacturing Company, Detroit, Michigan, circa 1903.
From American Memory, Library of Congress, Detroit Publishing Company Photograph Collection, LC-D4-43031 DLC (b&w glass neg.).

THE 100-YEAR-OLD WORKPLACE

Visitors transported in time from about 100 years ago would be utterly amazed by certain twenty-first century physical settings, but the typical office environment is not one of them. For example, the private office image in Figure 11.1 from Leland & Faulconer Manufacturing Company of 1903 bears a close resemblance to executive offices throughout the rest of the century. The familiar wood desk, desk lamp, and conference table for small group meetings are more ornate, perhaps, but not that different from the workplace of a modern executive in terms of furniture and layout. The executive office of the twenty-first century would have a computer in it, of course, but the introduction of that device didn't have spectacular effects on office design. Instead, it landed on the main desk, or found its way onto a nearby side table.

Below the executive suite, office managers and other knowledge workers have also not seen earth-shaking changes in their physical workspaces in

Figure 11.2. Cadillac Motor Car Company office workers, between 1900 and 1920.
From American Memory, Library of Congress, Detroit Publishing Company Photograph Collection, LC-D417-1407 DLC (b&w glass neg.).

many decades. Figure 11.2 shows the working environment for midlevel employees at Cadillac Motor Car Company, circa 1910. All had their own workspace, but no walls or barriers separated them. Common areas and shared resources such as filing cabinets were within easy reach. The rank and file were similarly housed in shared workspaces, albeit much more tightly packed. Figure 11.3 shows the workspace for clerks at the Chrysler Corporation in Michigan.

After World War II, office building and workspace design took a very functional turn. Architect James S. Russell, editor-at-large of *Architectural Record*, points out, "In the postwar era, business began to question whether architecture deserved a role in the workplace any more sophisticated than as a drafting service."[198] Ornate and distinctive designs, masonry, and terra cotta were gradually replaced by uniform steel and glass. Inside, the spaces

---

[198] Russell, J. S. (2000). Form follows fad: The troubled love affair of architectural style and management ideal. In D. Albrecht & C. B. Broikos, (Eds.), *On the job: Design and the American office.* New York, NY: Princeton Architectural Press and Washington, DC: National Building Museum.

Figure 11.3. Detroit, Michigan. Office workers at work at the Chrysler Corporation.
From American Memory, Library of Congress, Detroit Publishing Company Photograph Collection, LC-USW3-016395-C DLC (b&w film neg.).

were designed for interchangeability within levels of the hierarchy, but for clear distinction between those hierarchies. Large corner offices on top floors were for the top brass, and smaller private offices were for the organization men. The big open spaces housed row upon row of clerks, typists, filers, and data entry people (mostly women).

BÜROLANDSCHAFT, OFFICE LANDSCAPING, AND OPEN PLAN
Wolfgang and Eberhard Schnelle founded the Quickborner Consulting Group near Hamburg, Germany, and began promoting a workplace design that would deemphasize the corporate hierarchy. Instead of status-defining private offices, their designs incorporated curves and wide open spaces that would support more teamwork, cooperation, and wider participation.

The noise and distraction in such large, open spaces became a problem, but perhaps not as severe as the psychological effects of lack of privacy and a perceived loss of status. A middle manager who had private office would resist moving to a new corporate building designed in this fashion, and the original landscape designs quickly evolved to *open plan* workspaces. These are the rows of modular cubicles with interchangeable parts and noise-deadening movable barriers between them in order to permit some measure of privacy. Designers usually added large, well-lit common spaces with green plants, tables, sofas, or other amenities, to be shared by all for work or pleasure. Buildings still had private offices, though there were fewer of them, reserved for the higher echelons. In terms of the allocation of interior real estate and its connection to status, the middle and lower tiers in the corporate hierarchies were leveled and made more homogeneous. The highest ranking executives, however, retained their perks. This trend matches what I described in an earlier chapter about executive compensation and how it has pulled further and further away from much of the rest of the organization.

These open plan designs have great advantages for a corporation because of their lower cost and flexibility. The modules could be easily expanded and reconfigured as the corporation developed new initiatives, hired more employees, or moved people from one project to another. Though functional, they have certainly drawn their share of criticism for their potentially dehumanizing effects. For example, cartoonist Scott Adam created Dilbert in 1989 to satire life in the open plan workplace.

NETCENTRIC WORKPLACE DESIGNS

The existing open plans and private offices have been modified somewhat, or occasionally dramatically, to accommodate netcentric working styles. In workplaces with many telecommuters, smaller cubicles are reserved for *hoteling*, and the office concierge accepts reservations and delivers the worker's filing cabinets, personal photos, or other paraphernalia to the reserved space. Even smaller spaces or shared tabletops configured with electricity and jacks for Internet connectivity are for *motelers* who didn't have time to make a reservation but still need to stop in the office. The caves and commons approach stresses the distinction between workspace that requires quiet thought and dedicated individual effort and the area designed to support collaboration and teamwork. War rooms are also becoming more common as a means to energize and support a collocated team.

Support for mobility of all kinds is a central feature of netcentric workplace designs. Workstations designed for sitting or standing are on wheels so the employee can shove them around to different locations and then group them together in pods to conduct team sessions. Within the corporate campus, office designers have developed workstations that double as cars so they can be driven to different floors or nearby buildings. One design features a futuristic egg-shaped cart on wheels with interior seat, a joy stick to steer, and a four-screen computer display.

For people who travel beyond the corporate campus and away from home, other companies are stepping in to provide services. Hotels are increasingly providing broadband Internet access in rooms, a much needed improvement over dial-up access using the room's telephone. Airports and other public spaces used by travelers who want to stay connected are installing wireless networks so passengers can log in while waiting for the plane to depart. The widespread use of cell phones is making the public pay phone obsolete, and companies are thinking of ways to revitalize all those widely available pay phone "workstations" in innovative ways that will better support mobile workers. One, for example, is converting pay phone cubicles to cell phone charging stations, in which customers can lock their phone for half an hour and charge their phones (and credit cards). Public kiosks to charge PDAs or log them into a network to synch with corporate email systems are also on the horizon.

Will the workplace be dramatically different from what it is today because of the influence and diffusion of netcentric technologies? Though many office designers may suggest so, the workplace is not likely to change all that much. The physical changes that I just described would not appear very revolutionary to an early-twentieth-century knowledge worker, especially one who had a typewriter on the desk.

Nevertheless, the netcentric workplace can be improved in certain ways that will better accommodate knowledge work. One obvious improvement involves the size of the screen, the main window to the Internet, the corporate network, and most of the information assets knowledge workers use to accomplish their roles. This is the place where people focus their eyes much of the day, but it still is quite small relative to the size of the desk and the office. The size reflects the earlier notion that the computer would be one more piece of office machinery, albeit a very powerful one, that should be available in about the same way, from the standpoint of physical layout, as the typewriter had been. Emerging display technologies, however, enable the information display to be as large, small, and numerous as we need them to be. They can be projected on walls, on flexible paper-like materials, or as microdisplays embedded in eyeglasses, and workers will be able to change them easily at any time. The ability to expand the screen real estate so that the display is not a bottleneck or source of eyestrain will be a very welcome improvement.

Improvements for input devices are also underway. The mouse was an early addition that enabled people to easily interact with a graphical interface, and progress on using voice input or handwriting on tablets is also being made. The evolution of dictation in the office environment illustrates how working styles and habits change with the new input technologies. In the early version, a manager composed and spoke the contents of a letter while a secretary used special symbols – called *shorthand* – to document the words in a two-column writing tablet. The secretary would then type the letter on paper by translating the symbols back to words and give it to the manager for signature. The ability to dictate efficiently and create spontaneous letters with good grammar and clear content was an important managerial skill. Knowledge of shorthand, typically Gregg's version, was also an important skill that warranted higher pay, because it took some time to learn the arcane symbols. When voice recorders became common in offices, managers dictated into a microphone and secretaries used specialized dictation equipment to listen to it, with headphones and foot pedal to stop and start the tape. This was a major improvement, because the manager could dictate a document anywhere and at any time, regardless of whether a secretary skilled in shorthand was available. Once managers began using computers and keyboards, many stopped using dictation and began composing their own documents and email. Although the dictation skills of many managers may now be rusty (or nonexistent), voice input technologies may revitalize them. After a couple of hours of practice with the manager's voice and accent, the software can "type" with reasonable accuracy as the manager speaks, either live or from a recording. The keyboard and mouse will not disappear, at least not for a long time. But these improvements in input technologies will give workers many more options for interacting with the computer and network. They also, of course, disintermediate some lower level office positions whose roles are closely linked to the keyboard input device.

A number of innovations are vastly enhancing mobility. Improvements in wireless computing and battery power will make it even easier for workers to get up from their desks, taking their work and access to communication with them. The wearable technology movement is on the front lines of the mobility improvements, because a worker wearing a lightweight pair of glasses, a vest, or other garment linked to the network will be even more mobile than one who carries a laptop.

The rise of the paperless office has been predicted for decades, but it is far from reality in most workplaces. Because of limitations on screen real estate, workers must print out pages when they need to see information from many sources. Limitations on resolution also make reading tedious on the computer, though progress in electronic paper may alleviate these obstacles. As we streamline and digitize many components of the office – internal memos or purchase orders, for example – we make headway. Yet we are still so often hamstrung by pieces of the puzzle that are not so easily digitized, from the physician's prescription to the passport. When U.S. Airways was going bankrupt, analysts were strongly recommending that people who were holding e-tickets or e-summaries of their frequent flyer miles account should immediately try to get paper documentation from the company. Until people have more trust in digital documentation, the paperless office will face formidable obstacles. The quip about the office being a factory that produces paper will continue to amuse for some time to come.

The Internet in the Workplace: A SWOT Analysis

Every student of business learns the value of a SWOT, an analysis of a company's strengths, weaknesses, opportunities, and threats. Strengths and weaknesses are internal factors, such as core competencies, geographic location, or product line. A company that makes humorous greeting cards might list as strengths its strong design staff and its excellent reputation with the environmentally aware community because of its use of recycled paper. Bullets in the weakness quadrant might mention a shaky capital base or lack of distribution channels.

Opportunities and threats encompass the external factors that affect how a business performs and what strategy might work best to marry the strengths to the opportunities while avoiding the threats. For the greeting card company, an opportunity might be an offer on the table to merge with another company that makes cards with religious themes. A threat might be the rise of e-greetings, which are even more environmentally friendly than cards, regardless of what kind of paper the card maker uses.

SWOTs are analytical tools, often used for brainstorming and to understand the organization's position and environment. A SWOT focuses everyone's attention on the big picture rather than on the daily operational realities. It also is a way to help company executives avoid deluding themselves or engaging in groupthink about their own company. Although the Internet is not a company, it certainly has strengths, weaknesses, opportunities and threats. It is worthwhile to look at the Internet in the workplace within this context. For the net, however, it is more appropriate to use the SWOT approach somewhat differently and consider how each characteristic acts as both strength and weakness, or how each external force may present both opportunities and threats.

STRENGTHS AND WEAKNESSES

■ *The Internet provides the means to communicate quickly and cheaply with anyone who has access.*

The most obvious feature of the Internet, its support for rapid and inexpensive communications, is also its most important strength for the workplace. Businesses can launch Web sites to reach out to new customers with very little new investment in hardware or software, and they can communicate with their customers and suppliers very easily with email. Internally, the Internet is used to coordinate work and keep everyone informed. The marginal costs of adding another person to an email distribution list, or forwarding the digital communication history to a coworker who just joined the project, are trivial. Because the Internet's reach is global, distance is not a hindrance for this fast, cheap communication system. Internet communications reach my colleagues in India, Baltimore, and Germany at almost the same time. The Internet has done for communications what electricity did for power. In the workplace, the wall jacks for network connectivity are installed right along with the electrical outlets.

Fast and cheap communication is also a weakness, in the sense that it can easily be overused and trivialized. When communication becomes too fast and cheap, the recipients have far more difficulty sorting out the wheat from the chaff. This happens in organizations when people overuse the cc: line in email discussions and include coworkers in debates that just waste their time. It also happens with spam. Another reason "fast and cheap" can be considered a weakness is what makes it so fast and cheap – it lacks social presence and media richness. Nevertheless, people in the workplace use it routinely for communications that can easily be misconstrued without nonverbal cues, or whose meaning and impact are distorted by the impoverishment of the medium.

■ *The Internet's hourglass architecture supports openness and innovation.*

The open design of the network, with the emphasis on a small group of simple protocols that enforce certain standards for digital data transmission and ensure interoperability, leaves plenty of room for innovation at the network's edges. As long as devices, protocols, and new applications follow the simple rules, they can join the network and interact with everything else attached to it. A camera can be assigned an IP address and begin transmitting traffic images on the highway to everyone who logs in to the site. Some other company can quickly improve on that idea and launch a better device with more features, at lower cost. This is not like AT&T's telephone monopoly, during the time when customers could only buy their phones from Ma Bell. The outpouring of innovation and competition triggered by the net's architecture has led to many significant changes in the workplace, from new business models and new gadgets to changing organizational forms. It initiated a wave of creative destruction that has already transformed some industries, disintermediated workers, made many occupations virtually obsolete, and created new roles for employees. For other industries, the wave is just beginning and the impact from netcentric technologies lies ahead.

The Internet's design features also make it problematic to secure, regulate, and control the net. Although the proprietary network protocols of the past were difficult to interconnect, and thus never led to an integrated global network, they also were easier to protect and centrally manage. The Internet is seamless and global, so national boundaries and the laws passed for citizens within them are not easy to enforce. It is also a peer-to-peer style network, in which traffic can take many different routes without being centrally directed.

■ *Information is stored and transmitted digitally.*

The net's architecture requires information to be transmitted digitally, with zeros and ones. The way those two digits are represented within the transmission medium might vary, but the information itself has to be coded into patterns of zeros and ones using standard codes so they can be decoded later. The interest in adding more and more content to the Internet, and to transmitting that content, has led to a tremendous drive to digitize information, whether it is text, audio, graphic images, video, or multimedia.

One downside to this is that the digital information has to be stored in some format, and the technologies to translate the zeros and ones into meaningful information change quickly. For example, will books archived in a DVD format be readable fifty years from now? The book itself, if it survives, will be readable, but there may not be any technologies to convert the digital information back into readable text. Debates about how to create digital archives so they can outlast the technology used to create them are common, especially among librarians, archivists, and historians. The Library of Congress, for example, faces an enormous task of preserving early film reels, many of which are deteriorating in metal cans. They must be certain that future generations will be able to view them.

■ *The Internet is always on, and supports anytime-anywhere access.*

People can access the resources they need from their workplaces anytime of day or night, from wherever they are. And people can be reached anytime, as well. For a growing number of people, the workplace is no longer a specific place, nor is it a specific time of day with defined "hours of operation." It is becoming a fluid progression of "time slices" during which the worker focuses on work-related tasks, and which can occur anytime or anyplace. This feature enables flexible working hours, telecommuting, and productive use of time that was not easily put to use before, such as the commute to work. It has also led to many new elements in the workplace such as hot desks, hoteling, moteling, and the workplace concierge who organizes and coordinates the shared use of resources. The twenty-four-hour availability also means that information-based services and activities are always accessible; e-learning is one example.

The growing use of netcentric technologies has lessened any distinction between work and nonwork, and concerns about heightened stress levels, longer working hours, and effects on family life are mounting. People are increasingly engaged in multitasking and also cutting up their attention into smaller and smaller slices of time so they can switch from one activity to the next quickly. They did this before the net, of course, but netcentric technologies make cognitive overload much more likely. The long-term effects on the quality of work and life are unknown.

OPPORTUNITIES AND THREATS

The strengths and weakness of the Internet in the workplace have led to a fascinating combination of opportunities and threats. Its design characteristics and the way it has been implemented interact with the external environment – and I include human beings as part of that environment – in both predictable and surprising ways.

■ *The Internet promotes disinhibition.*

A byproduct of the characteristics of Internet communications is disinhibition, due especially to physical distance, lowered self-awareness, and the paucity of nonverbal cues that people ordinarily use to adapt their behavior in face-to-face settings. This can be a valuable opportunity in some contexts, as in online forums in which participants who would not normally contribute feel more relaxed and willing to voice their views. On balance, though, the disinhibiting influence of the Internet's communications environment has probably done more harm than good in the workplace. This is particularly true because so many people are unaware of how powerful the environment can be in its effects on behavior, and of how easy it is to misinterpret communications with low media richness.

■ *The Internet distributes power.*

The Internet alters power structures within organizations because of the way it facilitates new patterns of communications. As we discussed in previous chapters, Internet communications can easily bypass conventional organizational hierarchies and frequently do. Also, the net can be used in many novel ways to offset and counteract traditional power bases. A disgruntled employee can launch a Web site and collect anecdotes from visitors about corporate misdeeds. Also, a union leader can easily reach out to all the employees of an organization very quickly, disseminating information and getting feedback about a proposed work slowdown or walkout.

Changes in power distribution also occur in more subtle ways because of the net's lower social presence and its status-equalizing effects. High-status people are less likely to be able to dominate group discussions and decision making when most of the discussion occurs online. Shy people, or anyone for whom physical presence limits their contribution and influence, will participate more.

The distribution of power has been well received by employees but not always by managers or executive teams. Even in organizations in which decision making is often highly participative, the distribution of power can still be unsettling and disruptive to the usual ways of doing things.

■ *The Internet's design enabled unparalleled access to a rapidly growing body of information.*

The net's hourglass architecture was ideal for supporting very rapid growth in the sheer volume of easily accessible information. Standardizing the transmission protocols and reducing the complexity for displaying information by means of freely available browser software were forces that quickly attracted a critical mass. Once created, that critical mass attracted more people, more applications, and more content, and the value of the network grew exponentially. Every time a new user or new workplace was added, the network's value was further amplified like a snowball rolling downhill. With so many businesses and people using the network, no one is asking *whether* a business should invest in the development of a Web site any longer, regardless of where that business happens to be located. As the network grew, the volume of information about the ways in which people were using it exploded as well. The threat for the workplace is that more data do not necessarily lead to better information, nor are they likely to produce improvements in knowledge. If a worker is drowning in so much information that the individual has no hope of reading and analyzing it all, will that worker make better decisions? As we discussed earlier in this book, the volume itself is encouraging researchers to develop innovative tools to deal with such immensity. Data mining and knowledge management projects are two examples.

■ *The Internet's support for fast and cheap communications has led to far more communication.*

Behind this obvious fact are a great many opportunities and also very significant threats. On the opportunity side lies the potential for much more knowledge sharing, more virtual teamwork, closer coordination of supply chain relationships, timely communications with corporate stakeholders, and more efficient workplace activity in general. By comparison, postal mail, the fax machine, and even the telephone seem very cumbersome for communications in the Internet age.

More communication, however, is not necessarily a good thing. It becomes a threat when an employee receives dozens or even hundreds of emails or instant messages each day, many of which are not relevant to his or her work. The over-communication comes from many sources. One is simply well-meaning coworkers who want to keep people informed of many details, even if the recipients have very little involvement in the project. Another may be the company publications staff, who now publish newsy in-house e-zines to build esprit de corps and commitment on a weekly basis, instead of the monthly version that came out when the newsletter was printed on paper. On the surface, the e-zine seems to save the company money in printing costs, thanks to the fast and cheap Internet communications. However, the weekly e-zine costs more to produce in terms of staff time and four times more in terms of the extra time employees take to read it. A fair question to ask is whether the benefits of a weekly employee newsletter outweigh the hidden costs of the higher volume of communication.

Over-communication also emerges in the workplace because of e-commerce and the drive to manage customer relationships. Many companies have made egregious blunders in their eagerness to keep in touch with customers (who also happen to be workers somewhere else), and have wildly overused their newfound abilities to send out email newsletters, sale offers, and advertisements. Spam has emerged as a workplace nightmare, and states are rapidly passing laws in an attempt to control it and levy fines on the senders. Internet communications are *so* fast and cheap, from the standpoint of the sender, that a tremendous incentive exists to mine Web sites for any and every email address, build massive email marketing lists, and send out junk email as often as possible. For the employee struggling to do a job, this extra burden on attention can become intolerable.

■ *The Internet's design makes it easy to grow, but difficult to secure, protect, and maintain trust.*

The openness of this network has been an immense strength that led to many positive and innovative uses of the technology. It grew quickly, thanks to the many benefits it offers for communications and information access. No one is in charge, yet its routing schemes can easily find fast and reliable routes for packets, even when nodes are down or lines broken. Its design, however, and the fact that it is very difficult to develop policies to control what happens on the net – even if we wanted to – create enormous challenges for security and trust.

The productivity growth that should follow from better use of netcentric technologies in many industries, from old economy giants to health care, government, and education, could derail quickly if the network becomes unreliable. It can become unreliable in fact or in people's perceptions for a multitude of reasons. For example, the many viruses, worms, and other malicious code distributed through the network diminish trust and may destroy it if we are unable to protect against them. Robert Morris's worm, which he distributed over the Internet back in 1988, brought down more than half the hosts on the net for a time. He claimed that he just wanted to launch an experiment and never meant to do any damage. The Government Accounting Office estimated the event's cost to be anywhere from $10 to $100 million to clean up the mess. The price tag for the "I Love You" virus, launched in 2000 by a teen in the Philippines, was well into the billions. If the network is vulnerable to events like these, how secure will it be against a determined assault by terrorists?

A Social Dilemma

Although the net faces significant threats from external sources, it is also vulnerable to its most ardent enthusiasts. The net could simply become unusable, falling victim to a social dilemma like the tragedy of the commons.

Garrett Hardin described this dilemma in 1968, based on a pamphlet published in 1833 by amateur mathematician William Forster Lloyd.[199]

> "Picture a pasture open to all. It is to be expected that each herdsman will try to keep as many cattle as possible on the commons. Such an arrangement may work reasonably satisfactorily for centuries because tribal wars, poaching, and disease keep the numbers of both man and beast well below the carrying capacity of the land. Finally, however, comes the day of reckoning, that is, the day when the long-desired goal of social stability becomes a reality. At this point, the inherent logic of the commons remorselessly generates tragedy.
>
> As a rational being, each herdsman seeks to maximize his gain. Explicitly or implicitly, more or less consciously, he asks, "What is the utility *to me* of adding one more animal to my herd?" This utility has one negative and one positive component.
>
> 1. The positive component is a function of the increment of one animal. Since the herdsman receives all the proceeds from the sale of the additional animal, the positive utility is nearly +1.
> 2. The negative component is a function of the additional overgrazing created by one more animal. Since, however, the effects of overgrazing are shared by all the herdsmen, the negative utility for any particular decisionmaking herdsman is only a fraction of −1."

As more businesses and individuals use more of the net's capabilities, each will make individually rewarding, rational decisions. Collectively, however, the net may become less and less usable, just as the pasture did. Your email may be so filled with irrelevant messages at work that it becomes unproductive to sort through it. A search for information on the Web may be interrupted by so many pop-up ads or demands to "register" and provide personal information that the seeker gives up. Or the network itself and the servers on it may be plagued with unpredictable downtime and traffic so heavy that even broadband connections become barely usable.

What can be done to nurture the Internet's strengths in the workplace and pursue its opportunities? What can be done to reduce the threats that could limit the net's contribution to the workplace and to our working lives for the next generation? We are moving further along the wave of creative destruction the Internet prompted, and, so far, the ride has been both exhilarating and nerve-wracking. The wave metaphor, though, suggests that the net has its own momentum regardless of what we do. That assumption, based on technological determinism, is very risky. Neither the opportunities

---

[199] Hardin, G. (1968). The tragedy of the commons. *Science, 163,* 1243–1248.

nor the threats I described in the SWOT analysis are beyond our reach to influence.

The word "our" in the last sentence would have encompassed only a small number of people in the 1970s, millions by the 1990s, and many hundreds of millions in the 2000s. By 2010, it may encompass nearly all the businesses and government agencies, most of the people, and a growing number of nonhuman objects whose participation further amplifies the network's value. Though this exponential growth presented many challenges, both in numbers of users and in the kinds of applications being used, it is likely to be the most important factor in the Internet's long-term success.

Extending the Sphere

In the *Federalist Papers*,[200] James Madison advocated "extending the sphere" as a way to protect the society against certain kinds of dangers and social dilemmas. He was concerned that a governing body with a small number of parties and interests would be more likely to come to a "majority of the whole" whose common motive could be to damage or invade the rights of other citizens. He was not eager for a strong central government and wanted to promote measures to hinder factions or coalitions from gaining too much power, regardless of their purposes. By extending the sphere of participation to more and more parties with varied interests, motives, and agendas, it would become less likely that a majority would coalesce to take over.

Madison thought that the larger numbers would also inhibit communication among parties who might otherwise get together to wield undue influence toward what might be unjust purposes: "If such a common motive exists, it will be more difficult for all who feel it to discover their own strength, and to act in unison with each other." The Internet has pulled the proverbial rug out from under that piece of Madison's thinking. Finding others of like mind has never been easier, yet his basic argument is still sound. The more parties that have an interest in the Internet's long-term survival, the more motivation they will have to act in ways to ensure that survival, by developing policies, coordinating activities, creating uniform standards, and preventing abuses. Their diversity of viewpoints will help ensure that agreements to act are slow to emerge, and they will always have to balance different positions and find compromises.

[200] Madison, J. (1787). Federalist Papers, Federalist Number 10. Retrieved April 10, 2003, from The James Madison University Web site: http://www.jmu.edu/madison/federalist/fed10.htm

Extending the sphere has certainly affected debates about encryption, privacy, and the needs of law enforcement. It also affects debates about peer-to-peer computing, intellectual property, and technological innovations designed to protect copyrights. Now that the Internet plays a key role in the workplace, business, education, government, entertainment, and crime, that sphere has never been so large, nor the arguments more contentious. Extending it, as Madison advocated and which is almost certain to occur anyway, will further frustrate those who want rapid movement toward strong policies, tighter controls, and firm regulation. Parties with different motives and interests may eventually come to agreement, as they are doing in technological standards development, e-commerce practices, and many other arenas, but the process can be agonizingly slow. Nevertheless, extending the sphere has worked well so far for the Internet and is the best hope for its future.

Index